THE POETRY OF EXPERIENCE

ROBERT LANGBAUM has taught at Cornell University and is now James Branch Cabell Professor of English and American Literature at the University of Virginia. He is also the author of *The Gayety of Vision: A Study of Isak Dinesen's Art* and *The Modern Spirit: Essays on the Continuity of Nineteenth- and Twentieth-Century Literature*, and has edited Shakespeare's *The Tempest* and *The Victorian Age: Essays in History and in Social and Literary Criticism.*

THE POETRY
OF EXPERIENCE

*The Dramatic Monologue in
Modern Literary Tradition*

Robert Langbaum

The Norton Library
W · W · NORTON & COMPANY · INC ·
NEW YORK

To Francesca

W. W. Norton & Company, Inc. also publishes *The Norton
Anthology of English Literature*, edited by M. H. Abrams et al;
The Norton Anthology of Poetry, edited by Arthur M. Eastman
et al; *World Masterpieces*, edited by Maynard Mack et al; *The
Norton Reader*, edited by Arthur M. Eastman et al; *The Norton
Facsimile of the First Folio of Shakespeare*, prepared by Charlton
Hinman; *The Norton Anthology of Modern Poetry*, edited by
Richard Ellmann and Robert O'Clair; and the *Norton Critical
Editions*.

ISBN 0 393 00215 2

PREFACE

Since I have in 1971 the opportunity to write this preface to a new edition of a book that first appeared in 1957, I can only be grateful for the reception the book has had. There were a few errors in the 1957 hardcover edition; thanks to the friends and critics who pointed them out. Some of these errors were corrected in the first paperback edition of 1963, the rest are corrected here. I have also made, in the course of the two paperback editions, some small changes based on second thoughts of my own.

I would like to take this opportunity to answer the two main objections to my position that have emerged since 1957. The first has to do with my account of the dramatic monologue as deriving its special effect from the tension between sympathy and judgment. Several fine critics have objected to what they considered my implication that there are no moral judgments to be made in, say, Browning's dramatic monologues. Since these critics are well disposed towards *The Poetry of Experience,* the fault must be mine for not having made myself sufficiently clear; though I would have thought my readings of Browning's dramatic monologues—of *Andrea del Sarto,* to take only one—involve moral judgment at every point. Let me clarify, however, by saying that if there is to be a *tension* between sympathy and judgment, then both poles must be fully operative.

Sympathy, as I use it, has a technical meaning. It does not mean *love* or *approval;* it is a way of knowing, what I call romantic projectiveness, what the Germans call *Einfühlung,* what the psychologists call empathy. The difference between the dramatic monologue and other forms of dramatic literature is that the dramatic monologue does not allow moral judgment to determine the *amount* of sympathy we give to the speaker. We give him all our sympathy as a condition of reading the poem, since he is the only character there. The difference is that we split off our sympathy from our moral judgment. The dramatic monologue is most effective when the speaker is reprehensible; for we are then most acutely aware of the moral condemnation that is, not abolished, but temporarily split off from our sympathy. We take this excursion into sympathetic identification with the speaker in order to refresh and renew moral judgment. Because it depends on sympathy, the dramatic monologue is not the best vehicle for satire; although some of Browning's dramatic monologues contain satirical elements, none is pure satire. The dramatic monologue begins to do what the novel does even more conspicuously. Both modern forms teach us how to reinvalidate moral judgment in an empiricist and relativist age when no values can be taken for granted.

This leads to the second main objection to *The Poetry of Experience*—the objection to my reading of Browning's *The Ring and the Book* as a relativist poem. Certain critics have quite understandably taken off from the obvious difficulty that Browning dictates our judgments in Book I to argue that the poem is not relativist but mainly a demonstration of Guido's absolute wickedness and Pompilia's absolute goodness. The trouble with this argument is that it renders Browning's method supererogatory, since the reader has nothing to do but watch a demonstration through ten monologues of what is clearly established by Browning's account in Book I. It is surely a more workable hypothesis to take seriously Browning's innovating use of points of view, and conclude, as I originally did, that in forcing our judgment in Book I Browning did not carry his relativism far enough.

Our sympathetic identification with different points of view refreshes and renews moral judgment. That is how *The Ring and the Book* reasserts on a new relativist basis the Christian values originally questioned—the absolute reality of good·and evil. Far from being a flaw in the poem's relativism, the *right* judgments of Book I are—as I now realize and have recently explained[1]—a stroke of genius. For by giving us the sort of God's-eye view we never get in real life, Browning makes us understand how relative, on the one

[1] In *Essays in Criticism* (October 1970); thanks to the editors for permission to use these last two paragraphs.

hand, are human institutions and judgments, and on the other, that the relative is our index to the absolute. The question of relativism does not after all apply to God or a hypothetical ultimate reality; it applies to *knowable* reality. Browning says *human* institutions and judgments are relative, but that their fallibility throws us back on instincts which at their deepest connect with an absolute reality that can be felt though not known.

All the major characters arrive at this connection, but the process is most forcefully dramatized in Guido—who, when he imagines in his second monologue the horrors of his coming execution, lives through a hell that like Dante's substantiates and illuminates evil. When Guido finally speaks out of his deepest instinct, he recognizes in his own absolute evil and Pompilia's absolute goodness the reason for the fundamental antagonism between them. To watch Guido arrive at the truth through unpeeling, in his two monologues, layers of deception and then self-deception is for us the moral exercise that should renew the stale old words *good* and *evil*. Our return from the ultimate insights of Caponsacchi and Pompilia to the ordinary world of the lawyers, and from the ultimate insights of the Pope and Guido II to the mixed motives and distorted judgments of Book XII, reminds us with a shock that such insights are unrepresentative miracles in a world where the general rule is Fra Celestino's that "God is true/And every man a liar" (XII, 597-98). This is the relativist "moral" of the poem.

R.L.

Charlottesville, Virginia, June 1971

CONTENTS

Acknowledgments

I AM grateful for the help and encouragement I have received from Professors Jacques Barzun, Oscar James Campbell, Emery Neff and Lionel Trilling of Columbia University, and from Mr C. Day Lewis of Chatto and Windus and Mr Hiram Haydn of Random House.

Chapter III, "*The Ring and the Book: A Relativist Poem*," appeared originally in *Publications of the Modern Language Association*; Chapter V, "Character versus Action in Shakespeare," appeared in *The Shakespeare Quarterly;* and the part of the Conclusion dealing with Aristotle appeared as "Aristotle and Modern Literature" in *The Journal of Aesthetics and Art Criticism*. My thanks to the editors for permission to reprint these sections.

Thanks also to the following: George Allen and Unwin for permission to quote from Gilbert Murray's translation of Aeschylus' *Eumenides*; The Clarendon Press, Oxford, for permission to quote from Ingram Bywater's translation of the "Poetics" in the Oxford translation of *The Works of Aristotle* edited by W. D. Ross; Faber and Faber and Harcourt, Brace for permission to quote from T. S. Eliot's *Collected Poems* and *Selected Essays*; New Directions for permission to quote from C. F. MacIntyre's translation of Goethe's *Faust* (copyright 1949 by New Directions); Oxford University Press for permission to quote from the *Poems* of Gerard Manley Hopkins; Alfred A. Knopf and Faber and Faber for permission to quote from Randall Jarrell's *Poetry and the Age*; Mrs Maud Rosenthal and Macmillan of New York for permission to quote from W. A. Haussmann's translation of "The Birth of Tragedy" in the authorized English translation of *The Complete Works of Nietzsche* edited by Dr Oscar Levy; Ezra Pound for permission to quote from his *Personae* and *Letters*, and New Directions and Harcourt, Brace for permission to quote from the American editions of *Personae* (copyright 1926, 1952 by Ezra Pound) and the *Letters*, respectively; Macmillan of London and New York for permission to quote from W. B. Yeats's *Collected Poems*.

Finally, I want to thank the Faculty Research Grants Committee of Cornell University for their help with incidental expenses.

R. L.

Ithaca, New York, December 1956

INTRODUCTION

Romanticism as a Modern Tradition

"IN English writing we seldom speak of tradition," T. S. Eliot complained back in 1917.[1] Nowadays, thanks largely to Mr Eliot's influence, an opponent of his might complain, we seldom speak of anything else. But we do not have to be opponents of Eliot to recognize that the volume of talk about tradition has increased considerably since World War I, that the word which, as Eliot tells us, seldom appeared "except in a phrase of censure" now appears almost always in phrases of approval, phrases which mark the approver of tradition as a man of advanced ideas.

Why, we may well ask, should a word which used to carry associations of stale orthodoxy carry for us the shine of novelty? Because the word has been used, more frequently and emphatically than before 1917, to remind us that tradition is the thing we have not got, to remind us of our separation from the past, our modernity. The word helps construct for us that image of ourselves which constitutes the modern pathos, the image of ourselves as emancipated to the point of forlornness, to the point where each is free to learn for himself that life is meaningless without tradition.

> I can connect
> Nothing with nothing

says Eliot's modern equivalent for Ophelia, after she has been seduced. Ophelia is pathetic because her inability to make connections is a sign of madness. But the inability of Eliot's ruined lady to make connections is a sign of the times. It expresses perfectly the meaning of *The Waste Land*, as of all those poems and novels which ring most poignantly of the new age.

For we have used the contrast with tradition to define not only our separateness from the whole heritage of the West but

---

[1] "Tradition and the Individual Talent," *Selected Essays 1917-1932* (London: Faber and Faber, 1932), p. 13; (New York: Harcourt, Brace, 1938), p. 3.

to define also our separation from the immediate past, to define the special character of the twentieth century as an age distinct from the nineteenth. The curious thing about the twentieth century's reaction against the nineteenth is that we have levelled against the nineteenth century two apparently opposite charges. On the one hand, we have accused the nineteenth century of not being untraditional enough, of trying to compromise with the past, to cling through a false sentimentality to values in which it no longer really believed. On the other hand, we have accused the nineteenth century of breaking with the past, of rejecting *the* tradition, the "main current," to use Eliot's phrase, of Christian and humanist culture.

The apparent contradiction can be reconciled, however, once we realize the special nature of modern traditionalism, that it is built upon an original rejection of the past which leads to an attempt to reconstruct in the ensuing wilderness a new principle of order. If the nineteenth century ought to have swept away the sentimentally sustained debris of the past, it was because the debris hindered the work of discerning the really enduring patterns of human existence. Thus, Eliot's *Waste Land* and Joyce's *Ulysses* are at once more nihilistic and more deliberately traditional than any nineteenth-century works. In their accounts of the present, Eliot and Joyce show with uncompromising completeness that the past of official tradition is dead, and in this sense they carry nineteenth-century naturalism to its logical conclusion. But they also dig below the ruins of official tradition to uncover in myth an underground tradition, an inescapable because inherently psychological pattern into which to fit the chaotic present.

Eliot, in reviewing *Ulysses* for *The Dial* of November 1923, showed how modern anti-traditionalism clears the ground for modern traditionalism. Taking issue with Richard Aldington's condemnation of Joyce as a "prophet of chaos," Eliot calls *Ulysses* "the most important expression which the present age has found" precisely because Joyce has shown us how to be "classical" under modern conditions. He has given us the materials of modern disorder and shown us how to impose order upon them.

In using the myth, in manipulating a continuous parallel between contemporaneity and antiquity, Mr Joyce is pursuing a method which others must pursue after him. . . . It is simply a way of controlling, of ordering, of giving a shape and a significance to the immense panorama of futility and anarchy which is contemporary history. It is a method already adumbrated by Mr Yeats, and of the need for which I believe Mr Yeats to have been the first contemporary to be conscious. It is a method for which the horoscope is auspicious. Psychology (such as it is, and whether our reaction to it be comic or serious), ethnology, and *The Golden Bough* have concurred to make possible what was impossible even a few years ago. Instead of narrative method, we may now use the mythical method. It is, I seriously believe, a step toward making the modern world possible for art, toward that order and form which Mr Aldington so earnestly desires. And only those who have won their own discipline in secret and without aid, in a world which offers very little assistance to that end, can be of any use in furthering this advance.

The passage indicates the special nature of modern traditionalism in that Eliot does not talk about adherence to a publicly acknowledged tradition. He talks about a tradition which the past would not have recognized, a tradition tailored for a modern purpose by modern minds. And he talks, in the final sentence, of a sense of order won as a personal achievement in the face of external chaos.

The interesting thing is that both ideas, the idea of the past and of the superior individual as giving meaning to an otherwise meaningless world, derive from that same nineteenth-century romanticism against which Eliot is in reaction. Whatever the difference between the literary movements of the nineteenth and twentieth centuries, they are connected by their view of the world as meaningless, by their response to the same wilderness. That wilderness is the legacy of the Enlightenment, of the scientific and critical effort of the Enlightenment which, in its desire to separate fact from the values of a crumbling tradition, separated fact from all values—bequeathing a world in which fact is measurable quantity while value is man-made and illusory. Such a world offers no objective verification for just the perceptions by which men live, perceptions of beauty, goodness and spirit. It was as literature began in the latter eighteenth century to realize the dangerous implications of the scientific world-view, that romanticism was born. It was born anew in at least three generations thereafter as men of genius arrived intellectually at the dead-end of the eighteenth century and then, often through a total crisis of personality, broke intellectually into the nineteenth. As literature's reaction to the eighteenth century's scientific world-view, romanticism connects the literary movements of the nineteenth and twentieth centuries.

The nineteenth century is, for example, both anti-traditional and traditional in the same sense as the twentieth. Carlyle, in addressing Voltaire in *Sartor Resartus*, both accepts and rejects the eighteenth century. " 'Cease, my much-respected Herr von Voltaire,'" he says, speaking in the guise of the German Professor Teufelsdröckh,

'shut thy sweet voice; for the task appointed thee seems finished. Sufficiently hast thou demonstrated this proposition, considerable or otherwise: That the Mythus of the Christian Religion looks not in the eighteenth century as it did in the eighth. Alas, were thy six-and-thirty quartos, and the six-and-thirty thousand other quartos and folios, and flying sheets or reams, printed before and since on the same subject, all needed to convince us of so little! But what next? Wilt thou help us to embody the divine Spirit of that Religion in a new Mythus, in a new vehicle and vesture, that our Souls, otherwise too like perishing, may live? What! thou hast no faculty in that kind? Only a torch for burning, no hammer for building? Take our thanks, then, and——thyself away.'[1]

Thus, the nineteenth century accepts the iconoclastic contribution of the eighteenth. It starts with the acknowledgment that the past of official tradition is dead. But it seeks beneath the ruins of official tradition an enduring truth, inherent in the nature of life itself, which can be embodied in a new tradition, a new Mythus.

The famous romantic sense of the past derives its special character from the romanticists' use of the past to give meaning to an admittedly meaningless world. It is just the difference between the romantic and the classical sense of the past that the romanticist does not see the present as the heir of the past and does not therefore look to the past for authority as an ethical model. The romanticist sees the past as different from the present and uses the past to explore the full extent of the difference, the full extent in other words of his own modernity.

[1] Ed. C. F. Harrold (New York: Odyssey Press, 1937), Bk. II, Chap. IX, pp. 193-94.

Thus, Scott's sense of the past with its emphasis on costume, architecture and obsolete custom, on what is picturesquely peculiar to the past.

Such emphasis, curiously enough, helps to rescue from the past its core of life. For it is when everything else is as different as possible that we become most aware of the concrete life which remains our one point of contact with the past. Scott is often accused of projecting modern men into the Middle Ages, of making his characters aware of themselves as historical. We feel this in Scott because, reading him, we become aware of ourselves, with our modern historical consciousness, under the archaic costumes. It is, however, the whole point of the romantic use of the past to give us this sense of our own life in it. For it is our own life we feel when we feel the life of the past.

By giving us as exotic a past as possible, the romanticist gives us a past which, because it is inapplicable to the present, we can inhabit as a way not of learning a lesson but of enlarging our experience. It is just to the extent that we see the clothing of the past as a costume, as inapplicable to the present, that we project ourselves into the costume in order to feel what it would be like to live in the past. It is, in other words, when we no longer take the past seriously as an official tradition that we begin to "romanticize" it, which means that we rescue from beneath the ruins of the official tradition a more fundamental continuity, that core of life around which Carlyle would build his new Mythus.

Carlyle calls his philosophy of history a Clothes Philosophy. His point, as expressed in *Sartor*, is that the clothes of an age are symbolic of its institutions, which are in turn symbolic of its myth, its common faith. It is only by some miracle of common faith that the man in fine Red has the authority to condemn to the gallows the man in coarse Blue; while the spectacle of a naked Duke of Windlestraw addressing a naked House of Lords would be without any authority or significance whatever.[1] But the myth can give authority only as long as it is believed in. Once it is no longer believed in, clothes and institutions must be changed to accord with the new faith. In this sense, the Clothes Philosophy is relativist, asserting an anti-traditionalist principle of discontinuity in history.

[1] Bk. I, Chap. IX, pp. 60, 62.

It also asserts beneath the discontinuity, however, a fundamental continuity, the unchanging need of every age for clothes, for institutions and the myths which give them authority. The need itself is a sign that the changing myths are developing articulations of a truth inherent in the nature of human life. The Enlightenment had said that the past is dead and offers no model for the future. Carlyle admits that the particular articulations of the past are dead, but insists that the human need which they were designed to meet must still be met. The old Mythus may be dead, but mankind must have a new one to replace it. In this sense, the Clothes Philosophy is traditionalist and a corrective to the Enlightenment. It shows us how to be, as Eliot would say, "classical" under modern conditions, how to give meaning to the modern world by taking from the past not its dogmatic myth but the ground of life beneath it—the life of which the old myth was an expression and which we must try to express again in our own terms.

But how, without dogma, can the modern traditionalist hope to make the new Mythus? Here the superior individual performs his function. He brings to the new reconstructive task the critical or analysing intellect inherited from the Enlightenment, the faculty which rejects tradition. But he brings also a new creative or synthesizing faculty to which the romanticists gave the name of imagination. It was when superior individuals of eighteenth-century intellect discovered in themselves the new imaginative faculty that they became romanticists. It was when, confronted with a world rendered meaningless by the Enlightenment, they discovered in themselves the will and capacity to transform the world and give it meaning that they embarked on the reconstructive task of the nineteenth century. The new Mythus was to be made out of their imaginative insights into the three main aspects of reality—the past, nature and the self.

In describing through the thin disguise of Teufelsdröckh's autobiography his own intellectual transition from the eighteenth to the nineteenth century, Carlyle shows how the romantic quality of mind grows out of a total crisis of personality. He tells us what it was like to have arrived at the dead-end of the eighteenth century, to inhabit the mechanical universe of the Newtonian world-view, a universe without so much moral meaning as would render it even hostile. "'You cannot so much as believe in a Devil,'" he makes Teufelsdröckh complain. "'To me,'" Teufelsdröckh continues in the best-known passage of *Sartor*, "'the Universe was all void of Life, of Purpose, of Volition, even of Hostility: it was one huge, dead, immeasurable Steam-engine, rolling on, in its dead indifference, to grind me limb from limb.'" The problem was not merely intellectual. The inability to find meaning in the world leads to the inability to respond, to feel: "'Almost since earliest memory I had shed no tear.'"[1] It leads ultimately to the loss of desire to live.

Teufelsdröckh's period of emotional sterility has its parallel in Wordsworth's career at the point when he too arrives at the dead-end of the eighteenth century—when, having lost faith in the French Revolution and having lost through over-use of the analytic "knife" the ability to believe in anything and therefore to feel and live, he "Yielded up," as he tells us in *The Prelude*, "moral questions in despair." "This," he says referring to the eighteenth-century disease of analysis,

> was the crisis of that strong disease,
> This the soul's last and lowest ebb.   (XI, 305-07)[2]

The same crisis occurs in the career of even such a rationalist as John Stuart Mill at the point when, "in a dull state of nerves," he asked himself in his *Autobiography* the question that tests the value of his eighteenth-century radicalism. "'Suppose that all your objects in life were realized; that all the changes in institutions and opinions which you are looking forward to, could be completely effected at this very instant: would this be a great joy and happiness to you?'" The answer, he realizes, is "'No!'" Whereupon "my heart sank . . . I seemed to have nothing left to live for."

The first break in Mill's period of emotional sterility came when he found himself able to shed tears over an affecting passage in a volume of memoirs. "From this moment my burthen grew lighter. The oppression of the thought that all feeling was dead within me, was gone. I was no longer hope-

[1] Bk. II, Chap. VII, pp. 164-65.
[2] 1850 Text. See also Bks. XII and XIII, "Imagination and Taste, How Impaired and Restored."

less: I was not a stock or a stone."[1] For Teufelsdröckh, the break came through a similar discovery of his capacity to feel. But the feeling in his case was hatred, defiance of the mechanical universe. If the universe was a dead machine, then he was different from the universe. For he, as he discovered on that famous "sultry Dogday . . . along the dirty little *Rue Saint-Thomas de l'Enfer*," was alive and free enough to assert his superiority over it.

Thus, he discovered through defiance his own will. But he discovered along with it an opposing will in the universe, a something to defy, an "Everlasting No" which, if he declared himself alien from it, cast him out in return. "'The Everlasting No had said: "Behold, thou art fatherless, outcast, and the Universe is mine (the Devil's)"; to which my whole Me now made answer: "*I* am not thine, but Free, and forever hate thee!"'" If he had not yet discovered God in the universe, he had discovered the Devil; and the Devil was at least meaningful and alive. "'I directly thereupon,'" he says in words corresponding to Mill's, "'began to be a Man.'"[2]

It would be wrong to suppose that Carlyle and Mill have as yet at this point in their careers entered intellectually into the nineteenth century. They have reached at this point a stage equivalent to that of eighteenth-century sentimentalism, a stage we might call negative romanticism or, as the Germans call it, Storm and Stress. It is the stage of tears, of that deluge of tears on the tide of which the eighteenth century was quite washed away making place for the nineteenth.[3] And it is the stage of that posture of defiance which Byron made famous. It is the stage when the individual, after an iconoclastic period in which tradition has been rejected and conviction lost, first changes direction. The change of direction begins when he discovers his own feelings and his own will as a source of value in an otherwise meaningless universe. He is at this stage tearful and defiant because he is in the process of discovering his own life and freedom through exhibiting as much emotion and will as possible.

---

[1] Chap. V, "A Crisis in my Mental History" (London: Longmans, 1873), pp. 133, 134, 141; (New York: Columbia Univ. Press, 1944), pp. 94, 99.

[2] *Sartor*, Bk. II, Chap. VII, pp. 166-68.

[3] Although it is an occupation for wags to calculate by the numbers of buckets the tears shed in eighteenth-century novels, eighteenth-century sentimentalism is a movement of the profoundest significance, the birth pangs of the modern sensibility.

But he still believes in nothing but himself and his infinite capacity for experience, his capacity for feeling something about everything in the world, for absorbing the whole world into his centre of value. With all existing formulations abandoned, he is now ready to step forth like Adam and organize the world according to his own formulations. It is not, however, until he has begun to arrive at some positive formulations, it is not until he has begun to reconstruct the external world and to believe in it, that he can be called a romanticist, a man of the nineteenth century.

Thus Teufelsdröckh, after a period of travel and experience, comes to perceive the "Everlasting Yea" in the universe. He perceives not only that the world is alive but that the spirit pervading it is good. "'The Universe is not dead and demoniacal, a charnel-house with spectres; but godlike and my Father's!'"[1] In the same way Mill goes on, after having discovered feeling in himself, to read Wordsworth and follow him in formulating an ethics of the feelings. "The cultivation of the feelings became one of the cardinal points in my ethical and philosophical creed." Mill achieves a nineteenth-century position when he combines with his eighteenth-century rationalism that deliberate "culture of the feelings" which is its necessary corrective. "The delight which these poems [Wordsworth's] gave me, proved that with culture of this sort, there was nothing to dread from the most confirmed habit of analysis."[2]

Wordsworth himself, after giving up the habit of analysis, returned first to the world of nature as he had known it in childhood, when he had loved without reflection, he tells us in *The Prelude*, all he saw.

> I felt, observed, and pondered; did not judge,
> Yea, never thought of judging; with the gift
> Of all this glory filled and satisfied.
>
> (XII, 188-90)

But the return of sheer feeling dissociated from thought is a temporary phase necessary to cure the opposite habit of thought dissociated from feeling. He soon passes through this

---

[1] *Sartor*, Bk. II, Chap. IX, p. 188.
[2] *Autobiography*, pp. 101, 104.

phase to a renewed interest in man and to a new and higher kind of rationality.

> Thus moderated, thus composed, I found
> Once more in Man an object of delight,
> Of pure imagination, and of love;
> And, as the horizon of my mind enlarged,
> Again I took the intellectual eye
> For my instructor, studious more to see
> Great truths, than touch and handle little ones.

(XIII, 48-54)

The little truths are classified and re-classified by the analytic power. But the great truths are creatively perceived by a combination of thought and feeling, by "those sweet counsels between head and heart" (XI, 353) which Wordsworth in another place calls "Imagination" or "Reason in her most exalted mood" (XIV, 189-92).

It is the whole point of *The Prelude*, as of *Tintern Abbey*, to show how the achievement of this higher rationality inaugurates the period of Wordsworth's career which can properly be called romantic. He was not a romanticist before he left his native hills to plunge intellectually into the eighteenth century. Nor was he quite a romanticist upon his first return to nature after his rationalist period. In *Tintern Abbey* he achieves his characteristic position when, upon revisiting the banks of the Wye in 1798, he finds in nature a moral and religious meaning, a "still sad music of humanity" and a sense of divine presence, that was not there on his first visit five years earlier when nature was for him,

> An appetite; a feeling and a love,
> That had no need of a remoter charm,
> By thought supplied, nor any interest
> Unborrowed from the eye.

Tintern Abbey presents a biographical problem in that Wordsworth seems to equate with his pre-rationalist experience of nature an experience that took place in the year when, according to *The Prelude*, he was beginning to emerge from his rationalist period. There are two possible explanations for this. We can say that *Tintern Abbey* is not strictly autobiographical, that the poet has, for the sake of dramatic clarity, made the 1793 experience stand for his whole youthful as distinguished from his mature experience of nature. Or we can say, as one critic has suggested, that Wordsworth does distinguish his 1793 from his pre-rationalist experience of nature and considers the former unhealthy because regressive.[1] "Nature then," says Wordsworth referring to 1793,

> (The coarser pleasures of my boyish days,
> And their glad animal movements all gone by)
> To me was all in all.

But this was not good, for in 1793 he was

> more like a man
> Flying from something that he dreads than one
> Who sought the thing he loved.

The thing he was flying from was thought. We can therefore say, if this reading is correct, that in 1793 Wordsworth was using nature sentimentally, to put the head to sleep. But both readings lead to the same conclusion, that Wordsworth finds his characteristic subject when he finds in nature not merely sensation and emotion but a system of ideas as well, a whole religion.

It is the return to formulation which is characteristic rather than the formulation itself. For Wordsworth's formulations do not stop with the religion of nature. As early as 1802 he is saying in *Resolution and Independence* that nature is not enough, that there is something in the human spirit which man does not owe to nature. And he is in the same year already at work on the *Intimations of Immortality*, where he is to say that philosophy and Christian faith are other ways of arriving at the truths he used to know instinctively through his earliest experiences of nature. By the time he says in the *Elegiac Stanzas* of 1805 (the year *The Prelude* was completed) that nature can be hostile and man must place his faith elsewhere, he is only a step away from the Christian orthodoxy of the *Ecclesiastical Sonnets*, from the formulation of a new Mythus through the return to an old one. Not only is the return to formulation the subject of Words-

[1] C. H. Gray, "Wordsworth's First Visit to Tintern Abbey," *PMLA*, March 1934.

worth's greatest poetry but it is during the period when the return was in process (the period marked at one end by the volume of 1798 and at the other by the volume of 1807) that all his great, which is to say his romantic, poetry was written.

It makes no difference whether the romanticist arrives in the end at a new formulation or returns to an old one. It is the process of denial and reaffirmation which distinguishes him both from those who have never denied and those who, having denied, have never reaffirmed. Although many romantic careers look like a working back to what had been originally rejected, it would be a mistake to suppose that the position returned to could ever again be the same as the original position. For the position returned to has been *chosen*, and that makes it a romantic reconstruction rather than a dogmatic inheritance.

Teufelsdröckh, after having himself discovered the "Everlasting Yea," bids his readers close their Byron, turn from the most spectacular representative of negative romanticism, of sheer assertion of the will; and open their Goethe, turn to the Goethe of *Wilhelm Meister,* of work and self-renunciation.[1] But Carlyle forgot that the commitment of his hero and Goethe's has validity only because they have arrived at it through experience and self-realization. It is the whole point of *Faust* that the good man, as the Lord suggests in the Prologue, is the developing man. If there is any single morality of romanticism, it is that pronounced by the aged Faust who, after a career of experience, has arrived at his ultimate formulation:

> Yes! to this thought I hold with firm persistence;
> The last result of wisdom stamps it true:
> He only earns his freedom and existence,
> Who daily conquers them anew.[2]

The formulation is that formulation itself must never be allowed to settle into dogma, but must emerge anew every day out of experience. It must be lived, which is to say that it must carry within it its subjective origin, its origin in experience and self-realization.

Carlyle's mistake is repeated by those twentieth-century

[1] *Sartor*, Bk. II, Chap. IX, p. 192.

[2] Part II, V, vi, trans. Bayard Taylor (New York: Modern Library, 1930), p. 241. The complete *Faust Part II* appeared after *Sartor* was written.

traditionalists who not only forget the subjective origins of their own commitment to classicism and Christian dogmatism but would deny to others the same road to commitment. In thinking that they have broken with the nineteenth century, the twentieth-century traditionalists make the historical mistake of identifying romanticism with subjective denial. They forget the direction of romantic thought. They forget that in arriving themselves at an objective position they do not reverse but fulfil the direction of romantic thought. Their very rebellion against the last century is in the tradition of romanticism, which would have every man and every generation start again from the beginning. While the position they arrive at, no matter what it is, even if it includes the rejection of the romantic route by which they arrived at it, remains within the romantic tradition as long as it has been chosen.

For it is not this or that political, philosophical, religious or even aesthetic commitment that marks the romanticist. It is the subjective ground of his commitment, the fact that he never forgets his commitment has been chosen. The commitment is as a result absorbed into a certain atmosphere of mind and sensibility, the essential meaning of which is that the commitment, no matter how absolutist and dogmatic, remains subordinate to the chooser. This atmosphere of mind and sensibility is romantic because it emerges out of an intellectual experience of the eighteenth century, and therefore combines commitment with critical reservation.

Although one dreads reopening at this late date the quarrel over the definition of romanticism, it nevertheless remains impossible to talk long about modern literature without employing, whether explicitly or implicitly, some working definition of the term. Such a working definition can, I think, be achieved at the lowest common denominator of agreement, once we distinguish between romanticism as a permanently recurring characteristic of personalities and artistic periods, and romanticism as that unprecedented shift of mind and sensibility which began in the latter eighteenth century. In the first sense, romanticism is one pole of the eternal alternation between emotion and intellect, freedom and discipline. In the second, it is the attempt of modern man to reintegrate fact and value after having himself rejected, in the experience of the Enlightenment, the old values. Post-Enlightenment romanticism does, to be sure, make use of emotion and freedom, but only as means incidental to the main and, as far as one can make out, historically unique purpose of the movement, which is not in the end to reject intellect and discipline but to renew them by empirical means.

Post-Enlightenment romanticism is historically unique just to the extent that it uses for its reconstructive purpose the same scientific or empirical method which is itself unique to the modern world. Like the scientist's hypothesis, the romanticist's formulation is evolved out of experience and is continually tested against experience. The difference is that the scientist's experiment is a selected and analysed experience, whereas experience for the romanticist is even more empiric because less rationalized. It is what happens before selection and analysis take place. Romanticism is in this sense not so much a reaction against eighteenth-century empiricism as a reaction within it, a corrected empiricism. It is, as Mill suggested, the necessary corrective for the skeptical analytic intellect.

Thus the empiricist Locke, spelling out the philosophical implications of Newton's physics, says that the world of our ordinary perception is largely illusory, that the only objective reality consists of particles of matter moving in space. He gives us a world without aesthetic, moral or spiritual significance. Against such a world-view, the romanticist protests by appealing not to tradition but to his own concrete experience of nature, his own insight into "the life of things." It is *matter* which is the abstraction, the mere theoretical concept derived from an analysis of experience; whereas "the life of things" is what we perceive at the moment when experience is immediate and unanalysed.

"An atom," says Blake, is "a thing which does not exist."[1] For Blake, the "form" or "image," the object not in itself but as perceived, is the concrete fact. The object in itself is an abstraction, a rationalization after the fact, what Blake calls

---

[1] To George Cumberland, 12 April 1827, *Poetry and Prose*, ed. Geoffrey Keynes (London: Nonesuch Press, 1939), p. 927. See also Northrop Frye, *Fearful Symmetry: A Study of William Blake* (Princeton: Princeton University Press, 1947), Chap. I, "The Case Against Locke."

the "memory of an image," which is less certain than the "perception of an image." Wordsworth makes the same point in *The Tables Turned.* "We murder to dissect," he complains, meaning that nature is a living organism and you lose its truth, which is its life, once you analyse it. Goethe makes the same complaint in *Faust:*

> The man who wants to know
> organic truth and describe it well
> seeks first to drive the living spirit out;
> he's got the parts in hand there,
> it's merely the breath of life that's lacking.[1]

The romanticist is not against science. He is merely trying to limit the applicability of its findings. He is objecting to what Whitehead, in *Science and the Modern World,* calls the Fallacy of Misplaced Concreteness—the fallacy by which the eighteenth century mistook an analysis of reality, made because the intellect is too weak to comprehend it as a whole, with the concrete totality by which we must live. "To thee," says Wordsworth to Coleridge in *The Prelude:*

> Science appears but what in truth she is,
> Not as our glory and our absolute boast,
> But as a succedaneum and a prop
> To our infirmity. No officious slave
> Art thou of that false secondary power
> By which we multiply distinctions, then
> Deem that our puny boundaries are things
> That we perceive, and not that we have made.

> (II, 211-19)

"A man, born and bred in the so-called exact sciences," says Goethe, "will, on the height of his analytical reason, not easily comprehend that there is also something like an exact concrete imagination."[2] This "exact concrete imagination" Goethe employed not only for his poetry but for his scientific investigations as well.

Goethe used the same faculty for poetry and science because reality resided for him in what he called the "symbol," by

[1] Part I, "Faust's Study," trans. C. F. MacIntyre (Norfolk, Conn.: New Directions, 1949), p. 60.

[2] Quoted in Erich Heller, *The Disinherited Mind* (Cambridge: Bowes and Bowes, 1952), p. 26.

which he meant not a mere cipher for an abstract idea but the particular with its ideal meaning complete within it. Goethe's "symbol," like Blake's "form" or "image," is what really exists because it is both real and ideal. It is "the living revelation of the unfathomable" which can be comprehended only by what is itself unfathomable, "and the only truly unfathomable faculty of man is love."[1] Romanticism is both idealistic and realistic in that it conceives of the ideal as existing only in conjunction with the real and the real as existing only in conjunction with the ideal. The two are brought into conjunction only in the act of perception when the higher or imaginative rationality brings the ideal to the real by penetrating and possessing the external world as a way of knowing both itself and the external world.

"The great significance of Goethe in the history of the European mind," says Heller, "lies in the fact that he is the last great poet who lived and worked in a continual effort to save the life of poetry *and* the poetry of life."[2] Heller is not entirely right. For while it is true that no poet after Goethe dared intrude into the scientists' own realm, the effort to save the poetry of life, at least in the cultural realm, has continued into our own day along with the effort to save the life of poetry. In both efforts, the imagination has been the instrument of revelation; while the revelation itself has been that living organic reality which the imagination perceives through immediate experience of the external world. Such naturalistic revelation provides the living waters out of which the modern literary movement, from Goethe's time to our own, has sprung and to which it has continually returned for refreshment in its effort to restore the spiritual possibility in the post-Enlightenment world.

But why should immediate experience yield a living reality? Because the act of knowing spontaneously and completely is an act of imaginative projection into the external object, an act of identification with the object; so that the living consciousness perceived in the object is our own. If, in other words, the act

[1] Heller (p. 86), who cites the Goethean word *Anschauung*, which means "the mental process by which we spontaneously grasp, through observation aided by intuition, a thing in its wholeness. Goethe uses it as the opposite of analysis" (p. 58).
[2] p. 25.

of knowing analytically requires that we "murder" the object, treating it as something unlike ourselves, something unalive; the act of knowing organically requires that we imbue the object with life, finding in it the counterpart of our own consciousness.

In *Movements of Thought in the Nineteenth Century*, George Mead describes romantic thought as a way of knowing through playing roles. "For Descartes, I am conscious and therefore exist; for the romanticist, I am conscious of myself and therefore this self, of which I am conscious, exists and with it the objects it knows."[1] Descartes establishes the self on empiric grounds, but has to deduce the object. The romanticist, on the other hand, by projecting himself into the object, playing its role, knows himself in the object. He therefore knows both himself and the object empirically, through the reciprocal process of experience or self-objectification. Farther than this the doctrine of concrete experience cannot go. To know an object, the romanticist must *be* it.

The development of the role-playing or projective attitude of mind can, I think, be attributed to both the historical and psychological moment when the eighteenth-century iconoclastic purpose changes direction to turn into the nineteenth-century reconstructive purpose. For the free-wheeling critical intellect becomes the sympathetic intellect once, unfettered by traditional values, it tries to construct new ones by giving itself in an experimental spirit to every possibility, excluding none. There remains, however, the hard-headed critical awareness that the self is something other than the object, that the identification has been deliberately undertaken and is only temporary. It is this combination of nineteenth-century sympathy with eighteenth-century critical awareness that explains the role-playing attitude. For whether the romanticist projects himself into the past, nature, or another person, he never forgets that he is playing a role. The result is that the experience makes him more acutely aware than ever of his own modernity and his own distinctness from the external world. The process of experience is for the romanticist a process of self-realization, of a constantly expanding discovery of the self through discoveries of its imprint on the external world. Faust, in embark-

[1] Ed. M. H. Moore (Chicago: Chicago University Press, 1944), pp. 82-83.

ing on his career of experience, says that pleasure is not his purpose. He will close his heart, he says,

> to no future pain. I mean to enjoy
> in my innermost being all that is offered to mankind,
> to seize the highest and the lowest,
> to mix all kinds of good and evil,
> and thus expand my Self till it includes
> the spirit of all men—and, with them,
> I shall be ruined and perish in the end.[1]

How, then, does this lead to values? The romanticist discovers through experience the empiric ground for values. He does this by giving himself so completely to each object that the object is allowed to generate its own laws, creating the values compatible with its fullest existence. But since the romanticist finds in the object the values he puts there, he finds also the objectification of at least one aspect of the values compatible with his own fullest existence. The romanticist's sympathy with the object leads to an illumination of beauty and truth in the object—an illumination which involves at the same time an experience of recognition, recognition of this beauty and truth as values he has known potentially all along in himself. As an experience, the illumination is undeniably valid. But once the perception of value is abstracted from the immediate experience and formulated for application elsewhere, it becomes mere theory and therefore problematical. The formulation remains useful, however, as long as it returns us to experience, as long as we earn it, to paraphrase Faust, every day anew.

The romanticist is thus always in the process of formulating values, although he never arrives at a final formulation. Like Faust's, his career of experience ends not logically, with the formulated truth, but naturalistically, with death. What he does achieve, however, as a positive accomplishment, is an expanding potentiality for formulating values, an expanding area of sympathy and insight out of which values of increasing refinement can emerge and to which they can return.

Faust spends the whole poem evolving the law by which his actions are to be judged. His formulations evolve because he

---

[1] Part I, "Faust's Study," p. 55.

senses at each point that his understanding of the experience is inadequate to his total apprehension of it. He does not in the end articulate a general law, but the fact that he does finally arrive at his perfect moment indicates what is confirmed by his salvation after death, that his whole career of experience, even the harm done to Margaret, even the fact that his final bliss is based on a delusion, is justified by the necessity for self-realization, for self-discovery and self-development. Of course, he has known this intuitively from the start, which is why he continually rejects Mephistopheles' too facile formulation of his actions as merely evil. His career bears out the Lord's prediction in the Prologue:

> A good man, struggling in his darkness,
> will always be aware of the true course.[1]

In his total apprehension the good man will be aware of the true course, but his reason will at each point make a temporarily inadequate interpretation of the facts. For in making new values the romanticist employs two modes of apprehension, sympathy and judgment—sympathy being always ahead of judgment, and certain whereas judgment is problematical.

Once we understand that we are interested in romanticism not as a recurring phenomenon but as that movement in thought and art which followed the eighteenth century, it is not difficult to agree, in defining romanticism, on those qualities which could have occurred only after the eighteenth century. Nor is it difficult to account for most of those qualities as determined by the attempt to answer the central question posed by the Enlightenment—the question of tradition, of how, after the collapse of the traditional authority for values, to find and justify new values. It is when we think of romanticism as an attempt to answer this question, as in large measure literature's answer to science, that we can understand it as essentially a doctrine of experience, an attempt to salvage on science's own empiric grounds the validity of the individual perception against scientific abstractions.

The advantage of understanding romanticism in its post-Enlightenment character, as a doctrine of experience, is that we understand it as the movement which unites us to the last

[1] Part I, "Faust's Study," p. 4.

century instead of separating us from it. For we are still children of the Enlightenment. We are still trying to mark out a path through the wilderness bequeathed us by the Enlightenment; we are still seeking values in a world where neither tradition nor science offers much assistance to that end. If anything, the wilderness has grown wilder since the last century. Time, two world wars and universal social upheaval have removed us even farther from the traditional past; while the spread of technological culture has given science an increasing dominion over our lives. To bridge the increased gap between knowledge and value we ought to require, if our reasoning thus far has been correct, an even more extreme and articulated romanticism. The question even arises whether in the post-Enlightenment world, in a scientific and democratic age, literature, whatever its program, can be anything but romantic in the sense I mean. Are not, after all, even our new classicisms and new Christian dogmatisms really romanticisms in an age which simply cannot supply the world-views such doctrines depend on, so that they become, for all their claims to objectivity, merely another opinion, the objectification of somebody's personal view?

It would hardly be necessary to insist on this line of continuity with the nineteenth century, were it not that the rejection of romanticism has been the issue with which the twentieth-century literary movement, especially in poetry, has declared its independence of its nineteenth-century predecessor. The main charges against romantic poetry have been that it is subjective, that it is sentimental, that its diction is inflated, and that it lacks form. In regard to the first charge I have, I believe, already said enough to indicate that it is an historical mistake to accuse the romanticists of subjectivism. It is to misunderstand the *direction* of romantic thought. For subjectivity was not the program but the inescapable condition of romanticism. No sooner had the eighteenth century left the individual isolated within himself—without an objective counterpart for the values he sensed in his own will and feelings—than romanticism began as a movement toward objectivity, toward a new principle of connection with society and nature through the imposition of values on the external world. Wordsworth wrote

The Prelude, the model in English of the subjective or auto-biographical poem, not because he believed in autobiographical poetry but in order to prepare himself for a long philosophical poem treating of the "mind of man." He wrote it because he felt as yet inadequate to the objective undertaking, out of "real humility": "Here, at least, I hoped that to a certain degree I should be sure of succeeding, as I had nothing to do but describe what I had felt and thought."[1]

The whole conscious concern with objectivity as a *problem*, as something to be achieved, is in fact specifically romantic. Objectivity presented no problem to an age of faith like the Middle Ages, which considered the object and its value as equally *given*. Nor did it present a problem to a critical and rationalist age like the Enlightenment, the whole point of which was to undermine the established order of values by driving a wedge between the object and its value. It was the romanticists with their new reconstructive purpose who, starting with an inherited split between object and value and wanting to heal the breach, saw objectivity as desirable and as difficult to achieve. When subjectivity came to be called a disease (*la maladie du siècle*), the Romantic period had begun. "Look you, the end of this disease is death!" said Goethe,[2] who as early as 1774 sought to deliver himself from the disease by writing *Werther*. The complaint continued throughout the next century into our own. Goethe had his Faust pass through the *sickness* (subjectivity) of Part I in order to achieve the *health* (objectivity) of Part II. Coleridge suffered from subjectivity:

> Such punishments, I said, were due
> To natures deepliest stained with sin,—
> For aye entempesting anew
> The unfathomable hell within.[3]

Byron, "the wandering outlaw of his own dark mind," tried to exorcise the devil of subjectivity with the laughter of *Don Juan*. Carlyle preached Work as an escape from subjectivity. Arnold

---

[1] To Sir George Beaumont, 1 May 1805, *The Early Letters of William and Dorothy Wordsworth (1787-1805)*, ed. Ernest de Selincourt (Oxford: Clarendon Press, 1935), p. 489.

[2] Quoted in Karl Viëtor, *Goethe the Poet* (Cambridge, Mass: Harvard University Press, 1949), p. 28.

[3] *The Pains of Sleep*.

found in his own *Empedocles* the example of what was wrong with modern poetry—that it deals with situations

> in which the suffering finds no vent in action; in which a continuous state of mental distress is prolonged, unrelieved by incident, hope, or resistance; in which there is everything to be endured, nothing to be done.[1]

And in our own time a militant insistence upon objectivity characterizes the leading critical doctrines: Yeats' *mask*, that the poet must not write about himself but about the antithesis of himself; Eliot's *catalyst*, that the poet acts like a catalyst to bring the poetic elements into combination but remains himself outside the poem; and Eliot's *objective correlative*, that emotion cannot be stated as a description of subjectivity but must be presented through

> a set of objects, a situation, a chain of events which shall be the formula of that *particular* emotion; such that when the external facts, which must terminate in sensory experience, are given, the emotion is immediately evoked . . . this is precisely what is deficient in *Hamlet*. Hamlet (the man) is dominated by an emotion which is inexpressible, because it is in *excess* of the facts as they appear.[2]

One is reminded here of Arnold's strictures on *Empedocles*.

It should be clear, then, that the desire to overcome subjectivity and achieve objectivity is by no means peculiar to the twentieth century, but has determined the direction of poetic development since the end of the Enlightenment. Certain twentieth-century poets have, it is true, tried to escape the post-Enlightenment condition by attaching their poetry to dogmas. Yeats with his cosmology of cones and gyres, Eliot with his Anglo-Catholicism, the Auden circle of the 'thirties with their Marxism, all sought to create for their poetry the external condition enjoyed by the Middle Ages and the Renaissance. By positing an objective order of values, they sought to make their poetry not so much an externalization of

[1] Preface to the 1853 edition of his *Poems* (London: Oxford University Press, 1945), pp. 2-3.

[2] "Hamlet," *Selected Essays* (London: Faber and Faber), p. 145; (New York: Harcourt, Brace), pp. 124-25. For the *catalyst*, see "Tradition and the Individual Talent" in the same volume. For Yeats' doctrine of the *mask*, see T. R. Henn, *The Lonely Tower* (London: Methuen, 1950), and Richard Ellman, *Yeats: The Man and The Masks* (New York: Macmillan, 1948).

their own minds as an imitation of an external system of ideas.

Yeats, for example, once he had established his cosmology, was not in his own view making metaphors but, like Dante, describing objectivity. Yet Yeats can hardly be said to have succeeded in his aim, since his cosmology remained after all a private one; while the Auden circle, in renouncing Marxism, have admitted the failure of their aim. Eliot apparently rests secure on the rock of Christian dogma, but his success is no less characteristic of the romantic movement than the failure of the others. For if the others failed because of the romantic condition, he has apparently succeeded in accordance with the romantic prescription—in having intellectually worked his way back from the Enlightenment, in having achieved the goal of the romantic quest for commitment. His poetry is romantic in that it gives a history of that quest and is more consistent in its autobiographical development than any poetry in English since Wordsworth's.

Once we grant that the return to objectivity is a purpose distinctive of the literature since the Enlightenment, then the poetry of the last one hundred and seventy-five years or so can be understood as belonging to a single developing tradition in which the romantic idea, far from having been rejected, is being perpetually realized through isolation from incidental accretions—from eighteenth-century accretions in the nineteenth century, and from nineteenth-century accretions in the twentieth. It is, for example, as eighteenth-century accretions that we can explain the sentimentalism and inflated diction of which romantic poetry has been accused.

Sentimentalism is an eighteenth-century phenomenon in that it belongs to Locke's world where the push and pull of atoms was considered the only reality. In such a world the individual fell back upon the feelings, but with the fundamental acknowledgment that they did not reflect reality. Even today sentimentalism flourishes among the so-called Philistines—in just those circles, that is, where the Lockian world-view persists, where respect for beauty is at its lowest and the *real* is equated with the ugly and mechanistic, with whatever is antithetical to human wishes. But the romanticists were prepared precisely to take up the issue that the sentimentalists were content to let lie. They were out to transform reality, to show that it had no existence apart from the emotional apprehension of it. It is where the romantic transformation does not come off, where emotion remains opposed to an object that will not yield it back, that a poem falls into sentimentalism or bathos. But the point is that sentimentalism is the failure of romantic poetry not its characteristic. The sentimental poem has not achieved the romantic fusion, it has been unable to win out over the eighteenth century.

In the same way, there is nothing new or distinctively nineteenth-century in the inflated diction of which there was certainly plenty. To the extent that there were innovations in diction, they were in the direction of plainness and colloquialism, as in Wordsworth, Browning and Hopkins. The nineteenth-century poets who were not innovators of diction simply continued with the cluster of Spenser, Milton and the neo-classicists which had constituted the norm of mid-eighteenth-century style. It is that mid-eighteenth-century style which is most often meant when "romantic" diction is criticized. But to the extent that poets take over a conventional style, they are not being romantic at all but quite traditional.

It may be argued that the romanticists were responsible for the revival of archaic diction. But insofar as this was a revival of what had become extinct, as distinguished from a continuation of what was becoming stale, the archaic revival was surely as beneficial for refreshing the language and enlarging its resources as, say, the introduction of scientific words by twentieth-century poets. The use of archaic diction is sufficiently justified by *The Ancient Mariner*; while Eliot himself has shown how effective it can be, in *East Coker*: "In daunsinge, signifying matrimonie," and in that bewitching quotation in *Little Gidding*: "Sin is Behovely."

There remains still the charge of formlessness which has been levelled against romantic poetry. If, however, we consider form as existing not only around the edges of a poem but in the relation of all its parts, it is hardly possible for a poem which has meaning to be formless, to have no discernible relation between its parts.[1] It is possible for a poem not to adhere to established forms, or to have no relation (though this is un-

[1] For a discussion of this idea, see Jacques Barzun, "The Fetish of Form: An Example from Music," *Kenyon Review*, Winter 1950.

likely) to the forms of other poems. It is also possible for a poet not to be aware of the relation between one poem of his and another, or between his poetry and that of his contemporaries. It is possible for poets and critics not yet to have generalized the rationale of a new kind of poetry.

This is, I think, the case with the romantic poets and their critics. In making their new kind of poetry, many romanticists announced that they were sacrificing form in the interest of *sincerity*. They announced an ideal of artlessness—Coleridge finding the perfect poet in the Eolian harp which being played on by the wind makes music without intervention of art, Shelley finding him in the skylark which pours out its

> full heart
> In profuse strains of unpremeditated art,

Faust teaching the pedantic classicist, Wagner, that sincerity is the only effective rhetoric:

> but you'll never move others, heart to heart,
> unless your speech comes from your own heart.[1]

Yet the anti-rhetorical style is itself a rhetoric. For there remains, between the sincere feeling in the heart and the effect of sincerity on the page, the art of communication. Literary scholarship has by now discounted the popular illusion that the best romantic poetry sprang full-blown from the poet's heart, unrevised and unlaboured (that the illusion existed is a sign of the success of the romantic rhetoric). The point therefore in understanding the form of romantic poetry is to understand how the sincere, unpremeditated effect is achieved—the history of romanticism being largely the history of the attempt of poets and critics to arrive at that understanding. The fact that the so-called reactions against romanticism, from the Victorian reaction to the reaction of our own time, have all called for more objectivity and more form is a sign that they have been attempts to articulate a form potential in romantic poetry from the start.

For it is with form as with objectivity; at the same time that

---

[1] Part I, "Night," p. 13. See Coleridge's *The Eolian Harp* and Shelley's *To a Skylark*.

the romanticists broke away from both, they were also pre-occupied to a degree unknown before with working back to both. Goethe was for most of his career a professed classicist, who sought to emulate in his poetry the abstraction and pure formalism of Greek sculpture; and we owe to German romanticism generally the unprecedented glorification of Greece in modern times. It is too often forgotten that romanticism was as much responsible for a Greek as for a medieval revival, the former having had as a matter of fact the more widespread and enduring effect. It should also be remembered that the Greek interest of most nineteenth-century literary men was in the formal aspects of Greek aesthetics, as distinguished from the Renaissance interest in the Greek ethos. For the Renaissance, Greece offered an alternative way of life to Christian culture (Shelley's Greek interest was in this respect Renaissance); but for the nineteenth century, Greece came to represent objectivity and form as opposed to modern subjectivity and naturalism. Toward the end of the century, the aesthetic capital shifted for some people from Greece to Byzantium or Japan, because they found as they moved eastward a more extreme stylization.

Yeats' *Sailing to Byzantium* is less a reaction against Keats' *Ode on a Grecian Urn* than it is a more extreme articulation of Keats' essential idea. Where Keats sees in the formal perfection of Greek plastic art an idealization of nature, Yeats sees in the two-dimensional golden abstractness of the Byzantine mosaics a rejection of nature. The difference is of degree not kind. Both poets recognize the Lockian split between the real and the ideal, and both see that the artist must transform the real into the ideal. The difference is in the amount of transformation which each considered necessary. Yeats required a more radical transformation because he saw the split as wider. The fact that Yeats had to turn Keats' recognition of the split between art and nature into a belligerently anti-naturalistic position is a sign that his is, if anything, the more extreme romanticism, the more radical solution of the more radical problem.

For if romanticism gave rise to the poetry of artlessness spontaneity, and sincerity, to the "spasmodic" poets, Whitman and free verse; it also gave rise, and this has been its more enduring contribution, to Keats, the pre-Raphaelites, and the aesthetic and symbolist movements, to the poetry of art, even of artifice and insincerity. The doctrine of insincerity that characterized the aesthetic movement is a sign of the connection of that movement with romanticism and the doctrine of sincerity. Neither would have been conceivable as classical doctrine. The classical poet could afford to distinguish between the subjectivity of his lyric poetry and the objectivity of his narrative and dramatic poetry, because he had no trouble being objective when he wanted to be. It is only when meaning is in the epistemological sense a personal creation that the distinction between the subjective and objective statement breaks down and the poet feels it necessary to mask the subjective origin of his idea, to expend art to objectify it. *Insincerity* together with its offshoot Yeats' *mask*, in fact the whole literary attempt since the late nineteenth century to escape from personality, have created a literature in which sincerity and autobiography are encoded, written backwards.[1]

We would therefore require, to talk intelligently about the form of romantic poetry, a theory which could account for both the artlessness and the artifice, the sincerity and the insincerity, the subjectivity and the objectivity, of poetry since the Enlightenment. We would require, in other words, a theory to connect the poetry of the nineteenth and twentieth centuries, to connect romanticism with the so-called reactions against it. We are now in a position to advance such a theory. For having seen the poetry which set out to be different from romantic poetry, we can find in the core that remains unchanged the essential idea of romanticism. That essential idea is, I would suggest, the doctrine of experience—the doctrine that the imaginative apprehension gained through immediate experience is primary and certain, whereas the analytic reflection that follows is secondary and problematical. The poetry of the nineteenth and twentieth centuries can thus be seen in connection as a poetry of experience—a poetry constructed upon the deliberate disequilibrium between experience and idea, a poetry which makes its statement not as an idea but as an experience from

[1] For a discussion of the aesthetic movement's doctrine of insincerity in connection with Yeats' doctrine of the mask, see Ellman, *Yeats: The Man and the Masks*, Chap. VI.

which one or more ideas can be abstracted as problematical rationalizations.

Much could be learned from the isolation of a poetry of experience. It would reveal for the first time, in addition to the distinctively romantic sensibility and subject matter which we already know, a distinctively romantic form in poetry—a form of which the potentials are realized in the so-called reactions against romantic poetry, in the dramatic monologues of the Victorians and the symbolist poems of the moderns. Such a form, furthermore, if it were treated as a way of meaning, a way of establishing the validity of a poetic statement, would become the best index of a distinctively modern tradition. What better sign can there be, after all, of a culture's real belief than the principle by which it establishes the validity of its statements of value? And what better sign can there be of its coherence than the fact that it can make such statements, statements combining its unspoken convictions on the nature of truth, goodness and beauty? Form is a better index of a tradition than subject matter in that subject matter is often controversial; it is often an index of what people think they believe, whereas form is an index of what is believed too implicitly to be discussed.

Since a new culture, like a new art, looks disorderly until we discover its principle of order, and since the principle which gives order to a culture is intimately related to the principle which gives order to its art, the critic who finds the latter principle is by implication at least helping to find the former. If in addition to isolating the poetry of experience as a form, as a way of establishing in an anti-dogmatic and empiricist age a truth based on the disequilibrium between experience and idea, he could show that there emerges from this deliberate disequilibrium a correspondingly new moral and aesthetic symmetry—he would have suggested at least one line of coherence by which to discern in the bewildering heterogeneity of modern culture a distinctively modern tradition. Such a tradition would present a curious paradox in that it would have been created out of the rejection of tradition and the preoccupation with its loss. We would find that the artists and thinkers of the last one hundred and seventy-five years or so have, in proclaiming the freedom of modern life, actually laid down new rules for it, that they have, in proclaiming its meaninglessness and disunity, formulated for it a new meaning and a new unity.[1]

[1] The work of counting up the cultural treasure of the nineteenth and twentieth centuries and formulating from it a modern tradition may well fall upon the now emerging literary generation—a generation already recognizable as more critical than creative just because we of that generation have, I think, been rendered silent by our reverence for the immediate past, by our sense of having inherited a modern tradition, of having to master an impressive canon of modern "classics" before we can speak out in our own right.

The Dramatic Lyric and the Lyrical Drama

THE qualities which the twentieth century dislikes in the poetry of the nineteenth stem mainly from a dissociation, to use the phrase Eliot made famous, of sensibility from thought. "In the seventeenth century," says Eliot in his essay on the metaphysical poets, "a dissociation of sensibility set in, from which we have never recovered." Until about the middle of the seventeenth century, poets were able to think and feel together; they could, in Eliot's words, apprehend thought sensuously or re-create it into feeling, making of it an experience that modified the sensibility. But since that time poets have had to think or feel in turns. The sentimental age began with those poets who turned away from the purely cerebral alternative (chosen by Dryden and Pope) in order to make feeling possible. Their choice led in the eighteenth and nineteenth centuries to what Eliot calls a "reflective" poetry, a poetry alternating between thought and feeling and therefore to be distinguished from the "intellectual" poetry of Donne, the Elizabethan dramatists and Dante—from the poetry of *the* tradition. The difference between the poetry of Donne and the poetry of Tennyson and Browning is not "a simple difference of degree between poets. It is something which had happened to the mind of England."[1]

The thing which had happened was, as I have suggested, Newton, Locke and the Enlightenment. Thought and emotion were no longer complementary, they gave different, even opposite, reports on reality. In the conflict between thought and emotion we find, as Eliot recognizes, the unique condition of post-Enlightenment poetry. But we also find its unique form in the attempt to heal the breach—an attempt which began with sentimentalism.

The attempt began with those poets of the neoclassic age who in trying—as a counterpoint to the satirical and didactic

[1] *Selected Essays* (London, Faber), p. 273; (New York, Harcourt, Brace), p. 247.

poetry of the time—to be lyrical, found it necessary to give their lyrical poems a dramatic setting, to draw their feelings and reflections out of the observation of a scene remarkable for its beauty or picturesqueness. The result was a lyric type of which Gray's *Elegy in a Country Churchyard* is the best-known example and which Dr Johnson recognized as a "new scheme of poetry," describing it as "*local poetry*, of which the fundamental subject is some particular landscape to be poetically described, with the addition of such embellishments as may be supplied by historical retrospection or incidental meditation."[1] In this so-called topographical or meditative-descriptive type, post-Enlightenment poetry begins the search for its appropriate form. For what the meditative-descriptive poem tries to do is combine thought and feeling by providing an occasion which can give rise to both and can justify both as having an objective counterpart.

Take, for example, these lines from Denham's *Cooper's Hill* (1643), the poem which Johnson says is the original of the type. Johnson quotes the lines because they have been imitated, since Dryden commended them, by almost every poet for a century past.

> O could I flow like thee, and make thy stream
> My great example, as it is my theme!
> Though deep, yet clear; though gentle, yet not dull;
> Strong without rage, without o'erflowing full.

The epigrammatic quality of these particular lines would have appealed to Dryden. But the thing that distinguishes the poem from the usual neoclassic poem of epigrammatic statement is the poet's attempt to give the genesis of his moral reflection in an emotion which in turn proceeds from the river. Johnson, while praising the lines for their epigrammatic quality, puts his finger on their main fault. "Most of the words thus artfully opposed are to be understood simply on one side of the comparison, and metaphorically on the other; and if there be any language which does not express intellectual operations by material images, into that language they cannot be translated."[2]

[1] "Denham," *Lives of the English Poets*, ed. G. B. Hill (Oxford: Clarendon Press, 1905),I, 77.
[2] pp. 78-79.

In other words, the river remains a rhetorical device, an analogy. We do not believe in it as a perceived object, which is to say we do not believe that the thought proceeds from the emotion and that both proceed from the river. Thought, emotion and object are discrete quantities in mere juxtaposition. Since the river is expected to yield a significance which it in fact does not yield, the poem remains sentimental as do most of the meditative-descriptive poems of the seventeenth and eighteenth centuries.

Yet this was the poetry that Wordsworth began by writing, and that Coleridge admired in the sonnets of Bowles. In the original attachment of the two poets to the sentimental poetry of the eighteenth century and in their eventual break with it, we can see both the roots of romantic poetry and its distinctive contribution. For what Coleridge came to dislike in Bowles was his "perpetual trick of moralizing everything," of connecting natural appearances "by dim analogies, with the moral world." Nature "has her proper interest," says Coleridge; and "a poet's heart and intellect should be *combined*, intimately combined and unified with the great appearances of nature, and not merely held in solution and loose mixture with them, in the shape of formal similes." It is at least one way of understanding the romantic contribution in poetry to say that the thing romanticism had to do was fuse the elements of thought, feeling and perceived object, which in sentimental poetry were merely juxtaposed. The movement of mind which led Coleridge to reject Bowles was also responsible for the famous distinction—which he makes formally for the first time in this same passage—between the "fancy" or "aggregating" faculty, the faculty of a dissociated poetry whether cerebral or sentimental, and the "imagination" or "*modifying* and coadunating" faculty, the faculty of a traditionally integrated and a romantically re-integrated poetry.[1]

Wordsworth's poetic development from the sentimental *Descriptive Sketches* (1793) to the romantic *Tintern Abbey* (1798) is a development in fusion. The former poem, dealing in epigram-

[1] *Letters*, ed. E. L. Griggs (Oxford: Clarendon Press, 1956); ed. E. H. Coleridge (Boston and New York: Houghton Mifflin, 1895), I, 403-5. I have drawn for this paragraph upon M. H. Abrams, "Wordsworth and Coleridge on Diction and Figures," *English Institute Essays 1952* (New York: Columbia University Press, 1954), pp. 193-96.

matic couplets with the poet's walking tour of the Alps, combines descriptions of Alpine scenery with reflections on the virtues of nature, the natural life, Swiss history and Swiss freedom. Although the verse is skilful and the natural descriptions in many places superb, the ideas come ready made from sources outside the poem, with the result that their imposition on the landscape either strikes us as superfluous or reduces the landscape to a metaphor.

> And what if ospreys, cormorants, herons cry,
> Amid tempestuous vapours driving by,
> Or hovering over wastes too bleak to rear
> That common growth of earth, the foodful ear;
> Where the green apple shrivels on the spray,
> And pines the unripened pear in summer's kindliest ray;
> Contentment shares the desolate domain
> With Independence, child of high Disdain.
> Exulting 'mid the winter of the skies,
> Shy as the jealous chamois, Freedom flies,
> And often grasps her sword.

In a subsequent passage, however, we see promise of the romantic Wordsworth:

> Swoln with incessant rains from hour to hour,
> All day the floods a deepening murmur pour:
> The sky is veiled, and every cheerful sight:
> Dark is the region as with coming night;
> But what a sudden burst of overpowering light!
> Triumphant on the bosom of the storm,
> Glances the wheeling eagle's glorious form!
> Eastward, in long perspective glittering, shine
> The wood-crowned cliffs that o'er the lake recline;
> Those lofty cliffs a hundred streams unfold,
> At once to pillars turned that flame with gold:
> Behind his sail the peasant shrinks, to shun
> The *west*, that burns like one dilated sun,
> A crucible of mighty compass, felt
> By mountains, glowing till they seem to melt.

Here we can be sure the landscape is seen because it is in perspective, a sign that a located observer is seeing it in the present. The passage develops, not through relation to external ideas but dramatically, to an unexpected climax. The meaning is in the intensification of the glowing to the point where the observer apprehends it from inside the mountains—where he has, in other words, a revelation of his own sentience in nature, of the life of things.

The passage foreshadows the many passages of sudden revelation in *The Prelude*. Wordsworth tells, for example, how as a child he stole a boat and went rowing on a lake one moonlit night, when a high mountain, that suddenly became visible after he had rowed some distance from the shore, seemed to be following him. The sudden appearance so broke up his normal perspective that the mountain seemed to have a will of its own, to be approaching him when he was withdrawing from it. With "trembling oars," he turned around and put the boat back in its place. He was haunted for days afterward by a sense of "unknown modes of being," an atmosphere of "darkness" or "blank desertion" (I, 393-95). Or again, when ice-skating as a child, things would seem to spin around him. He would stop short suddenly, but things would go on spinning and he would have a revelation of the earth's motion:

> yet still the solitary cliffs
> Wheeled by me—even as if the earth had rolled
> With visible motion her diurnal round!
> Behind me did they stretch in solemn train
> Feebler and feebler, and I stood and watched
> Till all was tranquil as a dreamless sleep.

> (I, 458-63)

In both passages, the revelation proceeds from an optical illusion which, by disrupting the ordinary appearance of things, allows the imagination to transform them into significance. The effect of the revelation is to make us feel that so extraordinary a perspective is no less true to the reality of the object than an ordinary perspective, that it is even in a sense truer. For while the extraordinary perspective affords as limited an aspect of the object as the ordinary perspective, it does, by allowing our imagination an entry into the object, afford at least an intuition of the object in its ultimate reality—in its organic connection that is with the observer and, through the observer's innate conception of universality, with the universe. It is in their organic connection with Wordsworth's guilty conscience and sense of Deity in the first passage, and with his sense of the cosmos in the second, that the mountain and the spinning landscape come alive. But this identification with the object, this way of seeing it in its original concreteness before it has been abstracted from perception, is possible only when the "film of familiarity," in Coleridge's phrase, has been lifted from the eyes—or as Wordsworth puts it in the Preface to *Lyrical Ballads*, when a "certain colouring of imagination" is thrown over ordinary things by presenting them to the mind "in an unusual aspect."

The extraordinary perspective is a sign that the experience is really taking place, that the object is *seen* and not merely remembered from a public or abstract view of it. The experience has validity just because it is dramatized as an event which we must accept as having taken place, rather than formulated as an idea with which we must agree or disagree. Wordsworth will spend the rest of his career trying to understand such childhood experiences, but his formulations will never be adequate to the perception. The fact that the perception eludes final formulation is a sign of its concreteness, as is the fact that at the moment of experience the perception shades off into inarticulateness, into a numinous *atmosphere*.

Even where, as in *Tintern Abbey*, Wordsworth deals with a change in his ideas, the change of ideas is the incomplete articulation of a change in perception. The opening description of the landscape, with its emphasis on the physical sameness of the scene and its contrasting emphasis on the five long years that have passed since the poet's previous visit, raises a question. The poet's perception of the landscape exceeds his understanding; there is some change in the perception which the physical sameness of the scene renders unaccountable. He will spend the rest of the poem trying to understand his perception. He does this, first, by remembering what the landscape has meant to him in the intervening five years, then by hoping that it will have the same effect upon him in future. This makes him realize how much he has changed since the last visit, and then he understands that the new elements in his perception are "the still sad music of humanity" and the sense of a morally elevating "presence" in nature. His perception of nature now combines with the purely emotional response of the last visit an intellectual and moral response.

The poem is, in other words, about the dissociation of sensibility from thought and their reintegration. Having had to abandon his childhood intuitions for the sake of thought, and having had to abandon thought when he would recover (as in his last visit) an emotional response to nature, the poet has now managed to bind his days together, to see in his childhood intuitions the origin of his moral ideas and to find both in his unified response to the external scene. "Therefore" he is "still," in spite of the evolution of his thought, "A lover of the meadows and the woods," being "well pleased to recognize," he concludes in the final lines of the main section,

> In nature and the language of the sense
> The anchor of my purest thoughts, the nurse,
> The guide, the guardian of my heart, and soul
> Of all my moral being.

We should not suppose, however, that these lines are the climax of the poem, and the final passage in which the poet turns to his sister a mere postscript. If this were so, the original perception would have been completely formulated and the poem would be the equivalent of a true or false statement. The lines offer instead the partial articulation of a deeper, more mysterious perception which has now opened out from the first—a perception of a benevolent working of things which, if we fit our life into it, roots our most sophisticated idea in our most primitive impulse, uniting youth with age, the external with the internal, sense with idea, and matter with spirit.

It is as a way of expressing what formulation has left unexpressed that the poet makes the concretely dramatic movement by which he turns upon his sister the love and joy with which the perception fills him, and the vision which he carries over from the landscape. Now he sees in her what he once was, and sees in the difference between them what she shall be. He has a transforming vision of her as a child of nature blessed in all the stages of her life; and by identifying her future memory of this visit with his own and with his present memory of his last visit, he sees in the different stages of their development along the same line the rhythm and harmony of things. All this comes together in the graceful conclusion of the poem, where the poet turns his eyes back to the landscape:

> Nor wilt thou then forget
> That after many wanderings, many years
> Of absence, these steep woods and lofty cliffs,
> And this green pastoral landscape, were to me
> More dear, both for themselves and for thy sake!

thus connecting in one concrete vision himself, his sister and the landscape, their love for each other and for nature, nature's love for them, and past, present and future, time and timelessness. It is just because the poet now finds all this on returning to his original view of the landscape that we can measure the distance he has come, his gain in perception.

We find the same circular movement in Coleridge's *Frost at Midnight*, where in the unnatural silence of his cottage the poet becomes aware of the silent working of the frost outside:

> The Frost performs its secret ministry,
> Unhelped by any wind.

In trying to understand the "secret," the poet remembers his shut-up, lonely boyhood in a city school; then, turning to his sleeping baby whose breathings filling up

> the interspersèd vacancies
> And momentary pauses of the thought

seem part of that same mysterious process going on beneath the threshold of silence, he realizes with a thrill that his child will grow up amid far different surroundings than he did and will receive its education through harmonious union with this natural process. But the idea of nature as educator is not the point of the poem; it is a step toward a larger perception, a perception of the natural process itself. For the poet now sees his child, in a transforming vision similar to Wordsworth's vision of his sister, as a wanderer among natural beauties, a beloved child of nature; and in describing the seasons, all of which shall be sweet to this child of nature, he returns with a grace equal to that of *Tintern Abbey* to his original vision of the frost:

> whether the eave-drops fall
> Heard only in the trances of the blast,
> Or if the secret ministry of frost
> Shall hang them up in silent icicles,
> Quietly shining to the quiet Moon.

The meaning of the poem is in all that has accrued since the original vision, in the gain in perception. But the gain is rather in the intensity of understanding than in what is understood. The word "ministry" now includes the vision of the child of nature to give an intenser understanding than in its original occurrence of the beneficent and numinous quality of the natural process; while "trances of the blast" includes "unhelped by any wind" and "the interspersèd vacancies" to give an intenser understanding of the area of silence where the process goes forward. If there is in the final vision a new transforming element, it is the added detail of the last line which reveals in and through the mystery of process the still profounder mystery of permanence. This shift in the location of the mystery may account for the small *f* of the second "frost" as making way for the capital *M* of "Moon." For here, as in *Tintern Abbey*, the revelation is not a formulated idea that dispels mystery, but a perception that advances in intensity to a deeper and wider, a more inclusive, mystery. The sudden advance in intensity gives a dynamic effect, a sense of movement, of the moving, stirring life of the mystery. It is the whole purpose of the poem, its way of meaning, to give just this apprehension of life, to transform knowledge into experience.

Joyce has taught us, in connection with the latest form of the short story, to call this way of meaning an *epiphany*—a manifestation in and through the visible world of an invisible life. But the epiphany does not begin in literature with the short stories of Joyce or Chekhov. It is the essential innovation of *Lyrical Ballads* and the effect toward which the meditative-descriptive poems of the neoclassic period were striving. For the epiphany, in the literary sense, is a way of apprehending value when value is no longer objective—when it is no longer in nature, which is to say in a publicly accepted order of ideas about nature. The epiphany grounds the statement of value in perception; it gives the idea with its genesis, establishing its validity not as conforming to a public order of values but as the genuine experience of an identifiable person. It gives us the idea, in other words, before we have to pass judgment on its truth or falsity, before it has been abstracted from perception—while it is still in union with emotion and the perceived object.

The unified response of the epiphany differs from that of traditional poetry in being built upon, indeed achieved as a victory over, an original dissociation of thought and feeling. In traditional poetry, the unified response belongs to the poet as his normal equipment, as the appropriate response to an objective reality which combines fact and value. But it comes in the epiphany as the climax of a dramatic action, and lasts a moment only. We are then returned to the world of ordinary perception and left with the question whether the idea we carry away from the experience is true. It is in this distinction—this new disequilibrium between the moment of insight, which is certain, and the problematical idea we abstract from it—that we can discern a distinctively modern form of literature, a form imitating not nature or an order of ideas about nature but the structure of experience itself: a poetry of experience.

What Dr Johnson understood to be the "*local*" or located quality of Denham's "new scheme of poetry" is in fact the essential characteristic of a poetry of experience. For locating the statement of value makes it an occurrence, something which happens to someone at a particular time in a particular place. The problem in writing such a poetry, the problem which Denham and most of the meditative-descriptive poets of the neoclassic period failed to solve, is to keep the poem located—to keep the dramatic situation from turning into a rhetorical device and the landscape from turning into a metaphor for an abstract idea. It remained for the romanticists to solve this problem; and their solution suggests the technique for a poetry of experience, for whatever is new in the form of romantic poetry.

We have already seen that the difference between Wordsworth's pre-romantic and romantic poetry is largely in the organization of the latter within a particular, even an extraordinary perspective. The particular or, more emphatically, the extraordinary perspective keeps the landscape intact by giving evidence of its being looked upon. It locates the poem more firmly by specifically locating the speaker with reference to everything he sees and hears; and this establishes the concreteness not only of the landscape but of the speaker as well, thus keeping the dramatic situation intact as an exchange between two real identities. The authority of the perspective is, of course, reinforced by the autobiographical connection of romantic poetry, by the identification of the speaker as Wordsworth or Coleridge and of the location as places where they are known to have been.

But even more important, the particular perspective marks out the limits within which the poem has its existence. The landscape of *Tintern Abbey* is not seen, like a landscape in traditional poetry, as it is in itself, which is to say in its conventional aspect (front view and on a level plane). It is seen in the opening passage from above, so that we must stand where the poet stands and borrow his eyes in order to follow the consistency of the distortion:

> These plots of cottage-ground, these orchard-tufts, . . .
> These hedge-rows, hardly hedge-rows, little lines
> Of sportive wood run wild: . . .
>   and wreaths of smoke
> Sent up, in silence, from among the trees!

Since in borrowing the poet's eyes we borrow also the past experience behind them, we are ready to see what he sees right through to the ultimate vision. But the content and meaning of what he sees has existence and validity only within the limiting conditions of his gaze, which is why any idea we may abstract from the poem for general application is problematical. For not only is this a particular view of a particular landscape; but it is only Wordsworth, at that particular point in his life, with his particular problems and memories and with his sister beside him, who can see what he sees and find the meaning he finds. The emphasis on particularity (the autobiographical connection being one of the means of achieving it) is a guarantee that the poem is an authentic experience which gives birth to an idea rather than the illustration of a ready-made idea.

In Shelley the extraordinary perspective is often upward. Mont Blanc is so high that the climbing vision,

> the very spirit fails
> Driven like a homeless cloud from steep to steep
> That vanished among the viewless gales!

And the skylark, mounting like a "cloud of fire," seems to

"float and run" upon the sunset until lost to view, only its song remaining. What the poet does not see is as much a part of his perspective as what he does see. And the limitation of vision gives both materiality and spirituality to the mountain and the bird; just as, in *Frost at Midnight*, the workings of nature come alive because of what Coleridge does not hear, and Keats' nightingale is "seen" because it is not seen. In all these poems the perspective is the cord that binds the observer to the object, that indicates the presence in the object of his perceiving consciousness.

Keats describes a passage of his as "a regular stepping of the Imagination towards a Truth."[1] The phrase is applicable generally to the poetry of experience, the action of which is the observer's imaginative penetration of the object to arrive at a meaning which is in the end the informed object—the bird, the mountain, the landscape with the observer inside it. The symmetry or equilibrium of such poetry is dynamic. The extraordinary perspective is the sign of an original disequilibrium between the object in its conventional or understood aspect and the object as perceived by the observer, and the observer's business is to right the balance by understanding in the course of the poem his own perception. Here again Keats applies: "The Imagination may be compared to Adam's dream—he awoke and found it truth." The observer finds in the external world the knowledge he has himself brought to it. Involved in Keats' phrase about "coming continually on the Spirit with a fine Suddenness,"[2] that phrase so admirably illustrated in the sonnet on *Chapman's Homer* where Cortez stares outward while his men look at each other "with a wild surmise"—involved, indeed, in all epiphanies, is not only discovery but the shock of recognition.

For the observer does not so much learn as become something. Each discovery of the external world is a discovery of himself, of his identity with and difference from the external world. In imaginatively penetrating the skylark's flight and the nightingale's song, the observer in the *Odes* of Shelley and Keats discovers the contrast between the bird's freedom and his own

[1] To John Taylor, 30 January 1818, *Letters*, ed. M. Buxton Forman (London: Oxford University Press, 1952), p. 90.
[2] To Benjamin Bailey, 22 November 1817, p. 67.

subjection to material conditions. Keats speaks of the world as a "vale of Soul-making." We come into it as "intelligences" or pure potentiality, pure "God" as Keats puts it. To become souls, we must acquire an individual existence or identity. "And how is this Identity to be made? Through the medium of the Heart? And how is the heart to become this Medium but in a world of Circumstances?"[1] Each encounter with the external world gives us a chance to project ourselves sympathetically into the Other and, by identifying there another aspect of the spiritual Self, to evolve a soul or identity. It is not extravagant to say that the ultimate subject of all poetry of experience is just such an evolution.

The need for circumstances explains the essential situation of all poetry of experience, that the observer deliberately seeks out the experience of the poem. It also explains the unprecedented importance of nature in romantic poetry, as the most universally affecting of all circumstances—though the natural circumstance is not essential to the poetry of experience. Indeed, the success of the romanticists having turned nature into something of a *cliché*, nature poetry has since their time declined in importance. For what does matter in the poetry of experience is that the circumstance be capable of awakening fresh response, in other words that it exceed formulation. This explains the constant search of modern poetry for new settings (or at least perspectives) from which to evolve new meanings, as distinguished from the classical preference for traditional settings and meanings.

The fact that meaning is evolved and is itself only an incident in the evolution of a soul explains the dynamic equilibrium of the poetry of experience. For the informed object which, by answering the question of the poem, rights the original disequilibrium between the observer's perception and understanding is itself a new perception exceeding understanding. Keats, in trying in the *Ode to a Nightingale* to understand his mixed response to the bird's song, penetrates the song imaginatively—understanding it first as an increasingly intense sensuous experience, an experience which, moving from sight to smell and from light to "embalmed darkness," seems to be

[1] To George and Georgiana Keats, 14 February–3 May 1819, pp. 334-36.

regressive and to reach its climax, a climax reconciling the joy and pain of his response, in a voluptuous longing for death. Then, transcending sensuality and death, he achieves a new intensity of understanding by hearing the song down the long corridors of the past, the sad Biblical past of Ruth and the joyous pagan past of "emperor and clown"—until, in the vision of the "magic casements," he achieves the insight which includes all the others, which, including both joy and pain and standing both inside and outside the world of sense and time, is finally adequate to his original perception. But the insight is itself an enigma and lasts only an instant—when the fading away of the bird's song breaks the union of subject and object, returning us to the world of ordinary perception and leaving us with the question:

> Was it a vision, or a waking dream?
> Fled is that music:—Do I wake or sleep?

Does the poem, then, deny itself? What is left us in the end? The thing we are left with is the thing the observer is left with— a total movement of soul, a step forward in self-articulation. Like the observer in Keats' *La Belle Dame Sans Merci*, we cannot be sure that the knight's dream of the beautiful lady is true or that his dream within a dream of the pale and vanquished knights is true. But we do know that his movement from dream to dream has revealed to him first beauty and then its terrible ambivalence, that something has happened to him. He can never be the same again—just as Coleridge's mariner can never be the same, whatever the truth of his narrative: and Lycius, in Keats' *Lamia*, cannot live after losing the sight of Lamia's beauty, whether it be illusion or reality. Nor, where there is an observer, can he be the same. Coleridge's wedding-guest departs, after hearing the mariner's tale,

> like one that hath been stunned,
> And is of sense forlorn.

The lines apply equally to the reader, who has participated with the observer in the experience of the poem.

The ambiguity of circumstance tells a great deal about how the poetry of experience communicates—that it communicates not as truth but experience, making its circumstance ambiguously objective in order to make it emphatically someone's experience. This explains the importance of the observer or narrator or central character not only as the instrument of perception and maker of the meaning but also as the maker of the poem's validity. For there is a difference in degree of actuality between the observer and the object or circumstance, the latter being real to the extent that it is looked upon or experienced. Because the observer has the same function whether or not he bears the poet's name, we should not—in those poems where he is Wordsworth or Keats or Shelley—think of him as the man his friends knew and his biographers write about; we should rather think of him as a character in a dramatic action, a character who has been endowed by the poet with the qualities necessary to make the poem happen to him.

Jacques Barzun speaks of the "playwright's vision" of the romantic lyricist: "He is in effect a dramatist using his own self as a sensitive plate to catch whatever molecular or spiritual motion the outer world may supply."[1] And Frederick Pottle shows how even those poems of Wordsworth which have a basis in personal experience "show autobiography so manipulated that the 'subject' corresponds to nothing Wordsworth ever saw with the bodily eye."[2] His comparison of *I Wandered Lonely* and *Resolution and Independence* with what Dorothy's journal and a letter of Wordsworth's reveal of their basis in personal experience shows about as much autobiographical connection as you find when you uncover the germ of a play or novel. Yet the autobiographical illusion is nonetheless important as precisely the plot—a plot about the self-development of an individual with whom the reader can identify himself to make the poem an incident in his own self-development as well. For the poetry of experience is, in its meaning if not its events, autobiographical both for the writer and the reader. The observer is thus a character, not in the Aristotelian sense of a moral force to be judged morally, but in the modern sense of a pole for sympathy —the means by which writer and reader project themselves into the poem, the one to communicate, the other to apprehend it as an experience.

[1] *Romanticism and the Modern Ego* (London: Secker and Warburg, 1944); (Boston: Little, Brown, 1944), pp. 97-98.

[2] "The Eye and the Object in the Poetry of Wordsworth," *Wordsworth: Centenary Studies*, ed. G. T. Dunklin (Princeton: Princeton University Press, 1951), p. 24.

It is the dramatic nature of the romantic lyric which distinguishes it not only from the lyrics of the older poets but from the traditional lyrics of the romantic poets themselves. If we compare Wordsworth's *Ode to Duty* with his dramatization of a similar idea in *Resolution and Independence*; or if we compare Keats' description of the aesthetic experience in *Ode on Melancholy* with his dramatization of that experience in the *Nightingale* and *Grecian Urn*, we see the difference between the traditional lyric in which the poet sets forth his already formulated idea either epigrammatically or logically (proposing a question, say, and answering it), and the new kind of lyric in which the poet discovers his idea through a dialectical interchange with the external world. The common assumption is that the classical lyric is objective and the romantic lyric subjective; but the assumption is only half true. The truth is that the classical lyric (take Sappho and Pindar, Catullus and Horace as examples) is either subjective or objective. The poet talks, as in conversation, either about himself or about someone or something else; and he talks, as we do in life, either to himself or to someone or something else.

The romantic lyric or poem of experience, on the other hand, is both subjective and objective. The poet talks about himself by talking about an object; and he talks about an object by talking about himself. Nor does he address either himself or the object, but both together. He addresses the object in order to tell himself something; yet the thing he tells himself comes from the object. Shelley in *Mont Blanc* says that his mind

> Now renders and receives fast influencings,
> Holding an unremitting interchange
> With the clear universe of things around.

I know of no better way to describe the peculiar style of address of the distinctively romantic lyric than to compare it to one side of a dialogue, with the other side understood by its effect. The poet speaks through the observer of the romantic lyric the way a playwright speaks through one of his characters—in that the observer moves through a series of intellectual oscillations toward a purpose of which he is himself at each point not aware.

When we consider how dramatic the romantic lyric is, in the arrangement of its events, the role of its observer and the dialogue-like style of its address, we can only wonder whether it can properly be called a lyric at all—whether the poetry of experience is not itself a new genre which abolishes the distinction between subjective and objective poetry and between the lyrical and dramatic or narrative genres. If *Tintern Abbey* is to be thought of as a lyric dramatized, then how are we to think of a poem like *Resolution and Independence*? Is it in a class with *Tintern Abbey*, or is it a narrative with lyrical qualities?

Resolution and Independence is not only a narrative about a meeting of two people, it is also a lyric about the evolution of an observer through his evolving vision of an old man. There is the same difference of actuality between the observer and the old man that there is between the observer of *Tintern Abbey* and the landscape. The old man is neither unequivocally object-ive nor the personification of an abstract idea. He is neither one nor the other because he looks as he does and means what he does only to this particular observer, who has just passed from joy in identifying himself with nature to despair in realiz-ing his difference from nature.

Thus, the old man's appearance evolves with the observer's understanding of him. First he appears half inanimate, half animate—like an unaccountably situated boulder the life-like quality of which is compared to that of a sea-beast barely distinguishable from the shelf on which it reposes.

> Such seemed this Man, not all alive nor dead,
> Nor all asleep—in his extreme old age.

The ambiguity shows the old man's existence as mysterious. But the observer's penetration of the mystery shifts the ambigu-ity from the lowest reaches of life to the highest, to the line between nature and spirit.

> The old Man still stood talking by my side;
> But now his voice to me was like a stream
> Scarce heard; nor word from word could I divide;
> And the whole body of the Man did seem
> Like one whom I had met with in a dream;
> Or like a man from some far region sent,
> To give me human strength, by apt admonishment.

The answer to the observer's original question about man's relation to nature comes as the greatest mystery of all—as an archetypal vision of the old man, not unlike the vision in *Tintern Abbey* of Dorothy as a child of nature:

> Therefore let the moon
> Shine on thee in thy solitary walk;
> And let the misty mountain-winds be free
> To blow against thee.

But this is a vision of Man's tragic and triumphant disharmony with nature:

> While he was talking thus, the lonely place,
> The old Man's shape, and speech—all troubled me:
> In my mind's eye I seemed to see him pace
> About the weary moors continually,
> Wandering about alone and silently.

On the one hand, the poem is a narrative about a man who learns a lesson through a providential encounter. It even ends with a moral:

> "God," said I, "be my help and stay secure;
> I'll think of the Leech-gatherer on the lonely moor!"

On the other hand, it is a poem like *Tintern Abbey* and *Ode to a Nightingale* about a movement of perception, with the moral a merely partial and problematical abstraction from the final penetrating vision. The moral returns us to the world of ordinary perception in the same way as Keats' "Do I wake or sleep?"

Even Wordsworth's *Michael*, unquestionably a narrative poem, evolves out of the narrator's affectionate perception of a "heap of unhewn stones" in an idyllic natural setting, and returns us in the end to the same heap of stones at that point in the present where the poem begins. The moral about the goodness of the country and the badness of the city is absorbed in the total movement of perception by which we now see, in the heap of stones in the natural setting, a new meaning—a natural rhythm or process in which the human events of the poem take their harmonious place. The narrator moves through the story to return with new insight to an original mysterious perception, in the same way that the observers of *Tintern Abbey* and *Frost at Midnight* move through a sequence of memories and associations to return with new insight to the landscape and the frost. And the meaning of all three poems is much the same, an immediate apprehension of the life of things. Whether the poetry of experience starts out to be lyrical or dramatic, whether it deals with a natural or human object or a story that evolves out of someone's perception of a natural or human object, to the extent that it imitates the structure of experience, to the extent that its meaning is a movement of perception, it must be in final effect much the same—both lyrical and dramatic, subjective and objective: a poetry dealing with the object and the eye on the object.

Wordsworth called attention to the double nature of his new kind of poetry by naming the volume of 1798, *Lyrical Ballads*. "The feeling therein developed," he says in the Preface to the second edition, "gives importance to the action and situation, and not the action and situation to the feeling." He considered this a revolutionary departure, which surprises us because we think of him as a lyric poet. But he thought of himself, at least in *Lyrical Ballads*, as a teller of tales. The departure lay precisely in the word, *lyrical*, by which he could not have meant that the poems were to be sung but must have meant that they were lyrical in the sense of subjective, stressing feeling over action.[1]

It was to experiment with the merging of genres that Wordsworth and Coleridge collaborated on *Lyrical Ballads*. As described by Coleridge in Chapter XIV of *Biographia Literaria*, the plan was that Wordsworth would start with the natural and Coleridge with the supernatural but that both would come out in the end with much the same kind of poem. To understand why the poems were to come out the same, we must understand that they were to present, no matter which side the poet started from, an experience. The poet gives us an experience of the natural when he causes us to see it with a sensitive and sym-

---

[1] To measure the extent of the departure, we have only to consider what Kittredge says about the objectivity of the old ballads: "Not only is the author of a ballad invisible, . . . but the teller of the tale has no rôle in it. Unlike other songs, it does not purport to give utterance to the feelings or the mood of the singer. The first person does not occur at all, except in the speeches of the several characters. Finally, there are no comments or reflections by the narrator. He does not dissect or psychologize. . . . If it were possible to conceive a tale as *telling itself*, without the instrumentality of a conscious speaker, the ballad would be such a tale." (Introduction to F. J. Child, *English and Scottish Popular Ballads*, Boston and New York: Houghton Mifflin, 1904, p. xi.)

pathetic eye, an eye from which "the film of familiarity and selfish solicitude" has been lifted, so as "to excite a feeling analogous to the supernatural." And he gives us an experience of the supernatural when he transfers "from our inward nature a human interest and a semblance of truth sufficient to procure for these shadows of imagination that willing suspension of disbelief for the moment, which constitutes poetic faith"—when he gives to what is equivocal as objective fact a psychological validity. Thus, Coleridge's supernaturalism differs from that of the old ballads in the disequilibrium he creates between the supernatural as fact and as experience. It is to the extent that the poem happens to someone, to the observer in *Tintern Abbey* and the wedding-guest in *The Ancient Mariner*, that it can be both natural and supernatural. For the observer, by external-izing his feelings, makes the supernatural imprint on the external world at the same time that he makes the supernatural natural as an incident in his biography.

If the poet's presence in the romantic lyrical poem makes it dramatic, his presence in the romantic narrative or dramatic poem makes it lyrical. The poet takes on the name and char-acter of the narrator or hero of the romantic narrative and drama for the same reason that he gives his own name and character to the observer of the romantic lyric—in order to give meaning to the poem. It is a commonplace that Childe Harold and Faust are aliases for Byron and Goethe. But the observation is misleading unless we see that these fictitious characters are related and unrelated to their creators in the same way as the observers of the romantic lyrics, that Byron's narrative and Goethe's drama are also poems of experience.

Both poems deal with the evolution of a soul, with a man's quest for knowledge through self-realization, the poetic truth being in both poems what the hero becomes. It is significant that both poems are poems of travel in which the hero, like the observer in the dramatic lyric, seeks out the incidents. This means that there is no necessary sequence between the incidents (they simply occur at the will of the hero) and therefore no ending in the logical sense. *Childe Harold* and its sequel, *Don Juan*, end only because they were interrupted by the death of the author; while *Faust*, which Goethe finished almost with his last breath, ends with the death of the hero. Although Faust has his moment of happiness at the end, it is based on a delusion and cannot therefore be said to result from the incidents leading up to it or to offer the objective truth Faust was looking for. The meaning of *Faust* is not, I would say, that Faust has discovered the truth but that he has lived his life—he has evolved. The limits on the narrative or drama of experience are not logical but naturalistic. The poem ends because there is a physical limit on the amount of experience one man can have; and a limit on life itself, the author's no less than the hero's.

In this sense, the narrative or drama of experience can be said to approach in its structure a series of dramatic lyrics connected in biographical sequence. Indeed, the single identity of the observer in Wordsworth's dramatic lyrics gives to at least that selection of them which shows a clear evolution in thought and feeling a biographical sequence like that of lyrical drama. When Wordsworth tells us in his Preface to *The Excursion* that all his poems are to be considered as parts of a Gothic church with the poet himself the principle of unity, he is saying the same thing that Byron says when he tells us in the Preface to *Childe Harold* that he introduced his "fictitious character . . . for the sake of giving some connexion to the piece."

The extraordinary visual perspective, which is the sign in the dramatic lyric of the observer's organizing function, has its counterpart in narrative poetry in the sensitive eye of Wordsworth's narrator who can see a story in a heap of stones, and in that special sensitivity of Coleridge's wedding-guest which causes the mariner to recognize him as one to whom he must tell his tale. As regards the mariner himself or Childe Harold or Faust, the extraordinary visual perspective has its counterpart in their extraordinary moral perspective. We recognize this extraordinary moral perspective when we speak of the *satanic* hero of romantic drama. For the romantic hero is not quite the same as the satanic hero of Elizabethan and Jacobean drama. Although the romantic like the Elizabethan and Jacobean hero has been separated from the human community by some terrible crime, the crime gives the romantic hero not only the theatrical advantage it gives his predecessor but also a certain philosophical and moral advantage. Like Faust's pact with the devil, the crime is a sign that the romantic hero has passed intellectually through the eighteenth century. It alienates him from all traditions and conventions, thus making him suitable as an agent of experience.

The crime is also, like Carlyle's discovery of the "Everlasting No," the means by which the romantic hero discovers his will and therefore his capacity for experience and for discovering through experience a new, more genuine morality, an "Everlasting Yea." The romantic drama is not, like the Elizabethan and Jacobean, principally concerned with displaying the wickedness of the satanic hero and his eventual fall. It is rather concerned with his redemption, with the experiences which lead him after his original denial to a new affirmation. He may, like Faust or Schiller's Karl Moor, discover a moral principle. Or he may, like Byron's Manfred and Cain, make a morality of denial itself, of the fierce assertion of the self against the encroachment of principle.

Faust discovers the moral law in the imperative always to evolve it; and Karl Moor, the robber captain of Schiller's prose play, *The Robbers*, discovers it when he realizes that "TWO MEN LIKE MYSELF COULD RUIN THE WHOLE EDIFICE OF THE MORAL WORLD."[1] But Manfred and Cain have only their remorse to justify them, and resist all temptation to surrender to external commitment. Manfred dies triumphant because his moral self-sufficiency renders the machinery of heaven and hell unnecessary. To the Abbot who offers him hope of heaven, he says:

> The innate tortures of that deep despair,
> Which is remorse without the fear of hell,
> But all in all sufficient to itself
> Would make a hell of heaven.   (III, i, 70-73)

And he drives away the demons who come to take him to hell:

> I bear within
> A torture which could nothing gain from thine.

He is even more autonomous than Faust in that he claims full responsibility for his magical power and his sin:

> The mind which is immortal makes itself
> Requital for its good or evil thoughts,—
> Is its own origin of ill and end—
> And its own place and time.   (III, iv. 127-32)

[1] *Works: Early Dramas and Romances*, trans. Henry G. Bohn (London: George Bell, 1873), V, ii, p. 129.

Cain, too, will kneel neither to God nor Lucifer. Whereas in the Bible Cain complains of the severity of his punishment and God mitigates it by placing a protective mark upon his brow; not only does Byron's God give the mark of His own accord, but Cain asks for more drastic punishment and chooses for exile the most desolate way.

Both dramas appear to leave the ultimate judgment of the hero in question. "He's gone," says the Abbot of the dead Manfred. "Whither?" he asks in the final line, "I dread to think—but he is gone." And when Cain's wife says of the dead Abel, "Peace be with him!" Cain answers in the final line, "But with *me*!" It is only the Christian judgment which is in doubt, however. In what we might call the existential judgment, the judgment by which we have been sympathizing all along with Manfred and Cain, they are undoubtedly justified. For we are ready to say that if they are not justified in the Christian sense as well, the fault is God's. The result of such exemption from external judgment is to make the hero of romantic drama a character not in the Aristotelian sense but in the same sense as the observer of the dramatic lyric—to make him not an agent of the action, to be judged morally, but a pole for sympathy who determines what we see and the meaning of what we see.

Like the observer of the dramatic lyric, the hero of romantic drama gains his authority by imposing upon us his extraordinary perspective. Once we see in Byron's drama that we are to have the story of Cain not from the official perspective but from Cain's, or in Goethe's drama that Faust's rejection of the traditional rules has God's approval, we lose sight of conventional signposts and find ourselves in an unmarked wilderness with only Cain or Faust to guide us. Our only course is to build a new moral world with them, to see what they see and learn what they learn with as unreserved a sympathy as we give to Wordsworth in *Tintern Abbey* or *Resolution and Independence*.

Indeed, there is between the hero of romantic drama and the world outside him (the incidents and the other characters) a difference in degree of actuality such as exists between Wordsworth and the landscape or the old man. Like the object of the dramatic lyric, the incidents and the other characters seem half to materialize out of the need of the hero to learn objectively what he already knows potentially. Thus, Goethe's Mephistopheles and Byron's Lucifer are not simply antagonists to Faust and Cain. They appear because the heroes want them to, and articulate the reasoning and doubting, the eighteenth-century element of the heroes' minds. "Thou speak'st to me," Cain says to Lucifer,

> of things which long have swum
> In visions through my thought.   (I, i, 164-65)

Faust and Cain carry on their dialogues with the devil for the same reason that Wordsworth carries on his dialogues with the landscape and the old man, in order to realize the contradiction between them through an advance in perception. In the dramas, too, the contradiction is between articulation and perception, with the devil representing articulation; the hero knows that there remains a part of the case which the devil fails to understand, but he has himself to understand what it is. He employs a style of address like that of the dramatic lyric in that he seems in his dialogue with the devil to be standing in both places, to be addressing his words outward for his own benefit.

It is through their crimes that Faust and Cain come to understand the difference between themselves and the devil. For in suffering a remorse which has nothing to do with any personal disadvantage they have incurred through their crimes, they respond in a way impossible to the detached intelligence. Thus, they realize that they have in addition to the critical intelligence of the devil a certain right instinct which the devil neither shares nor understands. "I thirst for good," Cain says in trying early in the poem to understand the difference of motive which distinguishes his intellectual rebellion from Lucifer's (II, ii, 238). And God predicts in the Prologue that Faust will profit from his career of freedom:

> A good man, struggling in his darkness,
> will always be aware of the true course.

The fact that the hero's right instinct shows itself as remorse is a sign that he has himself evolved the moral law which imposes a limitation upon his freedom. But the evolution would be impossible without a combination of right instinct with critical intelligence—which is why Goethe's God created the devil:

> Man's active spirit easily falls asleep;
> he's much too readily seduced by sloth.
> Therefore, I gladly give him a companion
> who prods and twists and must act as a devil.[1]

Only the detached intelligence is, in fact, evil. The complete human being, with a capacity for sympathy and therefore for experience and development, cannot be evil. For the remorse he suffers when he has done harm to others makes his lawless act an incident in his moral evolution, an incident which cannot be judged until the whole story has been told. In *The Robbers*, Schiller contrasts two kinds of criminal rebellion—that of the hero, Karl Moor, a man of right instinct who turns robber as a protest against an unjust world, and that of his brother, the physically and emotionally deformed Franz, who under the guise of respectability commits crimes for self-interest. Schiller in the Preface calls Franz a "monster," because his is the vice which "destroys virtuous sentiments by dissecting them, and holds up the earnest voice of religion to mockery and scorn," the vice of one who has quickened "his understanding at the expense of his soul." But Karl's is "A mind for which the greatest crimes have only charms through the glory which attaches to them, the energy which their perpetration requires, and the dangers which attend them. A remarkable and important personage, abundantly endowed with the power of becoming either a Brutus or a Catiline, according as that power is directed." He must learn that "Erroneous notions of activity and power, an exuberance of strength which bursts through all the barriers of law, must of necessity conflict with the rules of social life."[2] We see the difference between Karl's romantic remorse for the harm he has done others and Franz's Christian "repentance" which comes when he is about to die and then, as a rationalist's hedge, just in case there might be something after all in the Christian doctrine of heaven and hell.

Wordsworth's *The Borderers*, which shows the influence of Schiller's play, turns about a similar contrast between Oswald and the hero, Marmaduke, both of whom, in enforcing what

---

[1] Part I, p. 4. [2] *Early Dramas*, p. xiv.

they think is justice, commit similar crimes. The difference between them is that Marmaduke suffers remorse; whereas Oswald, by stifling remorse, has made himself into a detached intelligence and tempts Marmaduke to do likewise with himself:

> You have obeyed the only law that sense
> Submits to recognize; the immediate law,
> From the clear light of circumstances, flashed
> Upon an independent Intellect.   (III, 1493-96)

The difference between Marmaduke and Oswald, Karl and Franz, Faust and Mephistopheles, and Cain and Lucifer, is the difference between eighteenth-century rationalist rebellion which denies the soul and therefore leads to moral destruction, and nineteenth-century romantic rebellion which affirms the soul and therefore leads to moral reconstruction. The difference depends not on what the characters *do* but on what they *are*. We sympathize with the hero because as a complete human being he is the counterpart of ourselves.

We find our counterpart in the hero as we cannot find it even in the girl he loves. For she is always in these plays pious and right. If the villain represents critical intelligence detached from right instinct, the heroine represents right instinct detached from critical intelligence. She has not been intellectually through the eighteenth century. In Faust's Margaret or Cain's wife and sister, Adah, mind is in harmony with faith, dogma and instinct; whereas mind, in the post-Enlightenment reader, is presumably at odds with faith and dogma and must learn to make its peace with instinct. That is why we find the counterpart of our own divided consciousness only in the satanic hero, who must achieve through experience a new harmony of mind and instinct.

Such an arrangement pits the hero against opposite abstractions, thus opening the way for a new kind of allegory in which villain and heroine represent conflicting aspects of the hero's self with the hero's problem to reconcile his internal conflict through self-development. The allegory is operative, however, only to the extent that the play is, like *Faust, Cain* and *Manfred*, a monodrama—to the extent that only one character is unequivocally actual, with the incidents and the other characters existing as occasions for his self-expression and self-development, as a means of objectifying an essentially internal action. The Margaret episode, for example, must be understood as an incident in Faust's career, not Margaret's; otherwise it is intolerable that he should leave the scene of her death to go on to bigger and better experiences. To the extent that it is intolerable, to the extent that Margaret and the action command an interest and significance of their own, it may be argued that the episode works against the general meaning of the poem, that the episode is a melodrama asserting a system of values at odds with those of the monodrama in which it is set.

Romantic drama cannot be, in the old sense, tragic. It turns either into monodrama or melodrama. For the internal polar oppositions of monodrama look merely extravagant and sensational when they are, as in *The Robbers* and *The Borderers*, externalized through a plot so complex as to make the incidents and the other characters no less actual than the hero. As poles of an internal conflict the meaning of which changes with the stage of Faust's development, Margaret and Mephistopheles have a valid significance. But as independently objective characters with a significance independent of Faust and Faust's stage of development, they would represent absolute categories of good and evil, thus contradicting what God says in the Prologue about the relative nature of good and evil. They would signify, in other words, a moral assumption in which we presumably no longer really believe, although we would go along with it for the sake of the plot. That is the price the dramatist pays in a relativist culture for a plot in the old sense, an unequivocally external action. The action becomes a mere concession to theatrical requirements and does not illustrate whatever of serious moral significance there may be in the ideas or characters.

Action can be significant only where romantic drama is both lyrical and dramatic—where action serves the self-expression of a central character, where it is not the illustration of a ready-made truth but, like the action of the dramatic lyric, the story of the making of a truth. Such a drama is monodramatic in that it exists as the perception of a single observer, showing that disequilibrium of actuality between the observer and his perception which is characteristic of the poetry of experience.

This disequilibrium marks a line of descent from the dramatic lyrics and lyrical dramas of romanticism to the dramatic monologues and symbolist poems of the so-called reaction against romanticism. The modern symbol is closer to the Wordsworthian object than to the symbols of Dante or Spenser, just because there is a disequilibrium between the modern symbol and its possible meanings. In the allegorical poetry of the Middle Ages and Renaissance, the symbol stands in a one-to-one relation for an external idea or system of ideas. But the modern symbol exists as an object for imaginative penetration. Although any number of ideas may be applied to it as problematical interpretations, its ultimate meaning is itself, its own "life," which is to say the observer's life inside it.

The aim of Mallarmé to reunite "music" with verse, or of Hopkins to portray "inscape," are no different from Wordsworth's aim to "see into the life of things." By "music," Mallarmé meant not musical sound but musical meaning; and by "inscape," Hopkins meant the individuality or *thisness* as opposed to the categorical *whatness* of a thing, its *selfness* as perceived through "That taste of myself, of *I* and *me* above and in all things."[1] All three, in other words, wanted to get beneath categorical meaning to the object itself, to that point in perception where the object is perceived from inside because perceived together with the self in one concrete experience.

It is this aim which makes the difference between a symbol in Dante and the same symbol as taken over by Eliot. F. O. Matthiessen speaks of Eliot's "desire for a paradoxical precision in vagueness." Whereas Dante uses the three beasts, Beatrice, the purgatorial mount to point (even if obscurely) to definite ideas; Eliot, in *Ash Wednesday*, presents the three leopards, the Lady, the winding stair with a precision learned from Dante, but lets their "indefinite associations unfold variously in different readers' minds."[2] Eliot's symbols invite penetration as

[1] See Eleanor Ruggles, *Gerard Manley Hopkins* (New York: Norton, 1944), p. 137; (London, John Lane, 1947), p. 107.
[2] *The Achievement of T. S. Eliot* (Boston and New York: Houghton Mifflin; London: Oxford University Press, 1935), p. 116.

Dante's do not, because Eliot's symbols put forth an atmosphere of unlimited meaningfulness. This atmosphere, which is the "music" or magic of modern poetry, is the atmosphere of that point in perception where the mind envelops the object in personal associations. It is the atmosphere of that mysterious ground from which the symbol emerges in the poet's self and with which it communicates in the reader's self.

"What is the modern conception of Art?" asks Baudelaire. "To create a suggestive magic including at the same time object and subject, the world outside the artist and the artist himself."[1] The curious thing is that the "suggestive magic" is achieved through the most individualizing possible depiction, the mark of the poet's eye upon the object. Whether it is Blake seeing into the internal burning of his Tyger, or Wordsworth seeing in and through a landscape or solitary figure an infinite vista, or Hopkins seeing in the individuality or inscape of an object its "design" or "pattern,"[2] the aim of modern poetry seems to be to open a channel from the individual object to its archetype by eluding the rational category of the type.

The difference between Wordsworth on the one hand, and Blake and Hopkins on the other, is in the degree to which we see the poet in the process of transferring value to the object. *Resolution and Independence* not only shows the poet getting to the point where he can see the significance of the old man, but it makes explicit the transition from ordinary to extraordinary perception:

> The Old Man still stood talking by my side;
> But now his voice to me was like a stream
> Scarce heard; nor word from word could I divide.

Hopkins' *Windhover*, on the other hand, begins with the informed object, with the poet inside the bird, feeling its powerful

---

[1] Quoted in W. H. Auden, *The Enchafèd Flood* (New York: Random House, 1950), p. 61; (London: Faber and Faber, 1951), p. 58.

[2] "But as air, melody, is what strikes me most of all in music and design in painting, so design, pattern or what I am in the habit of calling 'inscape' is what I above all aim at in poetry." (To Robert Bridges, 15 February 1879, *The Letters of Gerard Manley Hopkins to Robert Bridges*, ed. C. C. Abbott (London: Oxford University Press, 1935), p. 66.)

and exultant life and aware of its significance as the active principle:

> I caught this morning morning's minion, king-
> dom of daylight's dauphin, dapple-dawn-drawn Falcon, in
> his riding
> Of the rolling level underneath him steady air, and striding
> High there, how he rung upon the rein of a wimpling wing
> In his ecstasy!

and the meaning evolves through transformations of the object itself.

Yet here, too, the poet remains in the poem—not only in the first word but in the contrast, which emerges in the final lines of the octave, between the poet's participation in the bird's aggressive life and his awareness of his own passivity or withdrawal:

> My heart in hiding
> Stirred for a bird,—the achieve of, the mastery of the thing!

The contrast in union is a perception beyond the poet's understanding, a mystery which Hopkins like the romantic poets resolves by intensifying each side of the contradiction to the point where it is transcended—shifted through an advance in perception to a realm of being where passive and active, self and not-self are one. The mystery is resolved in profounder mystery.

For it is when the bird, having "Rebuffed the big wind," stands at the height of his mastery and is thus more intensely himself than ever, that the sestet begins:

> Brute beauty and valour and act, oh, air, pride, plume, here
> Buckle! AND the fire that breaks from thee then, a billion
> Times told lovelier, more dangerous, O my chevalier!

The fire is the revelation, prolonged through the analogies by which the poet tries to understand it in the last three lines:

> No wonder of it; shéer plód makes plough down sillion
> Shine, and blue-bleak embers, ah my dear,
> Fall, gall themselves, and gash gold-vermilion.

The moment when the poet is most intensely aware of the bird's active life is also the moment when he is most intensely aware of his own passive life, and therefore aware that active and passive are at their intensest equally self-justifying manifestations of a single glory, that each at its intensest contains the other. There seems to be also a necessary and splendid violence in the union of opposites by which the glory is achieved. Thus, a shine emerges from even the aggression of the plough upon the soil; and dying embers are both aggressor and victim, falling of their own accord and wounding themselves into triumphant gold and the vermilion of blood and martyrdom. "Gash gold-vermilion" transforms the regal sunlight setting of the opening lines into another more mysterious explosion of light, one which contains the subject-object conflict and therefore the accumulated meaning of the poem.

It is indicative of the way symbolist poetry communicates that this essentially is the pattern beneath most of the readings one sees of *The Windhover*, though hardly two readings agree as to the meaning of the pattern. The subtitle *To Christ our Lord*, together with what we know about Hopkins, suggests an allegory of the relation between Christ and the poet, the two aspects of Christ as Tiger and Lamb, and the active and passive, external and internal aspects of Christian virtue. Yet nothing in the poem itself makes such a reading inevitable, and it certainly cannot be equated with *the* meaning. More immediately apparent, for example, are allegories of conquest and sexual union (e.g. the phallic symbolism of the bird's flight and explosion into brilliance), as well as allegories of the aesthetic and biological as against the moral life, or of the process of perception itself. Since the poem takes both sides at once of any opposition we find in it, each formulation has a merely tentative validity which serves not to put the poem behind us, by accounting for it, but to lead us back to the experience itself. That is why all these allegories can be partly right as long as they proceed from the same apprehension.

The contiguous allegories are not, however, "levels of meaning" such as we find in Dante. That is, the allegories do not stand for discrete ideas or add up to *the* meaning, but each points inadequately to the whole poem. Nor is meaning transcended in the sense that it is in Dante at the point of his final beatific vision. The beatific vision is not presented in Dante, because it exceeds dogmatic formulation. But it is just because Hopkins presents more than he formulates or than can be formulated that he is, in spite of his Catholic orthodoxy, a "modern" poet.

For he is fulfilling, after all, Wordsworth's aim—only more so. If we agree that the aim of Wordsworth and the romanticists is to get at the experience that precedes ideas, then Hopkins would seem to go as far as intelligible language will allow in suggesting the simultaneity of word and experience. Absolute simultaneity is what the poem is trying to suggest through imagery, syntax and tense. The shift from the past tense of the octave to the present tense of the sestet suggests that the whole poem takes place during the moment of understanding; while the language catches the immediacy of the moment before conventional syntax has through its analysing function separated subject from object, thus turning experience into memory. There is, Hopkins insists, "an inscape of speech" too. "Poetry is . . . speech framed to be heard for its own sake and interest even over and above its interest of meaning."[1]

The connection between romanticism and symbolism is best illustrated by the case of Blake, who managed to be a symbolist before romanticism had started as a literary movement in England. Blake's symbolism is romantic rather than traditional not only because it is directed against Newton, Locke and the neoclassicists but also because its theory and practice could hardly have been conceived, much less understood, before the Enlightenment made it necessary to put together again a world split between fact and value. Blake heals the breach by treating truth as a quality and intensity of perception rather than as the thing that is perceived. It is in this sense that Blake sees all myths and rituals as symbols of the same truth, so that "Every thing possible to be believ'd is an image of truth."[2] And it is in this sense, a sense we have since the Enlightenment been learning to understand, that there is meaning in Blake's *Tyger*:

> Tyger! Tyger! burning bright
> In the forests of the night,
> What immortal hand or eye
> Could frame thy fearful symmetry?

[1] "Poetry and Verse," *A Hopkins Reader*, ed. John Pick (New York and London: Oxford University Press, 1953), p. 83.
[2] *The Marriage of Heaven and Hell*, "Proverbs of Hell."

or *Sick Rose*:

> O Rose, thou art sick!
> The invisible worm
> That flies in the night,
> In the howling storm,
>
> Has found out thy bed
> Of crimson joy,
> And his dark secret love
> Does thy life destroy.

or *Sun-flower*:

> Ah, Sun-flower! weary of time,
> Who countest the steps of the Sun,
> Seeking after that sweet golden clime
> Where the traveller's journey is done:
>
> Where the Youth pined away with desire
> And the pale Virgin shrouded in snow
> Arise from their graves, and aspire
> Where my Sun-flower wishes to go.

We have only to compare these symbols with Donne's *flea* to understand what is new in Blake's symbolism. Donne's symbol remains external to the poet and the meaning, it is an analogy. But Blake's symbol *is* the poem, the meaning of which we understand by penetrating the symbol to that point of intensity where opposites meet—where the fierceness of the Tyger meets the gentleness of the Lamb ("Did he who made the Lamb make thee?"), where the Rose meets its amorous destroyer, and the aspiration of the Sun-flower meets the aspiration of the dead Youth and Virgin to become an aspiration for a region that transcends both death and life. It is not enough to say that the *Tyger* praises revolutionary energy and the *Rose* and *Sunflower* condemn sexual frustration; for the oppositions conduct us beyond praise and blame to a ground of life which is sufficiently self-justifying before and without these and other possible meanings, including the meanings hypostatized in Blake's private mythology.

The case of Blake shows that, given the need to react against the Enlightenment, symbolism was in the cards from the start

—whether to be achieved through the immediate hypostatization of the individual perception, or evolved from a poetry dealing with the genesis of the individual perception. Although neither observer nor object is located, Blake's objects like those of the dramatic lyrics bear the mark of an observer's eye; and the style of address by which Blake reads himself into the object is that of the dramatic lyrics. If we substitute for the natural object a human object, we can see the relation of the dramatic lyric not only to the symbolist poem but to that other product of the so-called reaction against romanticism—the dramatic monologue, which was also in the cards from the start.

When Hopkins, in the same way that he reads himself into the windhover, reads himself into a character like Harry Ploughman, the poem is what we might call a mute dramatic monologue:

> Hard as hurdle arms, with a broth of goldish flue
> Breathed round; the rack of ribs; the scooped flank; lank
> Rope-over thigh; knee-nave; and barrelled shank— . . .
>
> He leans to it, Harry bends, look. Back, elbow, and liquid waist
> In him, all quail to the wallowing o' the plough: 's cheek crimsons; curls
> Wag or crossbridle, in a wind lifted, windlaced—
> See his wind- lilylocks -laced.

The meaning is similar to that of the octave in *The Windhover*. The poem is an evocation of strength; and its meaning derives from our experience of the poet's sense of the difference between himself and Harry and at the same time of what it feels like to be Harry. As an informed object, Harry gives back the meaning pictorially. If he gave it back through an utterance (as even a natural object does in Shelley's *The Cloud*), the poem would be a dramatic monologue.

Wordsworth shows the connection between the dramatic lyric and the dramatic monologue, when he turns his visionary stare upon a solitary figure with the same transforming effect as when he turns it upon a natural object. Sometimes, as in *Her Eyes Are Wild* and *The Last of the Flock*, the visual presentation introduces what is from then on a dramatic monologue. But since Wordsworth's genius is overwhelmingly visual, his visual presentations give more insight into his characters than their own utterances. This may be why Wordsworth never consciously discovered the dramatic monologue, though he is always hovering on the edge of the form. He is more successful in a poem like *The Solitary Reaper*, where the girl's song is in a language the observer does not understand; so that the observer reads himself into it—giving not the girl's utterance but his sense of it through an imagery which, like Hopkins' and Blake's, combines opposites.

The best example of the bridge between the dramatic lyric and the dramatic monologue is in one of Wordsworth's worst poems, *The Emigrant Mother*, where the dramatic monologue is introduced as follows:

> Once having seen her clasp with fond embrace
> This Child, I chanted to myself a lay,
> Endeavouring, in our English tongue, to trace
> Such things as she unto the Babe might say:
> And thus, from what I heard and knew, or guessed,
> My song the workings of her heart expressed.

It is as the articulation of a meaning coming back from the *informed* object, that the dramatic monologue differs from other first-person utterances where the speaker is not the author. Wordsworth is unable, however, to express his projected consciousness through the speaker's words alone. That is why poems like *The Complaint of a Forsaken Indian Woman* and *The Affliction of Margaret*—,where there is no observer, are still not in the modern sense dramatic monologues in that they are not substantially different in effect from all the laments and complaints of traditional poetry. The speakers of all three poems are simply spokesmen for an emotion. Since we are not aware of the poet inside them, there is no means of ingress for us either. There is nothing to apprehend through sympathy, no core of character that is beyond what the speaker says, and therefore no disequilibrium between the speaker's utterance and the meaning of the poem.[1]

---

[1] Wordsworth's prefatory notes to these two poems are more expressive than the poems themselves, for in the notes the poet turns his eye upon the speakers.

The dramatic monologue, in other words—inasmuch as we use the term to denote a distinctively modern form—must be a poem of experience. Only by connecting it with all the forms of the poetry of experience can we understand what was meant by the American poet and critic, Randall Jarrell, when he said in a lecture at Harvard in 1950 that the dramatic monologue has now become "in one form or another the norm" of modern poetry:

> How our poetry got this way [too difficult]—how romanticism was purified and exaggerated and "corrected" into modernism; how poets carried all possible tendencies to their limits, with more than scientific zeal; how the dramatic monologue, which once had depended for its effect upon being a departure from the norm of poetry, now became in one form or another the norm . . .—is one of the most complicated and interesting of stories.[1]

Since it has more obvious connections than the symbolist poem with both the dramatic lyric and lyrical drama of the romanticists: and since it has, in the relation it establishes between action and character and between dramatic structure and lyrical effect, connections with modern drama and fiction generally, especially with the modern short story which originated at about the same time—the dramatic monologue would seem to be the best possible vehicle for studying the transformations of romanticism through the evolution of a poetry of experience.

It is therefore to the dramatic monologue that we shall now turn our attention: first, by studying its characteristic subject matter and effect and relating these to nineteenth and twentieth-century culture, and then by studying its dramatic structure and relating it to the dissolution of traditional drama as the dissolution appears in the nineteenth century's psychologizing and lyricizing reinterpretation of Shakespeare. This will lead to a discussion of the lyrical effect of the dramatic monologue—a discussion showing the dramatic monologue to be, with its combination of dramatic and lyrical elements, an imitation of experience and the representative form of a poetry of experience. Finally, by comparing Aristotle and Nietzsche

---

[1] "The Obscurity of the Poet," *Poetry and the Age* (New York: Knopf, 1953), p. 13; (London: Faber and Faber, 1955), p. 23.

on the subject of Greek tragedy, we shall see through Nietzsche's reversal of Aristotle's definitions that the poetry of experience (Nietzsche's Dionysian poetry) is really a new romantic genre which replaces and combines the traditionally distinguished dramatic and lyric genres.

2

The Dramatic Monologue:
Sympathy versus Judgment

WRITERS on the dramatic monologue never fail to remark how little has been written on the subject—and I shall be no exception. The reason for the neglect is, I think, that no one has quite known what to do with the dramatic monologue except to classify it, to distinguish kinds of dramatic monologues and to distinguish the dramatic monologue from both the lyrical and the dramatic or narrative genres. Such classifications are all too easily made and have a way of killing off further interest in the subject. For they too often mean little beyond themselves, they close doors where they ought to open them.

The usual procedure in discussing the dramatic monologue is to find precedents for the form in the poetry of all periods, and then to establish, on the model of a handful of poems by Browning and Tennyson, objective criteria by which the form is henceforth to be recognized and judged. The procedure combines, I think, opposite mistakes; it is at once too restrictive and not restrictive enough, and in either case tells us too little. For once we decide to treat the dramatic monologue as a traditional genre, then every lyric in which the speaker seems to be someone other than the poet, almost all love-songs and laments in fact (*Lycidas*, *The Song of Songs*, *Polyphemus' Complaint* by Theocritus, the Anglo-Saxon *Banished Wife's Complaint*) become dramatic monologues; as do all imaginary epistles and orations and all kinds of excerpts from plays and narratives—e.g. all long speeches and soliloquies, those portions of epics in which the hero recounts the events that occurred before the opening of the poem, Chaucer's prologues to the *Canterbury Tales* and the tales themselves since they are told by fictitious persons: almost all first person narratives, in fact, become dramatic monologues.

While such a classification is *true* enough, what does it accomplish except to identify a certain mechanical resemblance?—since the poems retain more affinity to the lyric, the drama, the narrative than to each other.

But if we are, on the other hand, too restrictive, we do little more than describe the handful of Browning and Tennyson poems we are using as models. We come out with the idea that dramatic monologues are more or less like Browning's *My Last Duchess*, and that most dramatic monologues being rather less like it are not nearly so good. We are told, for example, that the dramatic monologue must have not only a speaker other than the poet but also a listener, an occasion, and some interplay between speaker and listener. But since a classification of this sort does not even cover all the dramatic monologues of Browning and Tennyson, let alone those of other poets, it inevitably leads to quarrels about which poems are to be admitted into the canon; and worse, it leads to sub-classifications, to a distinction between what one writer calls "formal" dramatic monologues, which have only three of the necessary criteria, and "typical" dramatic monologues, which have all four. As for poems with only the dramatized speaker and perhaps the occasion—poems like Tennyson's *St Simeon Stylites* and Browning's *Childe Roland* and *Caliban*, which are among the best and most famous of all dramatic monologues—this writer, in order to salvage her classification, calls them "approximations."[1]

The trouble with so narrow a criterion is that it suggests a decline of the dramatic monologue since Browning's time. It blinds us to the developing life of the form, to the importance of dramatic monologues in the work of such twentieth-century poets as Yeats, Eliot, Pound, Frost, Masters, Robinson and both Lowells, Amy and Robert (the form is particularly favoured by American poets). Robert Lowell's latest volume (*The Mills of the Kavanaughs*, 1951) consists entirely of dramatic monologues;

[1] Ina Beth Sessions in her book, *A Study of the Dramatic Monologue in American and Continental Literature* (San Antonio, Texas: Alamo Printing Co., 1933). An extract with revisions appears as "The Dramatic Monologue," *PMLA*, June 1947. For other examples of this approach, see the only other book-length study: S. S. Curry, *Browning and the Dramatic Monologue* (Boston: Expression Co., 1908); and papers by Claud Howard, "The Dramatic Monologue: Its Origin and Development," *Studies in Philology*, IV (Chapel Hill, N.C.: University of North Carolina Press, 1910), and R. H. Fletcher, "Browning's Dramatic Monologs [*sic*], "*Modern Language Notes*, April 1908.

while Pound, who in many places acknowledges his debt to Browning, has said of the dramatic monologues of Browning's *Men and Women* that "the form of these poems is the most vital form of that period,"[1] and has called a volume of his own *Personae.* Although Eliot has little to say in favour of Browning, the dramatic monologue has been the main form in his work until he assumed what appears to be a personal voice in the series of religious meditations beginning with *Ash Wednesday.* The dramatic monologue is proportionately as important in Eliot's work as in Browning's, Eliot having contributed more to the development of the form than any poet since Browning.[2] Certainly *Prufrock, Portrait of a Lady, Gerontion, Journey of the Magi, A Song for Simeon* and *Marina* do as much credit to the dramatic monologue as anything of Browning's; while in *The Waste Land* Eliot has opened new possibilities for the form by constructing with a *collage* of voices the dramatic monologue of a modern consciousness that is also a cultural memory.[3]

To understand the continuing life of the dramatic monologue, we must abandon the exclusive concern with objective criteria by which poems are either combined when they lack any effect in common, or else are separated when they have a common effect but lack the necessary mechanical resemblance. It is when we look inside the dramatic monologue, when we consider its effect, its *way* of meaning, that we see its connection with the poetry that precedes and follows Browning. We see, on the one hand, that the dramatic monologue is unprecedented in its effect, that its effect distinguishes it, in spite of mechanical resemblance, from the monologues of traditional poetry; and on

[1] Reviewing Eliot's *Prufrock and Other Observations* in 1917. Reprinted as "T. S. Eliot," *Literary Essays,* edited with an introduction by T. S. Eliot (Norfolk, Conn: New Directions; London: Faber and Faber, 1954), p. 419.

[2] "For the eventual writer of the literary history of the twentieth century, Eliot's development of the dramatic soliloquy, a form that has been called 'the most flexible and characteristic genre of English verse,' cannot be divorced from the impetus furnished by 'Men and Women' to 'Personae.'" (Matthiessen, *Achievement of Eliot,* p. 73, London: Oxford Univ. Press, 1935.)

[3] The merging of individual into collective consciousness accounts for Tiresias, who is "the most important personage in the poem, uniting all the rest. Just as the one-eyed merchant, seller of currants, melts into the Phoenician Sailor, and the latter is not wholly distinct from Ferdinand Prince of Naples, so all the women are one woman, and the two sexes meet in Tiresias. What Tiresias *sees,* in fact, is the substance of the poem." (Eliot's Notes on *The Waste Land,* III, 218.)

the other hand, we welcome as particularly illuminating just those "approximations" that distress the classifiers. We welcome them because, having without the mechanical resemblance the same effect as the so-called "typical" dramatic monologues, they show us what the form is essentially doing.

One writer on the dramatic monologue has managed to suggest what it is essentially doing; and he has done this at just the point where he abandons objective criteria to make an intuitive leap inside the form. In a Warton Lecture of 1925 which remains the best study of the dramatic monologue, M. W. MacCallum sees sympathy as its way of meaning:

> But in every instance . . . the object [of the dramatic monologue] is to give facts from within. A certain dramatic understanding of the person speaking, which implies a certain dramatic sympathy with him, is not only the essential condition, but the final cause of the whole species.[1]

Unfortunately, MacCallum does not pursue the implications of this insight. If he had, he would not be so disposed to isolate the dramatic monologue within the Victorian period, and he would not confine his consideration to its quality as a monologue. Although the fact that a poem is a monologue helps to determine our sympathy for the speaker, since we must adopt his viewpoint as our entry into the poem, the monologue quality remains nevertheless a means, and not the only means, to the end—the end being to establish the reader's sympathetic relation to the poem, to give him "facts from within."

The distinction may seem niggling unless we see that, by subordinating the dramatic monologue's quality as a monologue to the larger question of the reader's relation to it, we are able to understand the wider connections of the form. For to give facts from within, to derive meaning that is from the poetic material

[1] "The Dramatic Monologue in the Victorian Period," *Proceedings of the British Academy 1924-1925*, p. 276. See also an earlier paper which moves in the same direction, though not nearly so far: G. H. Palmer, "The Monologue of Browning," *Harvard Theological Review*, April 1918; and the three pages Bliss Perry devotes to the subject in *A Study of Poetry* (Boston: Houghton Mifflin, 1920), pp. 267-70. Stopford Brooke makes the pioneering remarks on the dramatic monologue in Chap. XIII of *Tennyson: His Art and Relation to Modern Life* (London: Isbister, 1895). But Brooke in his *Tennyson* and William Lyon Phelps in Chap. V of *Robert Browning, How To Know Him* (Indianapolis: Bobbs-Merrill, 1915), are more concerned with the content of individual dramatic monologues than with generic characteristics.

itself rather than from an external standard of judgment, is the specifically romantic contribution to literature; while sympathy or projectiveness, what the Germans call *Einfühlung*, is the specifically romantic way of knowing. Once we consider the dramatic monologue as a poetry of sympathy, we are in a position to see the connection not only between the dramatic monologues of the nineteenth and twentieth centuries but between the dramatic monologue and all that is unprecedented in poetry since the latter eighteenth century. We can see in the differences between the dramatic monologue on the one hand, and the dramatic lyric and lyrical drama of the romanticists on the other, the articulation of a form potential in romantic poetry from the start.

The standard account of the dramatic monologue is that Browning and Tennyson conceived it as a reaction against the romantic confessional style. This is probably true. Both poets had been stung by unfriendly criticism of certain early poems in which they had too much revealed themselves; and both poets published, in 1842, volumes which were a new departure in their careers and which contained dramatic monologues. The personal sting was probably responsible for Tennyson's decade of silence before 1842; it was almost certainly responsible for the disclaimer attached by Browning to his 1842 *Dramatic Lyrics*: "so many utterances of so many imaginary persons, not mine." Yet the reserve of the two poets cannot explain the coincidence that, working independently, they both arrived at the same form and produced at first try dramatic monologues so perfect (Browning's *My Last Duchess* and Tennyson's *Ulysses* and *St Simeon Stylites*) that they were never themselves to surpass them. We must look for precedents; we must suspect that they inherited a form which required only one more step in its development to achieve the objectivity they desired.

Browning's poetry before 1842 suggests by the manner of its failure the kind of precedent that lay behind the dramatic monologue, and the kind of problem that remained for the dramatic monologue to solve. His first published work, *Pauline* (1833), is the poem in which he too much revealed himself. It is transparently autobiographical (although the fictitious identity of the lady addressed provides a disguise of a sort), tracing the poet's intellectual development up to the age of twenty, the time of writing. It was of *Pauline* that John Stuart Mill said: "The writer seems to me possessed with a more intense and morbid self-consciousness than I ever knew in any sane human being"—a criticism Browning took so to heart that he would not allow *Pauline* to be published again until 1867; and then with an apologetic preface which repeats the disclaimer of 1842: "The thing was my earliest attempt at 'poetry always dramatic in principle, and so many utterances of so many imaginary persons, not mine.'" In spite of which disclaimer, he is reported to have said in his old age that "his early poems were so transparent in their meaning as to draw down upon him the ridicule of the critics, and that, boy as he was, this ridicule and censure stung him into quite another style of writing."[1]

We can follow his attempts at "another style" in *Paracelsus* (1835), a dramatic poem, and *Sordello* (1833-40), an historical narrative. There is, however, little enough drama in *Paracelsus*, and the narrative line is at best intermittent in *Sordello*; in both poems the style that takes over is the introspective, transparently autobiographical history of a soul in the manner of *Pauline*—the soul being in all three recognizable as the same passionately idealistic and endlessly ambitious, endlessly self-absorbed disciple of Shelley. In the preface to the first edition of *Paracelsus*, Browning says that he has reversed the usual method of drama:

> Instead of having recourse to an external machinery of incidents to create and evolve the crisis I desire to produce, I have ventured to display somewhat minutely the mood itself in its rise and progress, and have suffered the agency by which it is influenced and determined to be generally discernible in its effects alone, and subordinate throughout, if not altogether excluded.

And reflecting in 1863 on the failure of *Sordello*, he says in the preface dedicating the new edition of the poem to his friend,

[1] Quoted in W. C. DeVane, *A Browning Handbook* (New York: Appleton-Century-Crofts, 1955), pp. 46-47; (London: John Murray, 1937), p. 44. Just as the failure of *Pauline* is considered responsible for Browning's reluctance to speak in his own voice, so Tennyson seems to have been similarly wounded by the failure of his 1832 volume, especially by Croker's insulting review of it in the *Quarterly*. Harold Nicolson gives an amusing account of the *Quarterly* review, considering it as "undoubtedly one of the many causes of the silent and morose decade which was to follow." (*Tennyson* London: Constable, 1949, pp. 112-17.)

the French critic Milsand: "My stress lay on the incidents in the development of a soul: little else is worth study. I, at least, always thought so—you, with many known and unknown to me, think so—others may one day think so."

Did Browning forget that the romantic poets had thought so, that even Arnold, who disagreed, could hardly help but write poetry as though he too thought so, and that the enormous popularity of the "spasmodic" poets gave evidence that by mid-century almost everyone thought so? The question is perhaps answered by Milsand, who, in reviewing *Men and Women* for the *Revue Contemporaine* of September 1856, describes Browning's dramatic monologues in terms applicable to the whole of what I have been calling the poetry of experience. "What Mr Browning has attempted," says Milsand, "is the fusion of two kinds of poetry into one." And after citing Browning's remarks in the *Essay on Shelley* on the distinction between subjective and objective poetry:

> This alone indicates that he sympathizes equally with both kinds of inspiration, and I am inclined to think that from the beginning, and partly without his knowing it, his constant effort has been to reconcile and combine them, in order to find a way of being, not in turn but simultaneously, lyric and dramatic, subjective and pictorial. . . . [His poetry] would have us conceive the inner significance of things by making us see their exteriors.[1]

Compare these remarks of Milsand and Browning with Wordsworth's: "the feeling therein developed gives importance to the action and situation, and not the action and situation to the feeling," and with Pound's description of his own poetry:

> To me the short so-called dramatic lyric—at any rate the sort of thing I do—is the poetic part of a drama the rest of which (to me the prose part) is left to the reader's imagination or implied or set in a short note. I catch the character I happen to be interested in at the moment he interests me, usually a moment of song, self-analysis, or sudden understanding or revelation. And the rest of the play would bore me and presumably the reader.[2]

Add to the comparison Pound's idea that drama is less poetic than other kinds of poetry because "the maximum charge of

---

[1] pp. 545-46.
[2] To William Carlos Williams, 21 October 1908, *Letters 1907-1941*, ed. D. D. Paige (New York: Harcourt, Brace, 1950), pp. 3-4; (London, Faber and Faber, 1951), p. 36.

verbal meaning cannot be used on the stage,"[1] and Virginia Woolf's aim "to saturate" in her novels "every atom":

> I mean to eliminate all waste, deadness, superfluity: to give the moment whole; whatever it includes. . . . Waste, deadness, come from the inclusion of things that don't belong to the moment; this appalling narrative business of the realist: getting on from lunch to dinner: it is false, unreal, merely conventional. Why admit anything to literature that is not poetry—by which I mean saturated?[2]

And we see Browning's innovations as part of a general change of sensibility—a demand that all literature yield much the same effect, an effect of lyrical intensity.

When we have said all the objective things about Browning's *My Last Duchess*, we will not have arrived at the meaning until we point out what can only be substantiated by an appeal to effect—that moral judgment does not figure importantly in our response to the duke, that we even identify ourselves with him. But how is such an effect produced in a poem about a cruel Italian duke of the Renaissance who out of unreasonable jealousy has had his last duchess put to death, and is now about to contract a second marriage for the sake of dowry? Certainly, no summary or paraphrase would indicate that condemnation is not our principal response. The difference must be laid to form, to that extra quantity which makes the difference in artistic discourse between content and meaning.

The objective fact that the poem is made up entirely of the duke's utterance has of course much to do with the final meaning, and it is important to say that the poem is in form a monologue. But much more remains to be said about the way in which the content is laid out, before we can come near accounting for the whole meaning. It is important that the duke tells the story of his kind and generous last duchess to, of all people, the envoy from his prospective duchess. It is important that he tells his story while showing off to the envoy the artistic merits of a portrait of the last duchess. It is above all important that the duke carries off his outrageous indiscretion, proceeding

[1] *ABC of Reading* (New Haven: Yale University Press, 1934), p. 33; (London: Routledge, 1934), p. 31.

[2] *A Writer's Diary*, ed. Leonard Woolf (London: The Hogarth Press, 1953), p. 139.

triumphantly in the end downstairs to conclude arrangements for the dowry. All this is important not only as content but also as form, because it establishes a relation between the duke on the one hand, and the portrait and the envoy on the other, which determines the reader's relation to the duke and therefore to the poem—which determines, in other words, the poem's meaning.

The utter outrageousness of the duke's behaviour makes condemnation the least interesting response, certainly not the response that can account for the poem's success. What interests us more than the duke's wickedness is his immense attractiveness. His conviction of matchless superiority, his intelligence and bland amorality, his poise, his taste for art, his manners—high-handed aristocratic manners that break the ordinary rules and assert the duke's superiority when he is being most solicitous of the envoy, waiving their difference of rank ("Nay, we'll go/ Together down, sir"); these qualities overwhelm the envoy, causing him apparently to suspend judgment of the duke, for he raises no demur. The reader is no less overwhelmed. We suspend moral judgment because we prefer to participate in the duke's power and freedom, in his hard core of character fiercely loyal to itself. Moral judgment is in fact important as the thing to be suspended, as a measure of the price we pay for the privilege of appreciating to the full this extraordinary man.

It is because the duke determines the arrangement and relative subordination of the parts that the poem means what it does. The duchess's goodness shines through the duke's utterance; he makes no attempt to conceal it, so preoccupied is he with his own standard of judgment and so oblivious of the world's. Thus the duchess's case is subordinated to the duke's, the novelty and complexity of which engages our attention. We are busy trying to understand the man who can combine the connoisseur's pride in the lady's beauty with a pride that caused him to murder the lady rather than tell her in what way she displeased him, for in that

> would be some stooping; and I choose
> Never to stoop.

The duke's paradoxical nature is fully revealed when, having boasted how at his command the duchess's life was extinguished, he turns back to the portrait to admire of all things its life-likeness:

> There she stands
> As if alive.

This occurs ten lines from the end, and we might suppose we have by now taken the duke's measure. But the next ten lines produce a series of shocks that outstrip each time our understanding of the duke, and keep us panting after revelation with no opportunity to consolidate our impression of him for moral judgment. For it is at this point that we learn to whom he has been talking; and he goes on to talk about dowry, even allowing himself to murmur the hypocritical assurance that the new bride's self and not the dowry is of course his object. It seems to me that one side of the duke's nature is here stretched as far as it will go; the dazzling figure threatens to decline into paltriness admitting moral judgment, when Browning retrieves it with two brilliant strokes. First, there is the lordly waiving of rank's privilege as the duke and the envoy are about to proceed downstairs, and then there is the perfect all-revealing gesture of the last two and a half lines when the duke stops to show off yet another object in his collection:

> Notice Neptune, though,
> Taming a sea-horse, thought a rarity,
> Which Claus of Innsbruck cast in bronze for me!

The lines bring all the parts of the poem into final combination, with just the relative values that constitute the poem's meaning. The nobleman does not hurry on his way to business, the connoisseur cannot resist showing off yet another precious object, the possessive egotist counts up his possessions even as he moves toward the acquirement of a new possession, a well-dowered bride; and most important, the last duchess is seen in final perspective. She takes her place as one of a line of objects in an art collection; her sad story becomes the *cicerone's* anecdote lending piquancy to the portrait. The duke has taken from her what he wants, her beauty, and thrown the life away; and we watch with awe as he proceeds to take what he wants from the envoy and by implication from the new duchess. He carries all before him by sheer force of will so undeflected by ordinary compunctions as even, I think, to call into question—the question rushes into place behind the startling illumination of the last lines, and lingers as the poem's haunting afternote—the duke's sanity.

The duke reveals all this about himself, grows to his full stature, because we allow him to have his way with us; we subordinate all other considerations to the business of understanding him. If we allowed indignation, or pity for the duchess, to take over when the duke moves from his account of the murder to admire the life-likeness of the portrait, the poem could hold no further surprises for us; it could not even go on to reinforce our judgment as to the duke's wickedness, since the duke does not grow in wickedness after the account of the murder. He grows in strength of character, and in the arrogance and poise which enable him to continue command of the situation after his confession of murder has threatened to turn it against him. To take the full measure of the duke's distinction we must be less concerned to condemn than to appreciate the triumphant transition by which he ignores clean out of existence any judgment of his story that the envoy might have presumed to invent. We must be concerned to appreciate the exquisite timing of the duke's delay over Neptune, to appreciate its fidelity to the duke's own inner rhythm as he tries once more the envoy's already sorely tried patience, and as he teases the reader too by delaying for a lordly whim the poem's conclusion. This willingness of the reader to understand the duke, even to sympathize with him as a necessary condition of reading the poem, is the key to the poem's form. It alone is responsible for a meaning not inherent in the content itself but determined peculiarly by the treatment.

I have chosen *My Last Duchess* to illustrate the working of sympathy, just because the duke's egregious villainy makes especially apparent the split between moral judgment and our actual feeling for him. The poem carries to the limit an effect peculiarly the genius of the dramatic monologue—I mean the effect created by the tension between sympathy and moral judgment. Although we seldom meet again such an unmitigated villain as the duke, it is safe to say that most successful dramatic monologues deal with speakers who are in some way reprehensible.

Browning delighted in making a case for the apparently immoral position; and the dramatic monologue, since it requires sympathy for the speaker as a condition of reading the poem, is an excellent vehicle for the "impossible" case. Mr Sludge and Bishop Blougram in matters of the spirit, Prince Hohenstiel-Schwangau in politics, and in love Don Juan of *Fifine*, are all Machiavellians who defend themselves by an amoral casuistry. The combination of villain and aesthete creates an especially strong tension, and Browning exploits the combination not only in *My Last Duchess* but again in *The Bishop Orders His Tomb*, where the dying Renaissance bishop reveals his venality and shocking perversion of Christianity together with his undeniable taste for magnificence:

> Some lump, ah God, of *lapis lazuli*,
> Big as a Jew's head cut off at the nape,
> Blue as a vein o'er the Madonna's breast . . .

and again in *The Laboratory* where the Rococo court lady is much concerned with the colour of the poison she buys and would like

> To carry pure death in an earring, a casket,
> A signet, a fan-mount, a filigree basket!

To the extent that these poems are successful, we admire the speaker for his power of intellect (as in *Blougram*) or for his aesthetic passion and sheer passion for living (as in *The Bishop Orders His Tomb*). *Hohenstiel-Schwangau* and *Fifine* are not successful because no outline of character emerges from the intricacy of the argument, there is no one to sympathize with and we are therefore not convinced even though the arguments are every bit as good as in the successful poems. Arguments cannot make the case in the dramatic monologue but only passion, power, strength of will and intellect, just those existential virtues which are independent of logical and moral correctness and are therefore best made out through sympathy and when clearly separated from, even opposed to, the other virtues. Browning's contemporaries accused him of "perversity" because they found it necessary to sympathize with his reprehensible characters.

But Browning's perversity is intellectual and moral in the sense that most of his characters have taken up their extra-

ordinary positions through a perfectly normal act of will.
Tennyson, on the other hand, although less interested in novel
moral positions, goes much farther than Browning in dealing
in his successful dramatic monologues with an emotional perversity that verges on the pathological. Morally, Tennyson's
St Simeon Stylites is a conventional liberal Protestant attack upon
asceticism. But the poem is unusual because the saint's passion
for a heavenly crown is shown as essentially demonic; his
hallucinations, self-loathing and insatiable lust for self-punish-
ment suggest a psyche as diseased (we should nowadays call it
sado-masochistic) as the ulcerous flesh he boasts of. St Simeon
conceives himself in both body and soul as one disgusting sore:

> Altho' I be the basest of mankind,
> From scalp to sole one slough and crust of sin,

and there is in his advice to his disciples a certain obscene zest:

> Mortify
> Your flesh, like me, with scourges and with thorns;
> Smite, shrink not, spare not.

Browning would have complicated the case against asceticism,
he might have emphasized the moral ambiguity presented by
the saintly ambition which does not differ in quality from the
ambition for money or empire; or if he did simplify, it would
be to present the case against ascetic ritualism satirically as in
The Spanish Cloister. Tennyson, however, is more interested in
the psychological ambiguity, pursuing the saint's passion to its
obscurely sexual recesses.

Treating a similar example of religious buccaneering,
Browning has written in *Johannes Agricola in Meditation* a dramatic monologue of sheer lyric exultation. Johannes is, like St
Simeon, on a rampage for salvation and confident of attaining
it. But compare with St Simeon's the beauty of Johannes'
conception of his own spiritual position:

> There's heaven above, and night by night
> I look right through its gorgeous roof;
> No suns and moons though e'er so bright
> Avail to stop me; splendour-proof
> I keep the broods of stars aloof:

> For I intend to get to God,
>   For 'tis to God I speed so fast,
> For in God's breast, my own abode,
>   Those shoals of dazzling glory passed,
>   I lay my spirit down at last.

Although Browning clearly intends us to disapprove of Johannes' Antinomianism, he complicates the issue by showing the lofty passion that can proceed from the immoral doctrine. Nevertheless, the passion is rationally accounted for by the doctrine; Johannes is a fanatic, one who has gone to a philosophical extreme. A moral and philosophical term like *fanatic* will not suffice, however, to characterize St Simeon; we need also a term out of abnormal psychology. It is interesting to note in this connection that *Johannes Agricola* originally appeared together with *Porphyria's Lover* under the common heading of *Madhouse Cells*, but the poems were later separated and the heading abandoned. Without the heading, there is nothing in *Johannes Agricola* to make us suppose that the speaker is mad, that he is anything more than fanatically devoted to his Antinomian principles. That is because Browning does not, like Tennyson in *St Simeon*, pursue the passion downward to those subrational depths where lurk unsuspected motives.

In *Porphyria's Lover*, the speaker is undoubtedly mad. He strangles Porphyria with her own hair, as a culminating expression of his love and in order to preserve unchanged the perfect moment of her surrender to him. But even here, Browning is relying upon an extraordinary complication of what still remains a rationally understandable motive. The motive and action are no more unreasonable than in *A Forgiveness*, where we do not consider the speaker or his wife mad. She is unfaithful because of her great love for him, and he eventually forgives her by awarding her hate instead of contempt; she allows the life blood to flow out of her to help his hate pass away in vengeance. The motives in both poems are likely to demonstrate for us rather more ingenuity than madness; and it is generally true that extraordinary motives in Browning come not from disordered subconscious urges but, as in Henry James, from the highest moral and intellectual refinement.

Tennyson does not look for extraordinary motives, but presents emotion with an unnatural intensity that reveals it as morbid because in excess of rational motive. Even in *Rizpah*, where the emotion is mother-love and is approved of, Tennyson manages to suggest its animal source and to show what a lawless passion it can become: Rizpah has broken religious and social law in giving vent to her mother-love, and the excess of passion has unhinged her reason. The hero of *Maud* hates with cause the family that has ruined his life, but he nurses his hate to the point where it unbalances and almost destroys him. Even in his love for the daughter of the enemy house there is an over-intensity, a hysteria, which sends him on the rebound into total disintegration until he finally saves himself by plunging into frenetic action, war.

Most characteristic of Tennyson is a certain life-weariness, a longing for rest through oblivion. This emotional bias is all the more powerful because it appears to be subconscious. Not only does it conflict with the poet's often stated desire for personal immortality, but it even conflicts in a poem like *Ulysses* with what seems to be his intent. Yet Tennyson exploits this emotional bias beyond any English poet before him; it informs not only his best lyrics—*Break Break Break*, *Tears Idle Tears*, and the best of *In Memoriam*—but also his best dramatic monologues. The longing for oblivion is certainly an element in Keats' *Nightingale*; but it is kept in balance by a countervailing sense of the hard reality which must in the end be returned to, and is in every instance sublimated into the imaginative construction of a realm where death is defied—the regressive urge leads after all to the vision of the "magic casements." In Tennyson, however, the longing for oblivion is not a first step toward a vision of transformed being but an end in itself, overwhelming us and dispelling all other considerations. It is presented in *Tithonus*, where it is consonant with a poem about the mortal lover of the Dawn who, having been granted eternal life without eternal youth, withers away forever and longs to die; and in "The Choric Song" of *The Lotos-Eaters*, where it is also consonant with the song of men who have rejected life for an infantile voluptuousness. It is presented in both these dramatic monologues with an over-richness of landscape, imagery and cadence that mark it as poisonous though at the same time heady and irresistible wine. The opening lines of *Tithonus* allow us no reserve of judgment:

> The woods decay, the woods decay and fall,
> The vapours weep their burthen to the ground,

while the lotos-eaters argue us out of any speck of reserve that may linger:

> Let us alone. What pleasure can we have
> To war with evil? Is there any peace
> In ever climbing up the climbing wave?
> All things have rest, and ripen toward the grave
> In silence; ripen, fall, and cease:
> Give us long rest or death, dark death or dreamful ease.

The same weariness and longing for rest is the emotional bias of Tennyson's finest dramatic monologue, *Ulysses*; though here the emotion is couched in the contrasting language of adventure, giving an added complexity of meaning to the poem. To read *Ulysses* as a poem of strenuousness in the manner of Browning, as some critics have done, is to read with the head only and not the sensibility. For its music bears the enervated cadence of *Tithonus* and *The Lotos-Eaters*. The speaker is the old Ulysses whose glories are behind him; and though he has still the appetite for life that makes him dissatisfied with the domestic hearth, it is an old man's appetite exceeding potency. We miss the emotional meaning of his final journey unless we see that it is undertaken with a sense of diminished strength, as the last thing possible:

> Tho' much is taken, much abides; and tho'
> We are not now that strength which in old days
> Moved earth and heaven; that which we are, we are.

It is a mystical journey undertaken by night with an old crew. They are to sail beyond the limits of the world until they die, it is a journey to death. But death here is not the culminating experience that it is in Browning's *Prospice*; it is as much experience as is possible to old men. Nor is death a fight as in *Prospice*, "the best and the last," but a decline, a sinking below the horizon. The poet is inevitably moved toward death in *Prospice*, but in *Ulysses* death is deliberately sought for.

The story of Ulysses' final journey comes from Dante, whose account of it in the *Inferno* Tennyson follows so closely that his poem is in places a paraphrase. Yet the difference in emotional meaning is especially apparent just because the facts and even the thoughts are analogous. Ulysses' famous exhortation of his crew as they are about to cross the limit of the habitable world: "Consider your origin: you were not made to live like brutes, but to follow virtue and knowledge" (xxvi, 118), is admirably represented by Tennyson's lines:

> and vile it were
> For some three suns to store and hoard myself,
> And this gray spirit yearning in desire
> To follow knowledge like a sinking star,
> Beyond the utmost bound of human thought.

But the informing image and emotion of the passage are not in Dante—the *gray* spirit indicating an old man's tired yearning, and the *sinking* star directing the yearning toward disappearance, extinction.

What is incidental in Dante, that Ulysses is old, caught Tennyson's imagination to become the central fact from which his meaning emerges. There is no sign of diminished vigour in Dante's Ulysses. He is destroyed, as a matter of fact, as punishment for his too vigorous presumption in daring to sail beyond the limit assigned to man. The tempest that destroys him is the disaster he has risked in going adventuring. But even before embarking, Tennyson's Ulysses holds out death in one form or another as the inevitable goal of the journey. They may be washed down by the gulfs, or they may touch upon the Happy Isles of the dead; in any case his purpose holds

> To sail beyond the sunset, and the baths
> Of all the western stars, until I die.

Tennyson's Ulysses picks himself up from his Ithacan somnolence to make the choice for life; he will carry on, he will make the last effort, but with the same cry of pain that stirs Eliot's vegetable world in April, and with the same endurance of life only because it leads to death. Although the longing for oblivion informs most of Eliot's early poetry, Eliot is hardly thought of in connection with Tennyson. Yet there is no discontinuity of cadence or sensibility between

> The woods decay, the woods decay

of *Tithonus*, and

> April is the cruellest month

of *The Waste Land*; or between the opening lines of *Ulysses*:

> It little profits that an idle king,
> By this still hearth, among these barren crags,
> Matched with an aged wife

and

> Here I am, an old man in a dry month,
> Being read to by a boy, waiting for rain

of *Gerontion*, or Prufrock's

> I grow old.

Both poets seem to have been strangely sensitive in their younger years to the debility feelings of old age, and we can see in the slowly stiffening Gerontion and the slowly withering Tithonus (both early creations) products of similar sensibilities.

If we have overlooked the connection between the two poets, it is because we are still too much misled by the Victorian image of the Laureate to conceive Tennyson in any contemporary connection. To understand the essential Tennyson, the only Tennyson who can interest us, we must discard the Victorian image for the image, proposed by Harold Nicolson a generation ago, of the brooding recluse of the Lincolnshire wolds and the talented misfit of Cambridge. Had he let his feelings go, says Nicolson, he might have been "our supreme poet of despair."[1] He did not often let his feelings go after 1850. But his early poems, including the superb art lyrics of *The Princess*, are enough to establish his primacy on the far side of that subtle line which separates Coleridge and Keats from the English Decadents.

In the dramatic monologues, Tennyson's feeling for the pathology of the emotions makes for the same final effect as Browning's use of the extraordinary moral position. There is the same tension between sympathy and judgment; our experience of a longing to evade experience becomes itself the most

---

[1] He might have been "an earlier Swinburne" (*Tennyson,* pp. 9–10) . See also A. J. Carr, "Tennyson as a Modern Poet," *University of Toronto Quarterly,* XIX (1950) , 361-82.

intense of experiences to the extent that we realize how far from the norm we are departing. Sympathy adapts the dramatic monologue for making the "impossible" case and for dealing with the forbidden region of the emotions, because we must suspend moral judgment, we must sympathize in order to read the poem.

Extraordinary moral positions and extraordinary emotions make up the characteristic subject-matter of the dramatic monologues that follow Browning and Tennyson. Swinburne's dramatic monologues follow the style of Tennyson, exploiting extraordinary emotions, especially the Tennysonian longing for oblivion. If Swinburne sets forth an extraordinary moral position in his dramatic monologue of the first-century Roman who rejects the newly proclaimed Christian religion to stick by the old gods, the poem is still a *Hymn to Proserpine,* the goddess of death; and like *The Garden of Proserpine* (which is sheer emotional expression without much moral concern) expresses the longing for oblivion. The speaker of the *Hymn* prefers to die with the old order rather than be reborn with the new. Swinburne introduces more violent aberrations with his projection of masochism in the lover's reverie over a harlot's viciously beautiful face, in *Faustine,* and the adoration in *Dolores* of an anti-Madonna, an ideal "Lady of Pain," and with his projection of Sapphism (it is Sappho herself who speaks) in *Anactoria.*

But these are pathological extremes peculiar to Swinburne, who is himself at his best in *Itylus* which—while it preserves the choice against the renewal of life—is still within the bounds of usual experience, with its antagonism between sorrow and joy, memory and forgetfulness. The melancholy nightingale rebukes her sister, the swallow, for finding new joy in the spring and for having forgotten the terrible Greek events that transformed them into the birds they are. The American poets, Robinson and Masters, use dramatic monologues to make us sympathize with misfits of the American scene, and Frost uses the form (often first-person narratives) to expose aberrations of mind and soul in New England. Eliot writes of asexuality and fear of life in *Prufrock* and *Portrait of a Lady.*

The emotional difficulties of these early Eliot characters gain increasing moral significance as they become identified with problems of faith in the dramatic monologues that lead successively to the personal utterance of the *Four Quartets*. The dramatic monologues set forth successive positions on the road to faith—first, the recognition of the waste land of irreligion in *Gerontion*, *The Waste Land* and *The Hollow Men*, and then in *Journey of the Magi*, *A Song for Simeon* and *Marina*, the recognition of what must be believed in although the speaker still lacks the capacity to go all the way in believing. Even in *Marina*, where the speaker is on the point of final revelation, the affections of the poem still cling around the fog that obscures complete understanding, keeping the woodthrush invisible. These poems combine the emotional sickness of their speakers with moral and spiritual sickness.

Yeats sets forth an extraordinary moral position in the dramatic monologues of Crazy Jane. Far from being mentally or emotionally deranged, Jane in her attack upon the Bishop speaks for the healthy life of the instincts which Christianity forces underground. It is a sign of society's derangement that her position should be extraordinary, that it should be put into the mouth of a "crazy" speaker. At the other end of the scale, Yeats, in *Supernatural Songs,* uses the dramatic monologues of the early Irish Christian, Ribh, to fuse Christian, Druidic and later occultist ideas in accordance with Yeats' historical eclecticism. It is because we sense in both speakers a consciousness beyond what Jane can intellectually and Ribh can historically lay claim to, because we sense the poet's consciousness in them, that we sympathize with their points of view understanding them as experience. It can be said of the dramatic monologue generally that there is at work in it a consciousness, whether intellectual or historical, beyond what the speaker can lay claim to. This consciousness is the mark of the poet's projection into the poem; and it is also the pole which attracts our projection, since we find in it the counterpart of our own consciousness.

Pound actually makes dramatic monologues of his paraphrases from the personal utterances of ancient poets by intruding into them a modern consciousness. By employing an idiom and a tone so unmistakably contemporary as to give us an historical view of the utterance that the ancient poet could not himself have had, Pound uses the ancient poet as the speaker of a dramatic monologue. For he projects himself into the ancient poet's role, using him as a mouthpiece to dramatize an idea of the poet's time and civilization suitable to Pound's modern purpose.[1] This is the same historical point of view which Eliot achieves with mythological analogies in *The Waste Land*— with his use, for example, of Tiresias as speaker in a poem with a contemporary setting and in contemporary idiom; and which Yeats achieves with art symbols—with the mosaic settings of the *Byzantium* poems, and with those carved Chinamen in *Lapis Lazuli* who manage to convey the sense of fallen civilizations:

> Their eyes mid many wrinkles, their eyes,
> Their ancient, glittering eyes, are gay.

The historical meaning that emerges is beyond what Yeats' Chinamen could know of themselves, just as a specifically twentieth-century meaning emerges from the cadences of Pound's Propertius:

> A Trojan and adulterous person came to Menelaus
>> under the rites of hospitium,
> And there was a case in Colchis, Jason and that woman
>> in Colchis;
> And besides, Lynceus,
>>> you were drunk

or from the juxtapositions in Pound's Rihaku:

> The paired butterflies are already yellow with August
> Over the grass in the West garden;
> They hurt me. I grow older.
> If you are coming down through the narrows of the river Kiang,
> Please let me know beforehand,
> And I will come out to meet you
>> As far as Cho-fu-Sa.

Pound projects a similar point of view in his original dramatic monologue, *The Tomb at Akr Çaar*, in which a soul makes love to its mummified body, for whose return to life it has been waiting, lingering in the tomb, these five millennia. Integral

---

[1] "If one can really penetrate the life of another age, one is penetrating the life of one's own. . . . [Pound] is much more modern, in my opinion, when he deals with Italy and Provence, than when he deals with modern life." (Eliot's Introduction to Pound's *Selected Poems*, London: Faber and Faber, 1935, pp. xii-xiii.)

to the meaning is our modern awareness that the monologue takes place as the tomb is about to be opened, that this is the five-thousand-year-old situation the archaeologists will break into.

In these historical poems, the extraordinary moral position and the extraordinary emotion become historical phenomena. The past becomes, in other words, a means for achieving another extraordinary point of view. Since the past is understood in the same way that we understand the speaker of the dramatic monologue, the dramatic monologue is an excellent instrument for projecting an historical point of view. For the modern sense of the past involves, on the one hand, a sympathy for the past, a willingness to understand it in its own terms as different from the present; and on the other hand it involves a critical awareness of our own modernity. In the same way, we understand the speaker of the dramatic monologue by sympathizing with him, and yet by remaining aware of the moral judgment we have suspended for the sake of understanding. The combination of sympathy and judgment makes the dramatic monologue suitable for expressing all kinds of extraordinary points of view, whether moral, emotional or historical—since sympathy frees us for the widest possible range of experience, while the critical reservation keeps us aware of how far we are departing. The extraordinary point of view is characteristic of all the best dramatic monologues, the pursuit of experience in all its remotest extensions being the genius of the form.

We are dealing, in other words, with empiricism in literature. The pursuit of all experience corresponds to the scientific pursuit of all knowledge; while the sympathy that is a condition of the dramatic monologue corresponds to the scientific attitude of mind, the willingness to understand everything for its own sake and without consideration of practical or moral value. We might even say that the dramatic monologue takes toward its material the literary equivalent of the scientific attitude— the equivalent being, where men and women are the subject of investigation, the historicizing and psychologizing of judgment.

Certainly the Italian Renaissance setting of *My Last Duchess* helps us to suspend moral judgment of the duke, since we partly at least take an historical view; we accept the combination of villainy with taste and manners as a phenomenon of the Renaissance and of the old aristocratic order generally. The extraordinary combination pleases us the way it would the historian, since it impresses upon us the difference of the past from the present. We cannot, however, entirely historicize our moral judgment in this poem, because the duke's crime is too egregious to support historical generalization. More important, therefore, for the suspension of moral judgment is our psychologizing attitude—our willingness to take up the duke's view of events purely for the sake of understanding him, the more outrageous his view the more illuminating for us the psychological revelation.

In *The Bishop Orders His Tomb*, however, our judgment is mainly historicized, because the bishop's sins are not extraordinary but the universally human venalities couched, significantly for the historian, in the predilections of the Italian Renaissance. Thus, the bishop gives vent to materialism and snobbery by planning a bigger and better tomb than his clerical rival's. This poem can be read as a portrait of the age, our moral judgment of the bishop depending upon our moral judgment of the age. Ruskin praised the poem for its historical validity: "It is nearly all that I said of the Central Renaissance in thirty pages of *The Stones of Venice* put into as many lines"; but being no friend of the Renaissance, this is the spirit of the age he conceived Browning to have caught: "its worldliness, inconsistency, pride, hypocrisy, ignorance of itself, love of art, of luxury, and of good Latin."[1] Browning, who admired the Renaissance, would have admitted all this but he would have insisted, too, upon the enterprise and robust aliveness of the age. What matters, however, is that Browning has presented an historical image the validity of which we can all agree upon, even if our moral judgments differ as they do about the past itself.

In the same way, our understanding of the duke in *My Last Duchess* has a primary validity which is not disturbed by our differing moral judgments after we have finished reading the poem—it being characteristically the style of the dramatic monologue to present its material empirically, as a fact existing before and apart from moral judgment which remains

[1] *Modern Painters* (London: Routledge; New York: Dutton, 1907), iv, 370.

always secondary and problematical. Even where the speaker is specifically concerned with a moral question, he arrives at his answer empirically, as a necessary outcome of conditions within the poem and not through appeal to an outside moral code. Since these conditions are always psychological and sometimes historical as well—since the answer is determined, in other words, by the speaker's nature and the time he inhabits—the moral meaning is of limited application but enjoys within the limiting conditions of the poem a validity which no subsequent differences in judgment can disturb.

Take as an example Browning's dramatic monologues in defence of Christianity. Although the poet has undoubtedly an axe to grind, he maintains a distinction between the undeniable fact of the speaker's response to the conditions of the poem and the general Christian formulation which the reader may or may not draw for himself. The speaker starts with a blank slate as regards Christianity, and is brought by the conditions of the poem to a perception of need for the kind of answer provided by Christianity. Nevertheless, the perception is not expressed in the vocabulary of Christian dogma and the speaker does not himself arrive at a Christian formulation.

The speakers of the two epistolary monologues, *Karshish* and *Cleon*, are first-century pagans brought by the historical moment and their own psychological requirements to perceive the need for a God of Love (*Karshish*) and a promise of personal immortality (*Cleon*). But they arrive at the perception through secular concepts, and are prevented by these same concepts from embracing the Christian answer that lies before them. Karshish is an Arab physician travelling in Judea who reports the case of the risen Lazarus as a medical curiosity, regarding Jesus as some master physician with the cure for a disease that simulates death. He is ashamed, writing to his medical teacher, of the story's mystical suggestions and purposely mixes it up with, and even tries to subordinate it to, reports of cures and medicinal herbs. Yet it is clear throughout that the story haunts him, and he has already apologized for taking up so much space with it when he interrupts himself in a magnificent final outburst that reveals the story's impact upon his deepest feelings:

The very God! think, Abib; dost thou think?
So, the All-Great, were the All-Loving too—.

Nevertheless, he returns in the last line to the scientific judgment, calling Lazarus a madman and using to characterize the story the same words he has used to characterize other medical curiosities: "it is strange."

Cleon is a Greek of the last period; master of poetry, painting, sculpture, music, philosophy, he sums up within himself the whole Greek cultural accomplishment. Yet writing to a Greek Tyrant who possesses all that Greek material culture can afford, he encourages the Tyrant's despair by describing his own. The fruits of culture—self-consciousness and the increased capacity for joy—are curses, he says, since they only heighten our awareness that we must die without ever having tasted the joy our refinement has taught us to conceive. He demonstrates conclusively, in the manner of the Greek dialectic, that life without hope of immortality is unbearable. "It is so horrible," he says,

> I dare at times imagine to my need
> Some future state revealed to us by Zeus,
> Unlimited in capability
> For joy, as this is in desire for joy,
> —To seek which, the joy-hunger forces us.

He despairs because Zeus has not revealed this. Nevertheless, he dismisses in a hasty postscript the pretensions of "one called Paulus," "a mere barbarian Jew," to have "access to a secret shut from us."

The need for Christianity stands as empiric fact in these poems, just because it appears in spite of intellectual and cultural objections. In *Saul* there are no objections, but the need is still empiric in that it appears before the Christian formulation of it. The young David sings to Saul of God's love, of His sacrifice for man, and His gift of eternal life, because he needs to sing of the highest conceivable joy, his songs about lesser joys having failed to dispel Saul's depression. David "induces" God's love for Saul from his own, God's willingness to suffer for Saul from his own willingness, and God's gift of eternal life from his own desire to offer Saul the most precious gift possible.

"O Saul,
it shall be
A Face like my face that receives thee; a Man
like to me,
Thou shalt love and be loved by, for ever:
a Hand like this hand
Shall throw open the gates of new life to thee!
See the Christ stand!"

The speaker of *A Death in the Desert* is a Christian—St John, the beloved disciple and author of the Fourth Gospel, conceived as speaking his last words before dying at a very old age. He has outlived the generation that witnessed the miracles of Christ and the apostles, and has lived to see a generation that questions the promise of Christ's coming and even His existence. As the last living eye-witness, John has been able to reassure this generation; but dying, he leaves a kind of Fifth Gospel for the skeptical generations to follow, generations that will question the existence of John himself. It is an empiricist gospel. "I say, to test man, the proofs shift," says John. But this is well, since belief in God would have no moral effect were it as inevitable as belief in the facts of nature. Myth, man's apprehension of truth, changes; but the Truth remains for each generation to rediscover for itself. The later generations will have sufficiently profited from the moral effect of Christianity, so as not to require proof by miracle or direct revelation. They will be able to "induce" God's love from their own and from their need to conceive a love higher than theirs. Thus, Browning invests with dogmatic authority his own anti-dogmatic line of Christian apologetics.

In *Bishop Blougram's Apology*, the case is complicated by the inappropriateness of the speaker and his argument to the Christian principles being defended. Blougram, we are told in an epilogue, "said true things, but called them by wrong names." A Roman Catholic bishop, he has achieved by way of the Church the good things of this world and he points to his success as a sign that he has made the right choice. For his relatively unsuccessful opponent, the agnostic literary man, Gigadibs, the bishop is guilty of hypocrisy, a vice Gigadibs cannot be accused of since he has made no commitments. Since the bishop admits to religious doubt (Gigadibs lives "a life of doubt diversified by faith," the bishop "one of faith diversified by doubt"), Gigadibs can even take pride in a superior respect for religion, he for one not having compromised with belief. Thus, we have the paradox of the compromising worldly Christian against the uncompromising unworldly infidel—a conception demonstrating again Browning's idea that the proofs do not much matter, that there are many proofs better and worse for the same Truth. For if Blougram is right with the wrong reasons, Gigadibs with admirable reasons or at least sentiments is quite wrong.

The point of the poem is that Blougram makes his case, even if on inappropriate grounds. He knows his argument is not the best ("he believed," according to the epilogue, "say, half he spoke"), for the grounds are his opponent's; it is Blougram's achievement that he makes Gigadibs see what the agnostic's proper grounds are. He is doing what Browning does in all the dramatic monologues on religion—making the empiricist argument, starting without any assumptions as to faith and transcendental values. Granting that belief and unbelief are equally problematical, Blougram proceeds to show that even in terms of this world only belief bears fruit while unbelief does not. This is indicated by Blougram's material success, but also by the fact that his moral behaviour, however imperfect, is at least in the direction of his professed principles; whereas Gigadibs' equally moral behaviour is inconsistent with his principles. Who, then, is the hypocrite? "I live my life here;" says Blougram, "yours you dare not live."

But the fact remains—and this is the dramatic ambiguity matching the intellectual—that the bishop is no better than his argument, though he can conceive a better argument and a better kind of person. He cannot convert Gigadibs because his argument, for all its suggestion of a Truth higher than itself, must be understood dramatically as rationalizing a selfish worldly existence. What Gigadibs apparently does learn is that he is no better than the bishop, that he has been the same kind of person after the same kind of rewards only not succeeding so well, and that he has been as intellectually and morally dishonest with his sentimental liberalism as the bishop with his casuistry. All this is suggested indirectly by the last few lines of the epilogue, where we are told that Gigadibs has gone off as a settler to Australia. Rid of false intellectual baggage (the bishop's as well as his own), he will presumably start again from the beginning, "inducing" the Truth for himself. "I hope," says Browning,

> By this time he has tested his first plough,
> And studied his last chapter of St John.

St John, note, who makes the empiricist argument in *A Death in the Desert,* and whose Gospel concludes with the risen Jesus *feeding* the disciples and bidding them "Feed my sheep."

Although *Blougram* and *A Death in the Desert* are too discursive to communicate their religious perceptions in the manner of *Karshish, Cleon* and *Saul,* as the speaker's immediate experience, they make their case empirically because in non-Christian terms. They might be considered as setting forth the rhetorical method of the more dramatic poems, a method for being taken seriously as intelligent and modern when broaching religion to the skeptical post-Enlightenment mind. The reader is assumed to be Gigadibs (it is because the bishop is so intelligent that Gigadibs finds it difficult to understand how he can believe), and the poet makes for his benefit a kind of "minimum argument," taking off from his grounds and obtruding no dogmatic assertions.

Eliot addresses his religious poetry to the same kind of reader, communicating his religious perceptions in terms that fall short of Christian dogma. This is especially interesting in Eliot since his concern has been with dogmatic religion, whereas Browning was always anti-dogmatic. Of course, the method is in both poets not merely a deliberate rhetorical device but the necessary outcome of their own religious uncertainties, and a sign that they share like Blougram the post-Enlightenment mind. This is again especially apparent in Eliot, who has dramatized in his poetry his movement from skepticism to orthodoxy, whereas Browning's poetry shows no significant religious *development.* Nevertheless, there is something of the obtuseness of Karshish and Cleon in those speakers of Eliot's dramatic monologues whose religious perceptions fall short of the Christian truth— and with the same effect as in Browning, that the reader can give assent to the speaker's experience without having to agree on doctrine.

In *Journey of the Magi*, one of the Magi describes with great clarity and detail the hardships of the journey to Bethlehem, but cannot say for certain what he saw there or what it meant. The Magi returned to their Kingdoms, like Karshish and Cleon "no longer at ease here, in the old dispensation," but still without light. The old Jew Simeon, in *A Song for Simeon*, is somewhat in the position of Browning's David in *Saul*; he sees clearly the glory of Christianity, but is too old to embrace it— not for him "the ultimate vision," the new dispensation is ahead of his time. In *Marina*, the speaker apparently finds the ultimate vision in the face of his newly recovered daughter and in the woodthrush song through the fog, but the vision is still not intelligible, not translated into Christian terms.

In the earlier skeptical poems, the fog is even thicker and no song of revelation comes through it. But Eliot uses idolatrous or "minimum" analogues to the Christian myth to indicate the groping for meaning, his own groping and that of the characters within the poem. The characters in *Gerontion* and *The Waste Land* practise idolatries, aesthetic and occultist. *Gerontion* ends with an occultist vision of the modern, cosmopolitan, unbelieving dead whirled around the universe on a meaningless wind:

> De Bailhache, Fresca, Mrs Cammel, whirled
> Beyond the circuit of the shuddering Bear
> In fractured atoms.

Yet seen in the subsequent lines as a natural phenomenon, the wind has a certain meaning in that it unites the parts of nature, north and south, into a single living whole:

> Gull against the wind, in the windy straits
> Of Belle Isle, or running on the Horn,
> White feathers in the snow, the Gulf claims,

and there is, I think, the suggestion that the wind may be a cleansing wind, one which may bring the rain the aged speaker has been waiting for. The same wind that carries off the dead may bring renewal to the depleted living; that is as much meaning and as much hope as the speaker can achieve.

It is as much meaning as our pagan ancestors achieved in the primitive vegetation myths of death and renewal, and Eliot uses the analogy of these myths to give at least that much meaning to the jumbled fragments of *The Waste Land*. Just as the vegetation gods were slain so they might rise renewed and restore the fertility of the land; so the longing for death, which pervades the modern waste land, is a longing for renewal and, if the reader wants to carry the analogy a step farther, a longing for redemption through the blood of Christ, the slain God.

The analogy with the vegetation myths is maintained even in the *Four Quartets*, which are written from a solidly orthodox position. The religious perceptions of these poems are couched less in Christian terms than in terms of that mystical fusion of anthropology and psychology, of myth and the unconscious, that Jung effected.[1] One wonders if the *Four Quartets* are not, for all their orthodoxy, more satisfying to the skeptical than to the orthodox, since the latter might well prefer an articulation of religious truth no less explicit than their own convictions. Post-Enlightenment minds, on the other hand, are particularly fascinated by the mystique of myth and the unconscious as a way back, I think, to a kind of religious speculation which commits them to nothing while preserving intact their status as intelligent, scientific and modern. Myth and the unconscious are contemporary equivalents of Browning's pragmatism in making the "minimum" argument for Christianity.

Although not the only way to talk religion empirically, the dramatic monologue offers certain advantages to the poet who is not committed to a religious position, or who is addressing readers not committed and not wanting to be. The use of the speaker enables him to dramatize a position the possibilities of which he may want to explore as Browning explores the "impossible" case. The speaker also enables him to dramatize an emotional apprehension in advance of or in conflict with his intellectual convictions—a disequilibrium perhaps inevitable to that mind which I have been calling post-Enlightenment or romantic because, having been intellectually through the

[1] For a discussion of Eliot's use of Jungian ideas and symbols, see Elizabeth Drew, *T. S. Eliot: The Design of His Poetry* (New York: Scribner's, 1949; London: Eyre and Spottiswoode, 1950).

Enlightenment, it tries to re-establish some spiritual possibility. Browning's St John, in *A Death in the Desert*, defends religious myth as the expression of just this disequilibrium, of the emotional apprehension that exceeds formulated knowledge:

> "man knows partly but conceives beside,
> Creeps ever on from fancies to the fact,
> And in this striving, this converting air
> Into a solid he may grasp and use,
> Finds progress, man's distinctive mark alone,
> Not God's, and not the beasts'."

Even Eliot who professes to be against this "dissociation" of emotional apprehension from its formulated articulation (which for him is dogma), even in Eliot's poetry emotion is always a step ahead of reason—as for example the dim adumbrations of Christianity provided by the vegetation mythology of *The Waste Land*, or the disturbance of the Magi that exceeds their understanding, or that ultimate vision in *Marina* the articulation of which is obscured by the fog.

Not only can the speaker of the dramatic monologue dramatize a position to which the poet is not ready to commit himself intellectually, but the sympathy which we give the speaker for the sake of the poem and apart from judgment makes it possible for the reader to participate in a position, to see what it feels like to believe that way, without having finally to agree. There is, in other words, the same split between sympathy and judgment that we saw at work in our relation to the duke of *My Last Duchess*. The split is naturally most apparent in those dramatic monologues where the speaker is in some way reprehensible, where sympathy is in conflict with judgment, but it is also at work where sympathy is congruent with judgment although a step ahead of it. The split must in fact be at work to some degree, if the poem is to generate the effect which makes it a dramatic monologue.

Browning's *Rabbi Ben Ezra* is a dramatic monologue by virtue of its title only; otherwise it is a direct statement of a philosophical idea, because there is no characterization or setting. Because the statement is not conditioned by a speaker and a situation, there is no way of apprehending it other than intellectually; there is no split between its validity as somebody's apprehension and its objective validity as an idea. But in *Abt Vogler*, where the statement is also approved of, it is conditioned by the speaker's ecstasy as he extemporizes on the organ. His sublime vision of his music as annihilating the distinction between heaven and earth has validity as part of the ecstatic experience of extemporizing, but becomes a matter of philosophical conjecture as the ecstasy subsides and the music modulates back into the "C Major of this life." The disequilibrium between the empiric vision that lasts as long as the ecstasy and the music, and its philosophical implication, makes sympathy operative; and the tension between what is known through sympathy and what is only hypothesized through judgment generates the effect characteristic of the dramatic monologue.

Since sympathy is the primary law of the dramatic monologue, how does judgment get established at all? How does the poet make clear what we are to think of the speaker and his statement? Sometimes it is not clear. The Catholic reader might well consider Tennyson's St Simeon admirable and holy. Readers still try to decide whether Browning is for or against Bishop Blougram. Browning was surprised at accusations of anti-Catholicism that followed the publication of the poem, but he was even more surprised when Cardinal Wiseman (the model for Blougram) wrote in reviewing the poem for a Catholic journal: "*we should never feel surprise at his* [Browning's] *conversion.*" We now know, at least from external evidence if not from more careful reading, that Browning's final judgment is against Don Juan of *Fifine* and Prince Hohenstiel-Schwangau (representing Napoleon III). But the reviewers considered that he was defending the incontinent Don Juan and accused him of perversity; while of *Hohenstiel-Schwangau,* one reviewer said that it was a "eulogism on the Second Empire," and another called it "a scandalous attack on the old constant friend of England."[1]

But these are exceptional cases, occurring mainly in Browning and the result partly of Browning's sometimes excessive ingenuity, partly of a judgment more complex than the reader is expecting, partly of careless reading. Certainly Don Juan's

---

[1] Quoted in De Vane, *Browning Handbook,* (New York: Appleton-Century-Crofts), pp. 243, 369, 363; (London: John Murray), pp. 216, 327, 321.

desertion of his wife and return to the gipsy girl in the end—even though he says it is for five minutes and "to clear the matter up"—ought for the careful reader to show up his argument as rationalizing a weak character, although the argument contains in itself much that is valid. In the same way, the final reference to Gigadibs as starting from the beginning with a plough and the Gospel of St John ought to indicate that he is getting closer to the truth than Blougram. I have tried to indicate that more is involved in our judgment of the bishop than the simple alternatives of *for* and *against*. As the bishop himself says of the modern interest in character, which interest is precisely the material of the dramatic monologue:

> Our interest's on the dangerous edge of things.
> The honest thief, the tender murderer,
> The superstitious atheist, demirep
> That loves and saves her soul in new French books—
> We watch while these in equilibrium keep
> The giddy line midway: one step aside,
> They're classed and done with. I, then, keep the line
> Before your sages,—just the men to shrink
> From the gross weights, coarse scales and labels broad
> You offer their refinement. Fool or knave?
> Why needs a bishop be a fool or knave
> When there's a thousand diamond weights between?

There is judgment all right among modern empiricists, but it follows understanding and remains tentative and subordinate to it. In trying to take into account as many facts as possible and to be as supple and complex as the facts themselves, judgment cuts across the conventional categories, often dealing in paradoxes—the honest thief, the tender murderer. Above all, it brings no ready-made yardstick; but allows the case to establish itself in all its particularity, and to be judged according to criteria generated by its particularity.

In other words, judgment is largely psychologized and historicized. We adopt a man's point of view and the point of view of his age in order to judge him—which makes the judgment relative, limited in applicability to the particular conditions of the case. This is the kind of judgment we get in the dramatic monologue, which is for this reason an appropriate form for an empiricist and relativist age, an age which has come to consider value as an evolving thing dependent upon the changing individual and social requirements of the historical process. For such an age judgment can never be final, it has changed and will change again; it must be perpetually checked against fact, which comes before judgment and remains always more certain.

3

"The Ring and the Book": A Relativist Poem

IN the same sense that Dante's great poem can be said to derive its meaning from a Catholic, and Milton's from a Protestant, ethos—so Browning's *The Ring and the Book* derives its meaning from the relativist ethos predominant in Western culture since the Enlightenment. The first sign of the poem's relativism is in Browning's use of dramatic monologues to tell his story. For though he does not entirely succeed, his aim at least in telling the same story eleven times over through ten dramatic monologues and his own account in Book I was to replace the objective view of events of traditional drama and narrative with points of view. Such a method can be justified only on the relativist assumption that truth cannot be apprehended in itself but must be "induced" from particular points of view, and that there can be sufficient difference among the points of view to make each repetition interesting and important as a psychological fact.

Another sign of relativism is that Browning counted it such a virtue for his poem to be based on "pure crude fact." Facts figure as pure gold in the analogy of the ring, which Browning uses to justify stamping an interpretation upon the facts. The poet's imagination, the "something of mine," is likened to the alloy which the goldsmith uses to shape the gold into a ring. But the ring once made, the goldsmith bathes it in acid to free the gold from the alloy; so that in the end, we are assured, "the shape remains,"

> Gold as it was, is, shall be evermore:
> Prime nature with an added artistry.   (I, 28-29)

It is significant that Browning should have felt it necessary to justify a liberty of interpretation which has always been granted poets.

But it was just the imputation of poetic licence, relegating his work to the realm of fancy, entertaining but unimportant, that he did not want. His truth had to be taken seriously, which meant in a positivist age that it had to have the facts behind it, had to emerge from the facts. In answer to the difficult question, "Why take the artistic way to prove so much?"—Browning, speaking again in his own voice in the concluding passage of the poem, says the artistic way is best for criticizing a whole false view of things. Since falsehood is formulation that has got too far from the facts, to attack it with another formulation is to awaken resistance and have your true formulation judged false by the logical criteria that established the false formulation. "But Art," he says.

> may tell a truth
> Obliquely, do the thing shall breed the thought,
> Nor wrong the thought, missing the mediate word.
> So may you paint your picture, twice show truth,
> Beyond mere imagery on the wall,—
> So, note by note, bring music from your mind,
> Deeper than ever e'en Beethoven dived,—
> So write a book shall mean beyond the facts,
> Suffice the eye and save the soul beside.   (XII, 859-67)

Art, then, is truer than philosophical discourse because it is closer to the facts, taking into account more complexities, breeding the thought precisely. It shows the truth twice in that it shows the physical facts and the metaphysical meaning behind them—opening out an extra dimension "beyond . . . the wall" because it brings to the business of understanding the mind's deepest resource, imagination, what Wordsworth called "Reason in her most exalted mood." Above all, art is more convincing than philosophical discourse because, confronting false formulations with facts, it causes us to start again with the facts and construct the truth for ourselves.

Yet the judgments of *The Ring and the Book* are by no means "relative"—if we mean by the word that no one is either good or bad but a bit of both. Pompilia, Count Guido's young wife whom he murders, is presented in the final judgment as nothing short of a saint; while Guido is an incarnation of evil. His being evil remains as the real motive and the only one that can explain all the facts of his behaviour—when, after two monologues totalling more than 4500 lines, the complex layers of rationalized motivations have been finally stripped away.

What he comes to understand, and we along with him, is that he has hated Pompilia for no other reason than that she is good. Let no one, he says,

> think to bear that look
> Of steady wrong, endured as steadily
> —Through what sustainment of deluding hope? . . .
> This self-possession to the uttermost,
> How does it differ in aught, save degree,
> From the terrible patience of God? (XI, 1373-80)

And he cries out in an unguarded moment:

> Again, how she is at me with those eyes!
> Away with the empty stare! Be holy still,
> And stupid ever! (XI, 2076-78)

He hates her, he reveals, because she did not hate him in return, did not wish him harm. But not until the end, when the black-hooded Brotherhood of Death has come to take him to execution, when the railing and the spite are no longer of use, nor the steadily shifting arguments ever retreating toward confession of his wolf nature—not until the extreme moment does he strip himself bare in a desperate call for help. He calls, in psychologically ascending order, upon the Abate and Cardinal who have attended him in the death cell, upon Christ, Maria, God, and in the final line:

> Pompilia, will you let them murder me? (XI, 2427)

That cry is his salvation, acknowledging for the first time, without qualification or self-defence, Pompilia's goodness and his own evil. The implication is that he dies repentant.

Between the moral poles of Pompilia and Guido, the other characters are assigned no less definite places. Caponsacchi, the young priest who helps Pompilia escape from Guido, possesses the heroic as distinguished from the saintly virtues; he possesses, too, the weaknesses of the heroic character when its potentiality is unemployed—dandyism and gallantry with women. But being good in the purely human way, Caponsacchi has a capacity for development not required by Pompilia's unchanging perfection. She is for him the *donna angelicata*, providing him with the crucial opportunity of his life—the chance for heroic exploit and the chance to recognize in her, embodied goodness, and to be thus recalled to his priestly vows and the true meaning of Christianity.

Corresponding in moral position to Caponsacchi is the Pope, who represents the highest moral attainment of human wisdom as Caponsacchi represents the highest in manliness and courage. Although not vessels of Divine Grace, like Pompilia, it is their distinction to be the only ones (except for Guido in his final line) who recognize her pre-eminence and learn from her. It is the Pope in his capacity of final court of appeal for Guido, who pronounces all the authoritative judgments of the poem—"the ultimate/Judgment save yours" (I, 1220-21) Browning calls it, addressing the reader. But if the reader has read correctly, his judgments should coincide with the Pope's; and to allow no mistake Browning tells the main events of the story in his own voice in Book I, in such a way as to shape our judgments of the speakers before we have met them. The judgments of the poem are obviously not intended to be "relative"—if we mean by the word *indefinite* or *a matter of opinion*.

To be sure, there are the characters of indefinite moral position. They people the world in which the significant action of the poem takes place; they are the poem's common clay, its chorus. Browning dubs in the "world" by means of the three speakers who represent the three lines of Roman opinion, the pro-Guido, the pro-Pompilia, and the impartial; by means of the two lawyers, prosecution and defence; and although they never speak, by means of Pompilia's parents, the Comparini who, through their mixture of motives and consistent pettiness, make the mistakes that involve their daughter in tragedy. But if these characters are in themselves indefinite, the judgment of them is quite definite. The Pope condemns the Comparini in terms general enough to apply to all the small-souled, morally indefinite inhabitants of the "world." "Sadly mixed natures," he calls the Comparini, who troop

> somewhere 'twixt the best and worst,
> Where crowd the indifferent product, all too poor
> Makeshift, starved samples of humanity! (X, 1213-15)

Nor are they less culpable because indefinite:

> White shall not neutralize the black, nor good
> Compensate bad in man, absolve him so:
> Life's business being just the terrible choice. (X, 1236-38)

What the Pope understands about the whole tragic Pompilia story, and what Guido also acknowledges in his final moments, is that it is sheer miracle that just this once the good has been vindicated and Pompilia's true worth recognized. All the established institutions for distinguishing right from wrong—the law, the Church, the authority of parents and husband—all have been either entirely wrong, or if partly right have still missed the main point, Pompilia's absolute goodness and Guido's badness. The courts, the lawyers, the representative of the impartial line of Roman opinion, all have committed the "relativist" fallacy of supposing that there must be both right and wrong on each side. Caponsacchi complains to the court of their "relativist" obtuseness. If I insist, he says, that my motives in helping Pompilia to escape were entirely pure and Christian, you cry "absurd!" But if I

> own flaws i' the flesh, agree
> To go with the herd, be hog no more nor less,
> Why, hogs in common herd have common rights: (VI, 1722-24)

why then you are indulgent of what you consider my peccadillo with a pretty woman. For the Pope it is precisely the moral of the story that the good was vindicated by just the dandy priest doing what his vows and the laws of Church and State expressly forbid, running away with a married woman. "Be glad," says the Pope apostrophizing Caponsacchi,

> thou hast let light into the world
> Through that irregular breach o' the boundary. (X, 1205-06)

And this brings us to the proper sense in which *The Ring and the Book* can be called a relativist poem. It is relativist in that the social and religious absolutes are not the means for understanding the right and wrong of the poem; they are for the most part barriers to understanding. Pompilia is misled by all the constituted authorities, by "foolish parents" and "bad husband" as the Pope puts it, as well as by Church and State in the persons of the Archbishop and the Governor of Arezzo who send her back to Guido when she appeals to them for help. She even turns out to have been the offspring of vice, since Violante Comparini alleges in the course of the poem that she bought Pompilia from her real mother, a Roman prostitute. Neverthe-

less, in spite of all the wrong external influences, Pompilia finds
the right way because her instinct is right. The Pope marvels at
the flowering, just where the odds against it were greatest, of
this one shining example of goodness vouchsafed his reign,
while the plants so carefully nurtured by Church and respectability came to nought:

> While—see how this mere chance-sown cleft-nursed seed
> That sprang up by the wayside 'neath the foot
> Of the enemy, this breaks all into blaze,
> Spreads itself, one wide glory of desire
> To incorporate the whole great sun it loves
> From the inch-height whence it looks and longs! (X, 1041-46)

In the same way, the Pope sees that Caponsacchi was in the
position for "catching quick the sense of the real cry" just
because he had strayed, had his "sword-hand" on the "lute"
and his "sentry-station" at some "wanton's gate"; he had
therefore a fresh ear for the contrasting moral cry, while pious
Christians had grown "too obtuse/Of ear, through iteration of
command" (X, 1198-99). Caponsacchi did right not to reason
out the merits of Pompilia's case but to follow with passionate
spontaneity his immediate perception of the good. "Blind?"
asks the Pope,

> Ay, as a man would be inside the sun,
> Delirious with the plenitude of light
> Should interfuse him to the finger-ends—
> Let him rush straight, and how shall he go wrong? (X, 1562-65)

Caponsacchi himself tells the court how in deciding to rescue
Pompilia he came to see that what official morality called sin
was in this case virtue, that death was in this case life, salvation:

> Death was the heart of life, and all the harm
> My folly had crouched to avoid, now proved a veil
> Hiding all gain my wisdom strove to grasp. (VI, 954-56)

Not only are the judgments of *The Ring and the Book* independent of official morality, they are for the most part in conflict with it and in this sense *relative* to the particular conditions
of the poem and to the motives and quality of the characters.
Browning is not saying that all discontented wives are to be
rescued from their husbands, but just this particular wife from
her particular husband. Why? Because of what we understand

Pompilia and Guido to *be*. Hence the use of repetition and the dramatic monologue—not because the judgments are a matter of opinion but because we must judge what is being said by who is saying it. The point is that all the speakers are eloquent to a fault and make the best possible case consistent with their own prepossessions and the facts accessible to them. Our judgments depend, therefore, on what we understand of them as people—of their motives, sincerity and innate moral quality. Judgment goes on, in other words, below the level of the argument and hence the dramatic monologue, which makes it possible for us to apprehend the speaker totally, to subordinate what he says to what we know of him through sympathy.

Browning makes it clear, speaking in his own voice in Book I, that the judgments of the "world" are inadequate because of the personal inadequacies of the "worldly" speakers. The speaker who represents the Half-Rome that favours Guido is honest enough in his "feel after the vanished truth," but harbours all the same in that feel "A hidden germ of failure," "Some prepossession" that causes

> The instinctive theorizing whence a fact
> Looks to the eye as the eye likes the look. (I, 863-64)

In recognizing the inevitability of personal distortion, Browning does not mean, as I understand it, that there is no truth, but that truth depends upon the nature of the theorizing and ultimately upon the nature of the soul of which the theorizing is a projection. After all, Browning justifies by the analogy of the ring his own instinctive theorizing of the facts of the Roman murder case, and there is disparity between the accounts of even such admirable characters as Pompilia and Caponsacchi. But the pro-Guido speaker of the monologue called *Half-Rome* reveals a prepossession hardly adequate to understanding Pompilia's story. He reveals toward the end that he is a married man worried about his wife's fidelity, and that his whole account, with its emphasis on Guido's just revenge, is by way of a warning that he wants delivered to his rival.

The pro-Pompilia speaker of the monologue called *The Other Half-Rome* is, instead, a sentimental bachelor, yet no more adequate as a judge. He represents

> the opposite feel
> For truth with a like swerve, like unsuccess,—
> Or if success, by no skill but more luck
> This time, through siding rather with the wife,
> Because a fancy-fit inclined that way,
> Than with the husband.   (I, 883-88)

Critics have objected to this unfavourable introduction of a speaker who in his monologue strikes us as intelligent, sensitive and sincere; and it must be admitted that we would probably not discern the limitations of the pro-Pompilia speaker were we not specifically alerted to look for them. But it is to alert us that Browning speaks in his own voice in Book I; he wants us to see that the speaker's interest in Pompilia is sentimental and literary rather than moral, and hence a "fancy-fit." The speaker conceives Pompilia as the beautiful wronged heroine of what he himself calls the "romance-books." He characterizes her as

> the helpless, simple-sweet
> Or silly-sooth, unskilled to break one blow
> At her good fame, by putting finger forth.   (III, 805-07)

This is to miss the hard moral core of the saint, diluting her into mere negative and vapid weakness; the conception, in fact, matches Guido's when he pictures an Ovidian metamorphosis in which Pompilia will turn into water after her death (XI, 2050-55).

The speaker is preoccupied with Pompilia's beauty and the theatrical effect of her death-bed scene. He is as inadequate as the rest of the "world" in judging her relation with Caponsacchi:

> Men are men: why then need I say one word
> More than that our mere man the Canon here
> Saw, pitied, loved Pompilia?   (III, 880-82)

though he is too well-versed in the conventions of the romance-books to suppose, like the others, that their love has not been technically innocent:

> oh, called innocent love, I know!
> Only, such scarlet fiery innocence
> As most folk would try to muffle up in shade.   (III, 894-96)

Just as he casts Pompilia and Caponsacchi in the roles of romance hero and heroine, so he casts Guido as romance villain at some points, and at others as comic cuckold—in both roles Guido is to be hated by literary convention. Guido is himself aware of literature's antipathy to the betrayed husband, and complains that literary and stage precedents have turned opinion against him. The speaker of *The Other Half-Rome* is so much concerned with the melodramatic surface of the story, and so little with its moral meaning, that he makes no moral distinction between Pompilia and the Comparini, characterizing the parents along with the daughter as innocent lambs ravaged by the Franceschini wolves, Guido and his family.

Whether or not we grant that Browning has successfully dramatized the limitations of the pro-Pompilia speaker, we must agree that in its intention at least *The Other Half-Rome* is perhaps the poem's boldest stroke. For at the risk of confusing us utterly, the poet forestalls just the facile judgment the casual reader is likely to make; he takes a stand not only against wrong judgments but against the right judgment on the wrong grounds. "So, listen," he says in concluding his introduction of the pro-Pompilia speaker,

> how, to the other half of Rome,
> Pompilia seemed a saint and martyr both!   (I, 908-09)

and there is, in the context of what has preceded, a note of sarcasm in the last line. Yet the last line does not differ from the Pope's "ultimate judgment" of Pompilia. The point for us, the point that explains the use of the dramatic monologue in this poem, is that the judgments are different because the men who pronounce them are different.

If the first two Roman speakers go wrong through their prepossessions, Tertium Quid, the representative of cultivated Roman opinion, goes wrong through his attempt to evade moral judgment altogether. Browning introduces him with evident sarcasm:

> Here, after ignorance, instruction speaks;
> Here, clarity of candour, history's soul,
> The critical mind in short.   (I, 924-26)

The speaker's assumption that there is neither right nor wrong in the case, but self-interested motives on both sides, is itself a prepossession that, with his aristocratic bias, leaves him in the end as "wide o' the mark" as the other two.

As the institutional mechanism by which the "world" passes judgment, law and the lawyers cannot be ignored, though they are included only to be satirized. "Ignore law," asks Browning with mock surprise,

> the recognized machine,
> Elaborate display of pipe and wheel
> Framed to unchoke, pump up and pour apace
> Truth till a flowery foam shall wash the world?
> The patent truth-extracting process,—ha? (I, 1110-14)

Law is too mechanical to deal adequately with moral issues, while the lawyers are immediately disqualified as judges of the moral issue by the professional nature of their motives. They speak for hire and subordinate the truth-extracting process to winning the case and advancing their careers. Arcangeli, the Procurator of the Poor who defends Guido, has not only to win the case but also

> All kind of interests to keep intact,
> More than one efficacious personage
> To tranquillize, conciliate and secure,
> And above all, public anxiety
> To quiet, (I, 1138-42)

and to render absurd his mixture of motives, he has in addition domestic burdens, a birthday-banquet to prepare for his only son, "Paternity at smiling strife with law" (I, 1146).

His opponent, Bottini, the Fisc, because he is prosecuting Guido finds himself

> Pompilia's patron by the chance of the hour
> To-morrow her persecutor, (I, 1173-74)

her persecutor, we learn in a postscript to the poem in the last Book, when after Pompilia's death he prosecutes a suit for her property, which requires that he prove her to have been a fallen woman. In prosecuting Guido, however, his job is to vindicate Pompilia's fame; but even in doing this, he grants so much against her that his "best defence"—as is pointed out by

the Augustinian monk who heard Pompilia's last confession—
is itself a calumny. A bachelor, he has not the domestic preoccupations of Arcangeli, but is preoccupied instead with his
own eloquence and ingenuity and with the frustrating awareness that his masterly argument is only to be read by the court
and will never enjoy the advantage of his oral delivery. Bottini's
extra preoccupations, like Arcangeli's, obscure the moral issue:

> ah, the gift of eloquence!
> Language that goes, goes, easy as a glove,
> O'er good and evil, smoothens both to one. (I, 1179-81)

Arcangeli and Bottini disqualify not only as lawyers but as
men, and it was probably to reveal their personal inadequacies
that Browning gave their pleas private and dramatic settings.
(Arcangeli is doing a first draft of his plea at home; Bottini is
rehearsing his aloud at home.) Arcangeli is much too normal,
fat, domestic and contented to appreciate the emotional and
moral intensities of the case; while Bottini is the young-old man,
disproportioned between emotional and intellectual development, a child with an old and corrupt mind:

> Just so compounded is the outside man,
> Blue juvenile pure eye and pippin cheek,
> And brow all prematurely soiled and seamed
> With sudden age, bright devastated hair. (I, 1196-99)

With his intellectual virtuosity he manipulates passions and
moral meanings he cannot begin to understand.

No less than the lawyers, the representatives of Roman
opinion speak to show off their virtuosity. They all reveal at
the end of their monologues self-interested motives which disqualify them as judges of the moral issue. The pro-Guido
speaker has a vested interest in the authority of the marriage
bond; the pro-Pompilia speaker is a bachelor with a sentimental,
if not an active, interest in melodramatic violations of the
marriage bond; and Tertium Quid reveals in his last two lines
that he has been the whole time speaking to impress certain
Princes and Cardinals:

> (You'll see, I have not so advanced myself,
> After my teaching the two idiots here!) (IV, 1639-40)

he mutters after an Excellency and a Highness have departed.

By their motives shall ye know them! This is Browning's injunction throughout. In contrast to the inadequate motives of the "world," we have the Pope's high seriousness as he sits out

> the dim
> Droop of a sombre February day   (I, 1235-36)

> With winter in my soul beyond the world's.   (X, 213)

The Pope is aware of his responsibility as Christ's Vicar in making the ultimate judgment, and knows also that his judgment is fallible. He is confident, however, for even if it should turn out that he has made a mistake in judging Guido, he knows he has judged according to the light given him, that his motives have been pure:

> For I am ware it is the seed of act,
> God holds appraising in His hollow palm,
> Not act grown great thence on the world below,
> Leafage and branchage, vulgar eyes admire.
> Therefore I stand on my integrity,
> Nor fear at all.   (X, 272-77)

To add to the solemnity of the Pope's motives, he is eighty-six and aware that Guido's death may just precede his own, that his judgment of Guido may be his last official act, closely bound up with his own salvation.

The Pope's confidence in his judgment does not rest on the supposition that the truth is directly or easily apprehensible; but neither does he suppose that the truth cannot be found in the "pleadings and counter-pleadings" he has before him:

> Truth, nowhere, lies yet everywhere in these—
> Not absolutely in a portion, yet
> Evolvible from the whole: evolved at last
> Painfully, held tenaciously by me.   (X, 229-32)

Truth is not in any one argument but can be "induced" from the particular points of view, the way Browning expects us to "induce" it from the ten dramatic monologues. And the judgments the Pope pronounces as evolved truth are the kind the dramatic monologue offers—judgments of character. The Pope does not weigh argument against argument, fact against fact, but cuts right through the facts to a sympathetic apprehension of the motives and essential moral qualities behind the deeds. He relies not upon logic to make his judgments but upon talent, intuition, insight, the advantages of his own character gained through a long experience of life and people:

> dark, difficult enough
> The human sphere, yet eyes grow sharp by use,
> I find the truth, dispart the shine from shade,
> As a mere man may,

with "well-nigh decayed intelligence," if what the populace says of his senility is true, but "What of that?"

> Through hard labour and good will,
> And habitude that gives a blind man sight
> At the practised finger-ends of him, I do
> Discern, and dare decree in consequence,
> Whatever prove the peril of mistake.   (X, 1241-52)

Thus he decrees:

> First of the first,
> Such I pronounce Pompilia, then as now
> Perfect in whiteness: (X, 1004-06)

Caponsacchi sprang forth "the hero," and in spite of the compromising look of the facts,

> In thought, word and deed,
> How throughout all thy warfare thou wast pure,
> I find it easy to believe: (X, 1169-71)

while in spite of all the arguments and legal rights that Guido can adduce, "Not one permissible impulse moves the man" (X, 537).

All the morally significant characters of the poem cut through facts in the same way. As soon as Pompilia and Caponsacchi lay eyes on each other, each recognizes the other's distinction. And their subsequent relation is carried on by means of such intuitive perceptions. Guido forges letters of crude solicitation which he has carried between them in order to compromise Pompilia. But each knows the other incapable of such letters. "As I," says Caponsacchi,

> Recognized her, at potency of truth,
> So she, by the crystalline soul, knew me,
> Never mistook the signs.   (VI, 931-34)

Their relation develops by means of the letters in a direction contrary to the purport of the letters. In the course of receiving them and sending back refusals, Pompilia comes to realize that Caponsacchi is the honourable man she can trust to rescue her, while he comes to realize that she is the virtuous woman whom it would not be a sin to rescue. Guido himself cuts through his own false defences to see in the end the moral truth. He stands for this reason a better chance of salvation than the inhabitants of the "world" who, by flattening out the moral issue, miss the final truth.

Thus, truth is psychologized in the sense that the facts do not reveal it, nor is it arrived at by any external yardstick, whether legal, Christian, or conventional. The moral judgments are definite and extreme, but they depend upon our total apprehension of the characters themselves. What we arrive at in the end is not *the* truth, but truth as the worthiest characters of the poem see it.

Truth is historicized as well, the historical meaning running parallel to the psychological. Just as the facts and arguments do not adequately reveal the moral issue between Pompilia and Guido, so the legal and ecclesiastical machinery of the time proves inadequate to reveal and judge the moral issue. The Pope is distressed by the failure of the instituted machinery because he sees its significance in terms of historical dialectics. "We have got too familiar with the light" (X, 1794), he says comparing his own time, when Christianity is respectable and necessary for getting on in the world, with apostolic times, when as a minority sect it could attract no one not sincerely committed to its essential meaning.

The time is 1698, almost the end of the seventeenth century and of the pontificate of Innocent XII (died 1700); almost the end, as the Pope points out, of Christianity's period of triumph, of the age when for all the heresies and theological disputes the authority of Christianity itself remained uncontested. The Pope foresees a new age to be ushered into life by his death, and asks whether it will be the mission of that age "to shake"

> This torpor of assurance from our creed,
> Re-introduce the doubt discarded, bring
> That formidable danger back, we drove
> Long ago to the distance and the dark?   (X, 1853-57)

He draws from Pompilia's case both despair and hope. On the one hand, her case presented a challenge which the instituted machinery showed itself unable to meet. The machinery of Christianity showed itself to be by now almost completely at odds with the meaning of Christianity. For was it not by daring to break the Christian rules that Caponsacchi came to virtue's aid, while where, asks the Pope, were "the Christians in their panoply?" "Slunk into corners!" (X, 1566-71).

On the other hand, there is hope in the fact that Pompilia and Caponsacchi did find the right way in spite of all the wrong external guidance. Even in the anarchic age ahead when men shall reject dogma and declare themselves a law unto themselves, some one Pompilia will keep essential Christianity alive through sheer right instinct:

> At least some one Pompilia left the world
> Will say "I know the right place by foot's feel,
> "I took it and tread firm there; wherefore change?"   (X, 1885-87)

just as in the past Euripides anticipated Christian morality without benefit of Christian revelation. Thus, the Pope comes to see that the truth is something other than the machinery by which men try to understand it. He sees what is pointed out by St John in Browning's *A Death in the Desert*—that "the proofs shift," that myth, dogma, the machinery changes, but truth remains, never in equilibrium with the machinery and sometimes in direct conflict with it. He draws dialectical comfort from the necessary disequilibrium, for injustice shows up the old machinery as inadequate and helps

> to evolve,
> By new machinery in counterpart,
> The moral qualities of man.   (X, 1378-80)

In trying, in other words, to adapt the machinery of understanding to the truth, which remains always in advance of the machinery, man advances his moral understanding.

Just as, psychologically, the truth about a man is larger and always in advance of our formulated understanding of him; so, historically, truth is larger and in advance of the formulations and institutions of any age. Fra Celestino, the Augustinian monk who was Pompilia's last confessor, carries this idea beyond the possibility of dialectical comfort in a sermon, some paragraphs of which are quoted as execrable in a letter of Bottini in Book XII. Let no one suppose, says the Augustinian in his sermon, that Pompilia's vindication proves man capable of discerning truth or his judgments trustworthy. Let us rather draw from the case the contrary lesson that "God is true and every man a liar." For the fact that such a case has come to our attention should warn us of all the Pompilias who have died wronged and unknown. Nor is her vindication to the credit of human institutions, public opinion or

> The inadequacy and inaptitude
> Of that self-same machine, that very law
> Man vaunts,   (XII, 576-78)

but the work of the Pope's miraculous insight, as much a gift of God as Pompilia's goodness itself:

> What I call God's hand,—you, perhaps,—mere chance
> Of the true instinct of an old good man
> Who happens to hate darkness and love light,—
> In whom too was the eye that saw, not dim,
> The natural force to do the thing he saw,
> Nowise abated,—both by miracle.   (XII, 592-97)

The conclusion to be drawn both from the Pope's dialectical perception of the developing disequilibrium between truth and machinery, and Fra Celestino's somewhat Antinomian perception of their eternal opposition, is that fixed principles and the institutions which embody them can never be adequate to judge the truth. Judgment must remain what it is in the Pope —a matter of talent, insight and the essential moral quality of the judge. It must remain what it is in the dramatic monologue —a matter of total apprehension to which formulation is secondary and in some degree of disequilibrium. Truth in other words is relative—psychologically, to the nature of the judge and person being judged; historically, to the amount of disequilibrium in any given age between truth and the institutions by which truth is understood.

Not only does Browning show the inadequacy of most people to judge Pompilia, but he sets the action against a detailed historical background the purpose of which is to show how far the disequilibrium between truth and machinery has gone by 1698. From every side it is made clear that the Church has become a centre of wealth and power, attracting to its service men whose motives are anything but religious. Guido's two younger brothers are priests as the only means of livelihood for younger sons of an impoverished noble family, and it is only the need to produce an heir for the family that has kept Guido himself from turning priest. He has, however, taken minor orders and served for thirty years as toady to a Cardinal in the hope of making his fortune. It is when the hope fails that he marries Pompilia for her money. The Pope finds it indicative of the condition of the Church that Guido has the effrontery to claim clerical privilege in appealing to the Pope the decision of the secular court of Rome. The Pope sees that the clerical privilege is now being used to protect crime.

Guido also expected the nobleman's privilege: "Who, using the old licence, dreamed of harm" (XI, 780), he complains; and he cites as the kind of precedent he has in mind the brutal story of a stableman, Felice, who in the reign of the last Pope was beheaded for daring to strike a Duke who had abducted his sister. "Ah, but times change," Guido complains,

> there's quite another Pope,
> I do the Duke's deed, take Felice's place.   (XI, 276-77)

Both Guido and the Pope are aware that the general corruption of the time ought to have guaranteed Guido protection, and that justice in this case is unaccountable miracle, "luck" as Guido calls it:

> What was there wanting to a masterpiece
> Except the luck that lies beyond a man?   (XI, 1566-67)

The Pope knows that a routine bribe would unquestionably have obtained for Guido the scrap of paper necessary to leave Rome with horses and so escape to his native Tuscany, where the Grand Duke's court had already declared in his favour and the Papal court could not touch him. That Guido, a thirty-years' resident of Rome and wise to its inside track, should have neglected to provide for such an obvious contingency, the Pope can only attribute to an act of God. And Guido completes the story by telling how, in his frantic efforts to use bribery for obtaining horses without the necessary scrap of paper, it was his bad luck to have encountered just "the one scrupulous fellow in all Rome" (XI, 1639).

It is a nice stroke, however, that the same general corruption which ought to have protected Guido would in any case have undone him in the end. For it is revealed in the Pope's monologue and again in Guido's second monologue that the four peasants from Guido's estate, who helped in the murder, were planning to murder him on the road from Rome to Arezzo, because he had not paid them the money promised. Although in his first monologue Guido speaks of their feudal loyalty and keen sense of their lord's honour, which caused them to volunteer vengeance for his wife's infidelity, the Pope reveals that they cared no more for feudal loyalty and honour than did their lord. "All is done purely for the pay," says the Pope,

> which, earned,
> And not forthcoming at the instant, makes
> Religion heresy, and the lord o' the land
> Fit subject for a murder in his turn.   (X, 952-55)

And Guido, complaining in his second monologue of his bad luck, says that even if all else had gone well, there were still these "rustic four o' the family, soft swains," planning to cut his throat.

In this second monologue Guido again goes over the story of the murder, this time to show that he committed not a "crime" but a "blunder"; for the practice, as distinguished from the professed ideals, of his time gave him every reason to pursue the course he did. He complains of his trial in terms that make clear his disrespect for the legal machinery of the time. Were not his lawyers sufficiently "fools" to satisfy the "foolishness set to decide the case?" Did the lawyers lack skill in law, Latin, logic? Did they neglect to feign and flatter, and were not the judges clearly moved by the flattery? How then did the decision go against him? And in appealing finally to the Pope, had he not reason to expect indulgence from an old man about to die, who professed to be "pity's source and seat"? What is more to the point, he had every reason to expect

> A little indulgence to rank, privilege,
> From one who is the thing personified,
> Rank, privilege, indulgence, grown beyond
> Earth's bearing, even, ask Jansenius else! (XI, 1778-81)

Actually, Guido and the Pope make the same historical observations, though for opposite reasons and with opposite judgments. Both see the age, to the Pope's distress and Guido's encouragement, as corrupt from top to bottom, and the murder case as symptomatic of the corruption. But they also see in the murder case, to the Pope's comfort and Guido's chagrin, signs that the corruption of the old order is giving birth to a regenerated new order. The ultimate origin of the crime in the poverty and vice out of which Pompilia was born, and in the property system which caused the Comparini to acquire Pompilia in order to preserve their claim to an inheritance; the cynical marriage barter of Pompilia's money for Guido's title; the precedents of injustice and abuse of privilege that Guido relied on and that were amply fulfilled by the decision of the Tuscan court in his favour; the failure of Church and State authorities to help Pompilia, forcing her to turn to Caponsacchi; the shameful conduct of the Roman convent that sheltered Pompilia, then sought after her death to defame her in order to inherit her property; the presence in the Church of men like Guido and his brothers; the brutality of Guido's peasants, which Guido first used to his advantage then found turned against him—these are signs that the ecclesiastical and feudal sanctions have ceased to apply, that the old order has died from within though the dead machinery still grinds. On the other hand, the unexpected accidents of which Guido complains, the approximately right judgment of the Roman court and the precisely right judgments of Fra Celestino and the Pope, even the exceptional scruples of the official who refused Guido the horses—these are signs that within the old institutions themselves lie the seeds of regeneration.

Psychologically, the right instinct of Pompilia and Caponsacchi is a guarantee that truth maintains itself in the human heart *in spite of* history, of external change. But historically, the murder case shows that truth maintains itself *by means of* history. The general corruption that made Guido's crime possible would also have destroyed him in the end, as it is destroying the old order he relied on. In addition, his crime aroused the almost forgotten conscience of the age to condemn him and the old order. That Pompilia and Caponsacchi found the right way in spite of the age, as Euripides found it in a pre-Christian era and some other Pompilia will find it in the coming post-Christian era, means that truth is different from and anterior to any cultural expression of it, and that the cultural expression must be renewed by testing against truth's source in the human heart. But the dying order makes its own contribution to truth, by dying, and by summoning up its own conscience to condemn itself to death. By isolating the truth within itself against itself, the old order hands on essential truth to find embodiment in a new order.

The Pope is aware of the social and revolutionary implications of the murder case. He is aware that the privileged class expects him to uphold authority by declaring Guido to have acted within his rights as lord and husband. That is why the Pope has Guido executed not in the usual place but in the Square frequented by the nobility: "So shall the quality see, fear and learn" (X, 2114)—learn that the age of special privilege is over. The Pope sacrifices the social order, and even the Christian era to Christian truth. The act by which he condemns Guido and vindicates Pompilia is the great final act of his life, his gift a dying leader of the old order to the new order.

The historical meaning of the poem is symbolized by the references to Molinism, which recur like a leitmotif throughout. Molinism was a fashionable sect in Italy during the 1670's and 1680's; "the sect for a quarter of an hour," Browning calls it. Since it was declared heretical and its leader, Molinos, con

---

[1] See A. K. Cook, "Molinos and the Molinists," *A Commentary Upon Browning's "The Ring and the Book"* (London: Oxford University Press, 1920), Appendix VIII.

demned and imprisoned in 1687, it was undoubtedly by the
time of the murder case in 1698 a lost cause from which everyone would be naturally eager to dissociate himself, if indeed
people still spoke of it as ubiquitously as Browning makes out.
But the very question of Browning's historical accuracy in
giving so much emphasis in 1698 to Molinism is a sign that the
short-lived heresy had advantages for his historical meaning.
First, the restricted life of the heresy and its obscurity in the
modern recollection help localize the poem historically, supply-
ing the detail appropriate to no other time and place, and the
authentic detail, since there it was though now almost forgotten. Second, the nature of the heresy suggests the stirrings
within the Church that foreshadow the new order. Since
Molinos was a Quietist who taught direct apprehension of God
apart from ritual, Church, and even in certain instances the
intermediary contemplation of the humanity of Christ, the
heresy has affinities not only with Evangelical Protestantism
but more to the point with the kind of essential Christianity
that the Pope finds in Pompilia, Euripides and the future
Pompilia of the post-Christian era.

Actually, the poem tells us nothing directly about Molinos'
doctrine; we gather its purport indirectly from the characters
who condemn as Molinism actions which strike us as adhering
to the spirit, in opposition to the dogma and machinery, of
Christianity. It is this pejorative use of Molinism as a recognition that the times are evil, and as a scapegoat on which to
hang the evils of the time, that is its third and most important
advantage in the poem. Molinism and the murder case are
linked together as signs that "Antichrist surely comes and
domesday's near," Guido's crime cropping forth

> I' the course of nature when Molinos' tares
> Are sown for wheat.   (II, 175-76)

We can almost rank the characters morally by the degree of
their preoccupation with Molinism and the extent to which
they use it as a scapegoat. On the one hand, Guido, the lawyers,
and the pro-Guido speaker of *Half-Rome* find Molinists in every
bush. Guido links the case against him with Molinism; Arcangeli, in defending Guido, calls it Molinist doctrine that would
"bar revenge," the "natural privilege of man"; the Fisc,

Bottini, calls Fra Celestino's sermon, "Molinism simple and pure!" Caponsacchi's cynical old bishop, aware of the use to which charges of Molinism are put, half-jestingly accuses him of turning Molinist because he plays "truant in church all day long" from the more worldly duties laid upon him by the Church—duties of society priest and apostle to rich ladies. (To which Caponsacchi replies, "Sir, what if I turned Christian?") Pompilia, too, is jestingly accused of dipping into Molinist books, because she is reluctant to give herself up to Guido's loveless embraces.

On the other hand, Pompilia, Caponsacchi, Fra Celestino and the pro-Pompilia speaker of *The Other Half-Rome* talk little about Molinism and say nothing against it; and the Pope even defends it:

> Leave them alone . . . those Molinists!
> Who may have other light than we perceive.   (I, 315-16)

The Pope sees the Molinists as heralds of the new era, who break up "faith in the report" to return to "faith in the thing." Remembering how Christianity broke up the "old faith of the world," the Pope wonders if it will be necessary in the new era for everyone to deny "recognized truths," as the Molinists do now, in favour of

> some truth
> Unrecognized yet, but perceptible?—
> Correct the portrait by the living face,
> Man's God, by God's God in the mind of man?   (X, 1871-74)

Just as Guido and the Pope display the same historical understanding of the age, so both the characters who condemn and those who do not condemn Molinism understand it in the same way—as an attempt to purify religion and as a herald of revolutionary changes to come. Whatever Molinos' actual doctrine, Molinism in Browning stands for an anti-dogmatic, an empirical and relativist, a psychological and historical approach to religion. Faith in the report must be replaced by faith in the thing; and the thing, the unformulated but perceptible truth, "God's God in the mind of man," is a step ahead of formulated truth, "man's God." Truth's ultimate source is in the individual mind; so that judgment of truth rests on judgment of character. Thus, the Pope is impressed by Molinism because its adherents make their denials "at peril of their body and soul," while the motives of orthodox Christians are questionable since orthodoxy is prudent for body and soul.

Nor is Browning's Molinism an anti-historical heresy that condemns the past as a mistake. It makes its protest within the limited historical context of 1698, a time when the disequilibrium between the thing and the report had grown too great. The Pope sees Molinism and the post-Christian era it foreshadows as history's way of producing again

> the Christian act so possible
> When in the way stood Nero's cross and stake,—
> So hard now when the world smiles "Right and wise!"
>
> (X, 1832-34)

The Church's heresy-hunting impedes the historical process by obscuring the truth, but it also advances history by advancing the decay of the old order. For the Pope sees that while the Church concentrates its attention on the frontier between orthodoxy and heresy, the Christian mainland inside, "quite undisputed-for," decays (X, 1605-13). The historical point is that heresy was not required in Nero's time when no one was likely to profess Christian dogma who had not the faith, and will not be required in the new era when there will again be no disparity between dogma and faith. We hear of no new Molinist dogma to replace the old Church dogma. Browning's Molinism would seem to leave truth at its source in the individual mind, to develop where and as the man of right instinct finds it.

Thus, by precept and example, by its ideas and structure, *The Ring and the Book* achieves its meaning through meeting the conditions of modern psychological and historical relativism. If Browning's poem does not offer the same order of satisfaction as Dante's or Milton's, or for that matter Homer's or Virgil's, it must be remembered that he starts with an almost opposite set of conditions, conditions unprecedented in major poetry before *Faust*.

First of all, Browning starts with Goethe's condition that the poem is not to derive meaning from any external standard of judgment, but is to be the empiric ground giving rise to its own standard of judgment. (Faust spends the whole poem evolving the law by which his actions are to be judged, so that we have really to suspend judgment until the end.) Then Browning imposes upon Goethe's condition another still harder one, in that he does not take off from traditional categories, does not like Goethe give new meaning to an old myth, but draws his meaning out of "pure crude fact." He starts with history, and not even official history with its incrustation of myth, but with just the unmoralized and unhistoricized remains of the life that goes on below the level of history, with an old and forgotten scandal.

It is impossible to overemphasize the importance Browning attached to the crudely and even sordidly realistic quality of his story, since he himself recurs to its rock-bottom factuality over and over again in Book I as though he could not exult enough about it. In his exultation he tosses the Old Yellow Book into the air, catches it again and twists it about by the crumpled vellum covers, all because it is "pure crude fact," likened to the "pure gold" of a ring. It has the shape of a book, he says returning to the subject, but is

> really, pure crude fact
> Secreted from man's life when hearts beat hard,
> And brains, high-blooded, ticked two centuries since.
> Give it me back! The thing's restorative
> I' the touch and sight. (I, 86-90)

And again, with naive wonder, as though he could hardly believe in his good fortune:

> So, in this book lay absolutely truth,
> Fanciless fact, the documents indeed,
> Primary lawyer-pleadings . . .
> real summed-up circumstance. (I, 143-46)

The book is an index to a much larger life situation, and Browning exults because he has found for his magnum opus a subject out of life not literature.

In an experience of illumination, Browning saw through the jumbled facts to the truth of the real life situation. To do this he used the alloy of imagination, not as an interpretive but as a projective function: "I fused my live soul and that inert stuff."

> The life in me abolished the death of things,
> Deep calling unto deep: as then and there
> Acted itself over again once more
> The tragic piece.   (I, 520-23)

For the repristination, the separation of the alloy from the gold once the ring has been shaped, Browning says he retained the sense and manner of the documentation:

> I disappeared; the book grew all in all;
> The lawyers' pleadings swelled back to their size,—
> Doubled in two, the crease upon them yet;   (I, 687-89)

for Browning's purpose was to make us repeat his experience of seeing through the facts to the truth.

The reason for giving the story literary form is not to impose truth upon it but to make the truth accessible, as the smith makes the gold accessible by shaping it into a ring. For though the truth is all set down in the bookful of facts, what has hitherto come of it? Who remembers Guido and Pompilia?

> Was this truth of force?
> Able to take its own part as truth should,
> Sufficient, self-sustaining? Why, if so—
> Yonder's a fire, into it goes my book,
> As who shall say me nay, and what the loss?   (I, 372-76)

No loss because the poet adds nothing to the truth. In imitating in due proportion God's creativeness, man "Creates, no, but resuscitates, perhaps."

> Man, bounded, yearning to be free,
> May so project his surplusage of soul
> In search of body, so add self to self
> By owning what lay ownerless before,—
> So find, so fill full, so appropriate forms—
> That, although nothing which had never life
> Shall get life from him, be, not having been,
> Yet, something dead may get to live again,
> Something with too much life or not enough,
> Which, either way imperfect, ended once:
> An end whereat man's impulse intervenes,
> Makes new beginning, starts the dead alive,
> Completes the incomplete and saves the thing.   (I, 718-34)

Here is the new nineteenth-century theory of the nature and function of poetry. The poet is neither the "creator" of one traditional poetic theory, nor yet the "mirror" or "imitator" of another. For while he works only with extant facts, his meaning is not quite there for imitation; he must find his meaning by restoring to the facts a concreteness they have lost in the process of becoming facts, of being abstracted from their original human and historical situations. Thus the poet as "resuscitator" is the superlatively effective psychologist and historian, the arch-empiricist who works toward greater concreteness and not, as in traditional poetic theory, toward general truths. His talent lies in the "surplusage of soul" which enables him to project himself into the facts, apprehend them sympathetically in other words, and thus apprehend their life. His poem establishes a pole for sympathy, so that the reader, too, can project himself into the facts and apprehend their life. For both poet and reader, to "see into the life of things" is to see their meaning. Meaning comes not from theoretical interpretation but from the intensest concreteness.

Thus, meaning is not separable from the facts, and is in that sense psychological and historical, co-extensive with the facts of character and setting. Any formulation of the meaning in terms applicable beyond the conditions of the poem remains partial and problematical as an account of the poem. Even the Pope's interpretation of the events is presumably partial and problematical, though we favour it above other interpretations because of what we apprehend about him as a person. Hence Browning's use of dramatic monologues, to make clear that no point of view is identifiable with the truth. "The same transaction," Browning said of the poem, "seen from a number of differing points of view, or glimpses in a mirror."[1] Just as we perceive the third dimension because each eye gives a different report, so the disparity in points of view gives the lifelike effect. Our apprehension of the total three-dimensional picture is the meaning. But when we try to rationalize our apprehension, break it up into moral or legal judgments or even judgments of fact, we are reduced to partial views, the variegated refractions of truth in the mirror.

[1] Quoted in Betty Miller, *Robert Browning: A Portrait* (London: John Murray, 1952), p. 231.

These then are the unprecedented conditions of *The Ring and the Book*—not only that the poem was to be no mere illustration of an external principle from which the facts would derive meaning, but that the facts themselves, all of them, unselected and as they came to hand (their sordidness was all the better as a guarantee that they were unselected), were to yield the meaning. It can be argued that Browning does not entirely let the facts speak for themselves; for he not only speaks in his own voice in Books I and XII, but he makes the Pope too authoritative.[1] It is certainly a valid criticism of *The Ring and the Book* that good and evil are not sufficiently interfused. Our judgment is forced from the beginning, whereas it would seem to be peculiarly the genius of a poem treating different points of view toward the same story to treat each point of view impartially, allowing judgment to arise out of the utmost ambiguity.

But such a criticism raises the question whether facts really can speak for themselves; whether a poet can, with the mere accumulation of prosaic details and a workable middle style seldom rising to passages which can in themselves be called poetry, achieve the high transcendental meaning Browning wanted. For he wanted nothing less than to portray in Pompilia the most exalted saintliness (Dante's Beatrice was not, I should imagine, beyond his mark), revealing itself amid and by means of the ordinarily vicious human motives and judgments. The poetry, the total illumination, lies in the dynamism of the whole scheme, really in the backward glance, the reader's sense of having come a long way.

However we measure Browning's achievement, his aim—to make poetry rise out of prose and spirituality out of the world's common clay, to meet in other words the conditions for modern intellectual and moral conviction as Tennyson in the *Idylls*, Arnold in *Sohrab* and Morris in *Sigurd* do not—would have to be the aim, I should think, of any genuinely modern literature. If his method seems to pertain more closely to the novel than to poetry, so much the better for my point. For to judge Browning's poem adequately, we would want to know whether other

[1] Henry James, who saw a point-of-view novel in *The Ring and the Book*, considers dropping the Pope from his hypothetical novelized version—"as too high above the whole connection functionally and historically for us to place him within it dramatically." ("The Novel in 'The Ring and the Book'," *Notes on Novelists*, London: J. M. Dent, 1914, p. 316.)

poets have managed to pitch their meaning higher, given the same weight of clay; or whether the long poem is, for that matter, the vehicle for sublimating a weight of clay.

The relativist conditions for modern conviction might explain, for example, the decline of the long poem and the rise of the novel in the nineteenth century, as well as the almost universal retreat by twentieth-century poets into short poetry—the poetry of momentary illumination in which the illumination is made possible through a personal and temporary rejection of the facts, or rather of the prevailing system of ideas through which we perceive the facts. Certainly, the relativist conditions make the virtues of classical narrative and dramatic poetry difficult to achieve. The weight of clay makes difficult what Arnold, protesting against the effect on poetry of modern culture, called the "grand style"; while the differing points of view, the variegated refractions in the mirror are, according to the new *ars poetica*, a virtue—though a virtue quite opposite from that singleness of view Arnold admired and envied so much in Sophocles, "who saw life steadily and saw it whole."

4

The Dramatic Element: Truth as Perspective

TO see life steadily and whole, as Arnold tells us Sophocles saw it, is to see life with its moral and emotional meaning inside it. It is to see Truth. But it is precisely the modern condition that there is no publicly accepted moral and emotional Truth, there are only perspectives toward it—those partial meanings which individuals may get a glimpse of at particular moments but which, formulated as ideas for other moments and people, become problematical. The empiricism of the dramatic monologue, as demonstrated by its disequilibrium between sympathy and judgment, is a sign that it imitates not life but a particular perspective toward life, somebody's experience of it.

The particular perspective is especially apparent in the dramatic monologue, where we clearly adopt the speaker's point of view, both visual and moral, as our entry into the poem —the resulting limitation and even distortion of the physical and moral truth being among the main pleasures of the form. Followed through consistently, the particular angle of vision gives an unfamiliar view of familiar things, opening us to an apprehension of their meaning at the same time that it reminds us of their physical reality; while the consistency of the distortion gives unity to the poem by establishing the singleness of the point of view. Most important, however, the particular perspective is the visual expression of the meaning and, in its departure from the ordinary view, the sign of the presence of the speaker and of the new thing the poem is saying. By seeing what the speaker sees we are able to identify ourselves with him, stand in his position and thus inside the poem where meaning resides. Since the projective leap is more apparent the more different from our own the view we take, the communication is likely to be more emphatic, the more particular, the more extraordinary even, the perspective.

Thus, the dramatic monologue specializes in the reprehensible speaker because his moral perspective is extraordinary; and it specializes for the same reason in the extraordinary visual perspective as the objective counterpart of the extraordinary moral perspective. Tennyson's St Simeon Stylites views the world, visually and morally, from the top of a pillar; while Browning's Caliban views it, visually and morally, from the bottom of a swamp. In both poems we adopt a view of the world which breaks up our ordinary idea of it. St Simeon's view is distorted not only by his elevated position "betwixt the meadow and the cloud," but also because he has grown "half deaf" and "almost blind,"

> So that I scarce can hear the people hum
> About the column's base, . . .
> And scarce can recognize the fields I know;

all detail is blurred. Caliban, on the other hand, sees with an extraordinary sharpness of detail the mud-bound crawling side of nature we seldom notice:

> Yon otter, sleek-wet, lithe as a leech;
> Yon auk, one fire-eye in a ball of foam,
> That floats and feeds; a certain badger brown
> He hath watched hunt with that slant white-wedge eye
> By moonlight; and the pie with the long tongue
> That pricks deep into oakwarts for a worm,
> And says a plain word when she finds her prize,
> But will not eat the ants; and the ants themselves
> That build a wall of seeds and settled stalks
> About their hole.

The unusual minuteness and precision of proximate detail is as much a sign of myopia as the blur of distant detail; and their myopia makes superb poets of both speakers, accounting for the extraordinary visual perception of which their thought is a consequence. It is the blur of physical detail that accounts for St Simeon's vivid perception of the angel who comes with a heavenly crown:

> What's here? a shape, a shade,
> A flash of light. Is that the angel there
> That holds a crown? Come, blessed brother, come!
> I know thy glittering face. I waited long;
> My brows are ready. What! deny it now?

> Nay, draw, draw, draw nigh. So I clutch it. Christ!
> 'Tis gone: 'tis here again; the crown! the crown!
> So now 'tis fitted on and grows to me,
> And from it melt the dews of Paradise,
> Sweet! sweet! spikenard, and balm, and frankincense

while the concreteness of Caliban's perception accounts for his attributing to the god, Setebos, the moral and aesthetic standards of the swamp. He not only equates Setebos' creation with the swamp but considers Setebos less beautiful than the creatures of the swamp, whom He created to make what He "would fain, in a manner, be." It is to demonstrate His power over creatures whom He envies that Setebos torments or rewards them capriciously; just as Caliban, if out of a desire for wings he fashioned a bird of clay, would delight to remind himself that the bird is after all his creation to do with as he pleases. "'Thinketh,'" says Caliban referring to himself with the third-person verb, perhaps as a sign of his rudimentary mind, but also I think to satirize his absurd attempt at objectivity:

> such shows nor right nor wrong in Him,
> Nor kind, nor cruel: He is strong and Lord.
> 'Am strong myself compared to yonder crabs
> That march now from the mountain to the sea;
> 'Let twenty pass, and stone the twenty-first,
> Loving not, hating not, just choosing so.
> 'Say, the first straggler that boasts purple spots
> Shall join the file, one pincer twisted off;
> 'Say, this bruised fellow shall receive a worm,
> And two worms he whose nippers end in red;
> As it likes me each time, I do: so He.

Both poems are effective just because we do not direct our judgment merely against the speakers' ideas, which would be in themselves too arbitrary for judgment, but against a whole visual organization of the world in which we have participated with sympathy and enjoyment, thus allowing an adequate foil against which our adverse judgment can make an impact. For the speaker's point of view must be built up before it can be torn down, if there is to be an adequate tension between our enjoyment of the point of view for its own sake on empiric grounds, and our judgment of it on grounds of truth or morality. The particular perspective is the device by which this disequilibrium between sympathy and judgment is achieved, because it leads away from judgment, from general ideas, toward the intensest concreteness. It is the device by which life is projected into the facts, since the facts were after all originally looked at, limited and distorted by the view of a particular person in a particular time and place. To present in their original concreteness, to *evoke*, as we say, a person, idea or historical period, is the whole purpose of the dramatic monologue—of which purpose the particular perspective is the condition, and the disequilibrium between sympathy and judgment the consequence.

Disequilibrium and the particular perspective are criteria not necessarily of the poem's success but of its success as a dramatic monologue; they are more apparent the more the poem is generating the effect characteristic of the dramatic monologue. *Rabbi Ben Ezra* is a dramatic monologue by virtue of its title only, because there is no way of apprehending the poetic statement other than intellectually, there is no split between its validity as somebody's apprehension and its objective validity as an idea. The reason for the lack of disequilibrium is the lack of a particular perspective; the statement is not conditioned by a particular person in a particular time and place, the poem is not located or anything in it seen. "Grow old along with me . . . Then, welcome each rebuff . . . So, take and use thy work . . . Let age approve of youth, and death complete the same"—these are maxims put forward as universally applicable and deriving validity from the logical connection between them. They do not differ from the statements of any sermon or of Pope's *Essay on Man*. Call Pope's poem *Bolingbroke* (from whom most of its ideas derive), and you have the same kind of poem as *Rabbi Ben Ezra*.

It would be a mistake, however, to suppose that *Rabbi Ben Ezra* is not a dramatic monologue because it deals with ideas. Dramatic monologues may, as we have seen, deal with the most abstract ideas, but they make the kind of statement not open to dispute because limited in application to the conditions of the poem. The general idea emerges as an inference only, and is never identical with what the speaker says. What poem could be more abstract in idea than Browning's *Abt Vogler*, where music is presented as an expression of the Absolute, as emanating from the soul's deepest wish and therefore from the Divine Will? Yet the poem is a dramatic monologue rather than a philosophical statement, just to the extent that the statement rises out of an illusion, out of a visual organization of the world limited in duration to the speaker's ecstatic moment of inspiration as he extemporizes on the organ.

Abt Vogler *sees*, as his music mounts to a climax, an accumulating vision of totality—first, as a palace reaching from sordid fact up toward sublimity, constructed by the ascending and descending genii called forth by his musical notes:

> And one would bury his brow with a blind plunge down to hell,
>> Burrow awhile and build, broad on the roots of things,
> Then up again swim into sight, having based me my palace well,
>> Founded it, fearless of flame, flat on the nether springs.

> And another would mount and march, like the excellent minion
>> he was,
>> Ay, another and yet another, one crowd but with many a crest,
> Raising my rampired walls of gold as transparent as glass, . . .
>> Up, the pinnacled glory reached, and the pride of my soul was
>> in sight

then as a whole cosmic union in which heaven and earth yearn toward each other:

> In sight? Not half! for it seemed, it was certain, to match man's
>> birth,
>> . Nature in turn conceived, obeying an impulse as I;
> And the emulous heaven yearned down, made effort to reach the
>> earth,
>> As the earth had done her best, in my passion, to scale the sky:
> Novel splendours burst forth, grew familiar and dwelt with mine,
>> Not a point nor peak but found and fixed its wandering star;
> Meteor-moons, balls of blaze: and they did not pale nor pine,
>> For earth had attained to heaven, there was no more near nor
>> far

a cosmic union in which not only space is annihilated, but time, too, so that spirits of the yet unborn and of the long since dead walk in this re-created universe where possibility and actuality are identical:

> What never had been, was now; what was, as it shall be anon;
>> And what is,—shall I say, matched both? for I was made
>> perfect too.

Abt Vogler recognizes his vision as Absolute reality, because he recognizes it as his soul's wish flowing "visibly forth"; and because that wish is realized instantaneously and completely—without discernible "cause" for the "effect," without art—Abt Vogler recognizes his wish as an instrument of the Divine Will and his music as a materialization of the "finger of God, a flash of the will that can."

It is the transient irrecoverable quality of music, especially extemporized music, that gives it such high import. Painting and poetry (and presumably written music) remain in place to be analyzed, to be accounted for by laws of art, while the undivided absorption in the instant of Abt Vogler's music gives it the miraculous totality reflective of the Absolute. In the same way, it is the absorption in the instant of Abt Vogler's vision—its departure from those ordinary laws of experience which have been abstracted as a norm from a multiplicity of instants—that gives it its dramatic concreteness. We say of this poem that it *evokes* a musical rhapsody, by which we mean that it is just its most fantastic part we believe in, its vision within the ecstatic instant of a transformed universe; for the vision is the counterpart of the music, and therefore evokes it.

When the ecstatic instant is over ("Well, it is gone at last, the palace of music I reared"), Abt Vogler judges the vision to have been illusory, but re-establishes its validity with a moral sentiment—that the illusion was an image of bliss to come:

> On the earth the broken arcs; in the heaven, a perfect round.

> All we have willed or hoped or dreamed of good shall exist;
> Not its semblance, but itself.

The speaker has shifted to a more ordinary perspective, and concomitantly moved into a more ordinary instant. The vision which was building before our eyes now exists in the past, through recollection. Only its moral meaning, not its empiric actuality, can be generalized, carried over in the "C Major of this life"; and its moral meaning is problematical. Yet even these final stanzas are conditioned by the speaker's emotional attachment to the vision ("Gone! and the good tears start, the praises that come too slow"), so that the moral meaning itself rises out of a new particular perspective and is dramatically concrete to the extent that we share the speaker's emotion.

What we have, in other words, is not a vision located in time, followed by a speculation unlocated in time; but rather the speculation is itself dramatized, conditioned by the nostalgic instant following the ecstasy. We have two particular perspectives and therefore two present tenses, the particular perspective being the visual sign of the present tense. We have really, to make the point clear, two dramatic monologues about the same event, each taking place at a temporally and psychologically separate instant. And, as in *The Ring and the Book*, we judge between the two points of view according to their relative intensity.

For the vision is the centre of certainty, the empiric fact out of which the whole poem rises. We are most closely identified with the speaker, accepting his point of view with least reservation, within the perspective of the ecstasy; while his shift to a more ordinary perspective opens the way for argument and speculation on our part as well as his. His final doubt of the vision's objective validity actually reinforces its validity as a fact of experience, since such a development imitates the structure of our own experience in which illuminations burn at the centre with certainty and then shade off into ambiguity and doubt. Abt Vogler's instant of doubt makes the ecstatic instant believable by providing it with a recognizable setting, at the same time that it sets off the ecstatic instant by showing its incompatibility with ordinary judgment. Far from weakening our confidence in the vision, the incompatibility throws us back upon the more intense instant as the primary certainty; while the judgment that proceeds from the less intense instant appears as a problematical speculation. Although the disequilibrium between sympathy and judgment is handled in *Abt Vogler* in three declining steps of intensity instead of the usual two, here as elsewhere the poetic statement is as much as is absorbed within a particular perspective—the more particular, the more extraordinary even the perspective, the more positive and convincing the statement; while we enter the realm of speculation and finally move beyond the poetic statement altogether, as the perspective approaches and finally reaches the ordinary and unparticularized.

By moving away from the general truth toward the eccentric particular, the dramatic monologue communicates with precision and concreteness the most general and tenuous ideas—making tangible such intangibles as the "spirit" of an age, of a work of art, of a world-view. Perhaps the best example of the evocative power of the particular perspective is Browning's *Master Hugues of Saxe-Gotha*, which evokes not only the musical but also the historical atmosphere of a dry, dusty and difficult old organ fugue. I say best example because the music is evoked not as in *Abt Vogler* by visualizing the invisible, so that the word *perspective* applies only figuratively, but by giving a particular and *less* than usually spiritual view of a church—so that perspective is used, as in an extreme angle-shot in photography, to derive unusual meaning from a usual scene by exaggerating its realistic or homely aspects.

It is after hours in the church and the sacristan is extinguishing the candles preparatory to locking up for the night, as we sit with the old organist in his organ-loft atop the "rotten-runged rat-riddled stairs," below the cobweb-covered roof. From the organist's vantage, the church is "our huge house of the sounds"; for the scene beyond his three claviers is dominated by "yon forest of pipes," while the "our" includes the composer, Master Hugues, the enigma of whose intricate organ fugues the organist has spent a lifetime trying to penetrate. The organist sees Master Hugues peeping in the shade of the forest of pipes, and sees his face in the bars and notes of his score. As the poem begins, the organist calls down to the sacristan for five minutes more of light, then starts to play again one of the master's fugues imploring him to yield his meaning this time "Quick, ere my candle's a snuff."

Both the quality of the fugue and the character of the organist are revealed simultaneously through the unusual details appropriate to a church attendant's view of a church and to the distorted view from the organ-loft. The details are all of obsolescence and neglect, of dust, rust, rats and spider-webs while the view of the church as a place to play music in combines with a view of it as a place to sweep up. For the organist church life occurs after hours when only he and the sacristan are about, and he conceives the church as having a life of its own at night when no one is about. Then, the sculptured saints leave their pedestals and, "with the moon to admire," go their rounds as superior church attendants, "Put rats and mice to the rout,"

> Order things back to their place,
> Have a sharp eye lest the candlesticks rust,
>   Rub the church-plate, darn the sacrament-lace,
> Clear the desk-velvet of dust.

In spite of the homely details, such a vision shows large imagination—the same imagination that can sense life behind the outmoded aridities of Master Hugues' music. For the details of obsolescence and neglect apply at every point to the music, which is more than once compared to an intricate spider-web:

> So your fugue broadens and thickens,
>   Greatens and deepens and lengthens,
> Till we exclaim—"But where's music, the dickens?
>   Blot ye the gold, while your spider-web strengthens
>   —Blacked to the stoutest of tickens?"

The "gold" is the meaning which lies obscured behind the formal structure of the music, as the gilt roof of the church is obscured by spider-webs. Just as the two shabby old men left behind in the neglected church melt into the spirit of the place; so forgotten himself, and left alone with his forgotten composer, the organist penetrates the composer's life. But though the organist believes that Master Hugues' music has meaning, he has never been able to make out what it is. He thinks he is coming upon it as he plays a fugue over again this time— coming upon the golden roof behind the spider-webs, as he puts it—when the sacristan extinguishes the last candle and the organist stops playing to grumble at him. You obviously want to find me, when you come to sweep up one morning, dead at the foot of your "rotten-runged rat-riddled stairs." By what light am I to get down? "Do I carry," he complains in the final line, "the moon in my pocket?"

A superb question, for of course the organist does carry his own light with him. The sculptured saints and the music have come alive in the moonlight of his imagination. For all its homely detail, the organist's vision is objectively as question- able as Abt Vogler's. What is certain is the strength and consistency of the imagination, of the master passion or master illusion which the organist reveals all unconsciously through his absorption in his own particular perspective.

It is this absorption in the particular perspective that makes the speaker's self-revelation incidental to his purpose; and it is the incidental nature of the self-revelation that distinguishes the dramatic monologue from the form which is most often confused with it, the soliloquy. The difference is that the soliloquist's subject is himself, while the speaker of the dramatic monologue directs his attention outward. Since talking about one's self necessarily involves an objective stance, the soliloquist must see himself from a general perspective. It is not enough for him to think his thoughts and feel his feelings, he must also describe them as an observer would; for he is trying to understand himself in the way that the reader understands him— rationally, by relating his thoughts and feelings to general truths.

That is why we get self-analysis and internal debate in the soliloquy but not in the dramatic monologue. The soliloquist is concerned with truth, he is trying to find the right point of view; while the speaker of the dramatic monologue starts with an established point of view, and is not concerned with its truth but with trying to impress it on the outside world. The meaning of the soliloquy is equivalent to what the soliloquist reveals and understands, the poetic statement being as much as he has been able to rationalize, to see in terms of the general perspective. But the meaning of the dramatic monologue is in disequilibrium with what the speaker reveals and understands. We understand the speaker's point of view not through his description of it but indirectly, through seeing what he sees while judging the limitations and distortions of what he sees. The result is that we understand, if not more, at least something other than the speaker understands, and the meaning is conveyed as much by what the speaker conceals and distorts as by what he reveals.

Pope's *Eloisa to Abelard* is a good case in point. Although it is often cited as a dramatic monologue and deals with the moral and emotional ambiguities appropriate to the dramatic monologue, it is essentially a soliloquy because written from a general perspective—or, as Professor Tillotson puts it, because Eloisa is "the 'artist' of emotion rather than the experiencer of it."[1] Eloisa writes a letter from her convent to Abelard in his, imploring him to come and telling him how she is torn between love and religious duty. She tells how her sinful dreams at night reveal her true desires, and how Abelard's image steals even into her prayers to claim the devotion meant for God. Her very penances are suspect, for she wonders whether she sighs for her sins or her lost love:

> Assist me heav'n! but whence arose that pray'r?
> Sprung it from piety, or from despair?
> Ev'n here, where frozen chastity retires,
> Love finds an altar for forbidden fires.

She breaks the self-description at intervals to bid Abelard come to her for reasons that alternate along with her emotions. He is to come as lover to seduce her from her religious duty; ah no, he is to come to instruct her in her religious duty. She finally bids him come, at the moment when her penance is sincerest and grace is dawning in her soul, to snatch her from salvation. Then recoiling in horror from the blasphemous thought, she bids him fly her and renounce her for the sake of both their souls. The poem ends with Eloisa's reconciliation to her religious duty. She looks forward to her own and Abelard's salvation and to their burial together in the Monastery of the Paraclete, where they will serve as a warning to future lovers and where sympathetic visitors may be moved to pity and forgive them. She also hopes that some future bard will be inspired by his own unhappy love to tell their story.

The poem is a soliloquy rather than a dramatic monologue to the extent that the paradox is in the moral problem rather than in the character of Eloisa, to the extent in other words that the paradox is stated rather than enacted.

> I ought to grieve, but cannot what I ought;
> I mourn the lover, not lament the fault

is not the language of a woman in the midst of internal conflict but of one who has clearly put the experience behind her, since

[1] Twickenham edition of Pope, Vol. II: *The Rape of the Lock and Other Poems*, ed. Geoffrey Tillotson (London: Methuen; New Haven: Yale University Press, 1954), p. 289.

she is able to analyse it into two neatly defined alternatives. The epigrammatic style does not in itself prove the poem to be no dramatic monologue; it merely confirms what we gather from the content as well—that Eloisa understands everything, even her own self-deceptions and submerged motives, that she understands herself as an observer would understand her. The fact that she can debate between love and religious duty means that she is not so committed to either alternative as to have her point of view conditioned by it, that she judges by a third principle, the general perspective.

She chooses religious duty in the end because it is identical with the general perspective. The sign of this is that the religious alternative has really had the victory from the start, as evidenced by the values assigned the alternatives. Love is always spoken of as sin and religion as virtue. Eloisa does, to be sure, speak of a time when she was willing to "Curse on all laws but those which love has made"; and if the poem had taken place at that time, it might have been a dramatic monologue since love might then have arisen out of its own intellectual and moral view of the world. As it is, that time is spoken of through recollection and from the point of view of a quite alien law which has since been embraced. All of Eloisa's description of her emotional conflict is recollected, which is why she understands everything about it. For she is not, as she writes the letter, absorbed in her emotions; she is judging them from the *right* perspective. She is telling the *truth* about them.

This does not mean that dramatic monologues cannot discuss past action. But the utterance about the past must have a strategic significance within a present-tense situation. The utterance must be conditioned by the effect the speaker wants to create at the moment, so that its truth is of less concern than its success as strategy. The distortion or deviation from truth of the particular perspective is the sign of the speaker's absorption in his strategy, and therefore the sign that the utterance is, even if about the past, in the present tense.

Browning's Andrea del Sarto describes to his wife, Lucrezia, the long years of conflict between his artistic conscience and his love of her. But Andrea is using his account to make love to Lucrezia, to persuade her to spend the evening home with him rather than go out to meet the "Cousin" who whistles for

her in the street below. He is trying to impress her, on the one
hand, with all that he has sacrificed for her in the way of
artistic accomplishment; and on the other, with how important
a painter he nevertheless is. We see of course that his musings
on art and his self-pity do not interest the lady, that he is talking
entirely too much about himself for successful love-making.
He half-sees this too:

> You don't understand
> Nor care to understand about my art,

and he demonstrates his awareness of her purely pecuniary
interest in his art, when he assures her that if she would sit
thus by him every night,

> I should work better, do you comprehend?
> I mean that I should earn more, give you more.

What he does not see, however, is that he cares less to make
love than to indulge in self-pity—that he enjoys degrading
himself before his wife, enjoys making clear his awareness of
the "Cousin" below and his awareness that she stays with him
only for the money he promises, money with which to pay for
"this same Cousin's freak." He does not realize that he enjoys
playing her victim since it means that he has resigned his will
to her and can blame her for his moral failure in art. "Had you
not grown restless . . ." he suggests in a timid, unfinished
sentence, he would not have left the protection of the French
King Francis, where he had been doing his best work. And had
she enjoined upon him "the play, the insight and the stretch,"
which his work for all its technical perfection now lacks,

> Had you enjoined them on me, given me soul,
> We might have risen to Rafael, I and you!

Had she as his model, with all her physical perfections intact,

> but brought a mind!
> Some women do so. Had the mouth there urged
> "God and the glory! never care for gain.
> The present by the future, what is that?
> Live for fame, side by side with Agnolo!
> Rafael is waiting: up to God, all three!"
> I might have done it for you.

He has not even the moral courage to make his accusation squarely, so as to antagonize her and cause her to defend herself. Each time he makes the accusation he withdraws it immediately, taking the blame upon himself but in such a way as not to invalidate the accusation and to make him feel considerate, self-castigating and infinitely injured. "So it seems," he continues,

> Perhaps not. All is as God over-rules.
> Beside, incentives come from the soul's self;
> The rest avail not. Why do I need you?
> What wife had Rafael, or has Agnolo?

The question is ambiguous, with at least one meaning unfavourable to Lucrezia. It is this meaning that Andrea takes up again at the end, where he fancies himself competing in heaven against Leonardo, Raphael and Michelangelo:

> the three first without a wife,
> While I have mine! So—still they overcome
> Because there's still Lucrezia,—as I choose.
>
> Again the Cousin's whistle! Go, my Love.

He deceives himself by his acknowledgment of having chosen. For the pretence of self-understanding prevents him from seeing how much he has chosen—that he has chosen, indeed composed as for a painting, all the details of the poem. He starts by describing the poem's setting as he would paint it— as a "twilight-piece" in which "A common grayness silvers everything" and "autumn grows, autumn in everything," while Lucrezia would figure as the moon, beautiful and cruelly unresponsive. But he does not see that he is a voluptuary creating the ideal conditions for his pleasure—that the hour, as he sees it, washes away with an enchanting vagueness all moral issues, while both season and hour stimulate soft regret and self-pity. In such a picture, the "Cousin" as symbol of Andrea's degradation is by no means an unwelcome figure; and Andrea does not realize that he introduces and re-introduces the "Cousin" deliberately, even using him in the final line as the final excruciating pleasure and to set the seal upon the special kind of victory he wins over Lucrezia in those last four lines.

Self-deception on this scale is not to be found in Pope's poem, and we must therefore read the two poems differently. We cannot understand Eloisa as we do Andrea, in a way other than she understands herself; for her self-description is true, it is expository. This is both the result and the sign of the fact that she does not use her self-description strategically to manipulate Abelard, as Andrea uses his to manipulate Lucrezia and secure his own gratification. The only passages in Pope's poem which correspond to Andrea's utterance are those in which Eloisa breaks her self-description to bid Abelard come to her. There, she is directing herself to a present-tense situation and is, significantly, for that space self-deceived. She bids Abelard come for a variety of reasons in each of which she believes while she is giving it, although we understand, as she for that space cannot, that her reasons are all rationalizations of the same sexual motive. When Eloisa says

> Oh come! oh teach me nature to subdue,
> Renounce my love, my life, my self—and you.
> Fill my fond heart with God alone, for he
> Alone can rival, can succeed to thee

she supposes that she has broken through to the right reason, after having urged Abelard to come as her lover. But we see still the same reason, for we see that Abelard will be hardly her most effective teacher of renunciation.

The poem is in these few passages a dramatic monologue, and would be a dramatic monologue in its entirety if the strategy of these passages were reinforced, instead of counteracted, by the self-description. As it is, Eloisa shows in describing herself that she understands as much as we do about the self-deception in the above passage. It is she who has alerted us to it by telling us, in one epigram after another, how ubiquitous love usurps every time the emotion which starts out to be religious: "Thy image steals between my God and me."

Perhaps the major sign of Eloisa's incomplete commitment to her strategy—or in other words, her incomplete absorption in a particular perspective—is the fact that she changes her mind at the end of the poem. After temporizing in many ways with her desire to have Abelard come, she finally reverses the desire and bidding him fly her, renounce her, comes to the *right* conclusion. Now it is significant that the speakers of dramatic monologues never change their minds. Even when it looks as though they might, as in the case of Don Juan in *Fifine*, it is only a bluff to be followed by a more daring assertion than ever of their original position. This unlooked-for and almost superfluous self-assertion in the end replaces in the dramatic monologue the kind of climax supplied by the conversion in Pope's poem. Thus Don Juan proves to his wife, Elvire, that his flirtation with the gipsy-girl, Fifine, is not incompatible with his love for her. Then in a surprise ending, he returns for "five minutes" to Fifine, even revealing that things between them had gone farther than we had supposed. There is no reversal in this, the surprise comes from an intensification of what we already knew, in that Don Juan is being even more himself than we had calculated.

When in the last two and a half lines the duke of *My Last Duchess* makes his insolent, trivial, egotistical and hyperaesthetic pause before that bronze by Claus of Innsbruck, he manages to add a new shock to the shocks we have already endured. We have seen him as all these things, but not until now with such compression. Even in Browning's *A Forgiveness*, where the betrayed husband forgives his wife after a long period of hatred, there is no reversal in his kind of forgiveness. The wife has to earn his forgiveness by letting the life blood flow out of her, so that his hate may be satisfied and pass away into love. And in telling the story, the husband shows himself to be the same vindictive person still: he tells it in the confessional, as we learn in the last stanza, to the monk whom he knows to have been his wife's lover, in order that the monk may not hope to elude "My vengeance in the cloister's solitude." Not even in the religious dramatic monologues do the speakers convert. The already uneasy paganism of Karshish and Cleon is simply made more uneasy by their exposure to Christianity; while the only effect on Tennyson's Rizpah of the evangelical lady's preaching is to confirm Rizpah's belief that her love for her son is more important than religion.

Andrea del Sarto makes clear from the beginning his expectation that Lucrezia will not spend the evening with him, and that in his internal conflict love will win again over the claims of artistic conscience. Both expectations are realized, yet the foreshadowed victory of Andrea's expectation does not have the same effect as the foreshadowed victory of the general perspective in *Eloisa to Abelard*. For there is no reversal in Browning's poem, and there is a reversal in Pope's. Although the general perspective establishes its judgment from the beginning of Pope's poem, Eloisa struggles against it until her final change of mind; whereas Browning's poem begins and ends with Andrea's perspective.

Andrea begins by surrendering to Lucrezia in the first line: "But do not let us quarrel any more," blaming her for his loss of artistic integrity:

> I'll work then for your friend's friend, never fear,
> Treat his own subject after his own way,
> Fix his own time, accept too his own price,
> And shut the money into this small hand

and ends by conceding artistic defeat even in heaven, "Because there's still Lucrezia,—as I choose." The development is one of simple intensification. The unlooked-for leap, which is the climax, is supplied by no change of direction but by a final revelation that brings into startling focus our accumulated suspicions, surprising us into certainty. Our sympathy for Andrea (self-pity is one of the best poles for sympathy, as witness the fondness for Werther, Childe Harold and Prufrock) suppresses our apprehension of his culpability until suddenly, in the end, he reveals flaws more definitely criminal than the mere weaknesses we have hitherto noted. He alludes to having swindled King Francis and allowed his parents to die of want. But even for these crimes he refuses to take moral responsibility: "I regret little, I would change still less." "It is true," he says of the wrong to Francis, and "all is said"—as though acknowledgment were enough. And of the wrong to his parents, "Some good son," he says,

> Paint my two hundred pictures—let him try!
> No doubt, there's something strikes a balance.

The "something" is not only his art. It takes on a new meaning in the next line where he justifies himself again, according to the pattern already established in the poem, by subtle transition to Lucrezia. "Yes," he says appearing to change the subject abruptly, "You loved me quite enough, it seems tonight." But the "Yes," which stands alone between the two lines, serves double duty. He uses it to answer what is probably Lucrezia's impatient request to be gone. But he also uses it to confirm his own speculation, the "no doubt" of the previous line, by relating it to Lucrezia and her request. "Yes," he says even as he gives her permission to betray him, she is the "something" that "strikes a balance," the price he pays for his sins.

When we see him shift to Lucrezia the blame not this time for his weaknesses but for his crimes, our suspicion hardens into certainty; we see clearly the use he has been making of her throughout the poem, as the penance offered in place of moral responsibility. Even in heaven, he goes on to say, I would choose, Lucrezia; even in heaven I neither could, nor would I choose to take steps to save myself. Such a position is, after all, impregnable. There is in it a mixture of self-abasement and pride, of pride in self-abasement, which is the weak man's heroism. It explains the sense Andrea has of himself as both heroic and pathetic when he makes that final gesture of surrender: "the Cousin's whistle! Go, my Love." The gesture dramatizes the whole basis of his self-justification, the pretence of knowing the worst about himself. But intent as he is on his strategy of self-justification, and without introducing any other perspective—indeed, because he is so absorbed in his own perspective—he yet reveals himself as more contemptible and yes, as in a way more attractive too (his absorption is attractive, it is a pole for sympathy) than he is aware.

This kind of climax, through an intensified and succinctly dramatized restatement of what has already been said, is the most effective climax in dramatic monologues. That is because the dramatic monologue is organized around a single perspective and must therefore move in a single direction. The reversal, as we find it in Eloisa's change of mind, requires the introduction of another perspective by which the character judges his own and to which he eventually converts. The reversal brings about the *right* conclusion, and there can be no *right* conclusion where there is only the speaker's perspective. There can be only self-revelation climaxed by the self-revelation that strips the mask even from self-revelation, revealing its strategy and thus revealing character with a concreteness beyond what we had thought possible.

I have called *Eloisa to Abelard* a soliloquy rather than a dramatic monologue just because it has this *rightness*, this meaning independent of character by which character is judged. Character bears the same relation to meaning in Pope's poem that it would in a play, for Eloisa speaks only part of the time for herself and most of the time for the general perspective or meaning. She wants Abelard to come to her, but she must also make it clear that this is the wrong thing to want and that it will be a good thing when she finally changes her mind. The result is that Eloisa speaks more often like the soliloquy than like the dialogue of a play. She exposes the meaning more often than she pursues her own strategy. The final sign of this is in the ending, where Eloisa adopts the storyteller's hindsight as to the subsequent fame of the lovers—a perspective not *characteristically* hers.

The dramatic monologue, on the other hand, in spite of its obvious resemblance to the soliloquy, corresponds in its style of address to the dialogue, where each speaker is absorbed in his own strategy. In the most typical dialogues, of course, each speaker is counteracted by the other, so that no single perspective prevails as in the dramatic monologue. Nevertheless, the style of address is the same in that the speakers in dialogue and in the dramatic monologue communicate with the audience indirectly. They neither speak *to* the audience, nor are they concerned to describe themselves *truly*, that is for the benefit of the audience; they are concerned only to exert force on the scene around them. Yet the audience are not mere eavesdroppers, the speakers do address them in that they communicate to the audience something which is not quite the same as what they say in the dramatic scene. The speakers communicate to the audience in spite of their absorption; their absorption is, in its intensity and direction, among the things they communicate.

The style of address is much more complicated in the dialogue and dramatic monologue than in the soliloquy. For the soliloquist, like the speaker in the traditional lyric, follows the style of address of ordinary conversation. He turns to the audience when he wants to tell them something and, when he wants to describe himself, he stands outside himself and talks about himself. There is no disparity between what he says and what he intends to say. He is as much aware as we are of the meaning of his utterance, and his utterance can therefore be judged as true in the same way that we judge the statements of ordinary conversation.

There is a discernible shift in the style of address between those passages in which Eloisa speaks the truth about herself and those few passages beginning with "Come!" in which she is so absorbed in her design upon Abelard that we understand her utterance as she cannot. But Andrea's style of address is consistent because he is absorbed at every instant in his design upon Lucrezia. Browning's *Soliloquy of the Spanish Cloister* is for the same reason not a soliloquy at all but a dramatic monologue. Although Brother Lawrence does not hear the imprecations directed against him, the speaker is entirely absorbed in them and manages to communicate about Brother Lawrence and himself something quite other than he intends. The utterance of Tennyson's St Simeon is also a dramatic monologue, though no one hears it; for it, too, is strategic (St Simeon is praying and arguing his way into heaven) and to be understood in a way other than he intends. The bias in the style of address corresponds to the particularity of the perspective. Both make clear that the utterance is to be understood not as true or false but as characteristic. And both make necessary our double apprehension within and without the bias or perspective, our apprehension through sympathy and judgment.

The style of address and the perspective both show the utterance as incomplete, and make it impossible for the dramatic monologue to achieve that logical completeness which we traditionally expect in dramatic poetry. Since the dramatic monologue is in its style of address really one voice of a dialogue, it lacks the logical completeness not only of the soliloquy but also of the dialogue. It lacks the conflicting voice of the dialogue and consequently the final judgment that resolves the conflict. The final judgment, which is impossible where there is only one voice of a dialogue, corresponds to the reversal, which is impossible where there is only a single perspective.

Without reversal or final judgment there can be no logical completeness, no *right* conclusion.

When Eloisa finally changes her mind, she solves the problem of the poem; we feel that the problem will never occur again. But Andrea has talked this way before to Lucrezia, and will talk this way again with the same result. In the same way, the duke of *My Last Duchess* has been showing the duchess's portrait to visitors and will go on showing it, and the speaker of *The Spanish Cloister* has always growled at Brother Lawrence and will go on growling at him. If St Simeon Stylites does not go on pleading his case with God, and Browning's bishop does not go on ordering his tomb, it will be because they have died. The whole point of the dramatic monologue is to present not the Aristotelian complete action but habitual action.

This means that the dramatic monologue has no *necessary* beginning and end but only arbitrary limits, limits which do not cut the action off from the events that precede and follow but shade into those events, suggesting as much as possible of the speaker's whole life and experience. They are naturalistic limits, imposed not by logical necessity but by physical conditions such as location and perspective and ultimately by the physical limitations on life and experience. Since the speaker's death is the only ultimate conclusion of a dramatic monologue, the dramatic monologue must be read not as a definitive unit, a complete action, but as a characteristic and characterizing episode in the speaker's career.

The Ring and the Book, of course, and Tennyson's *Maud* tell a complete story. But they achieve completeness through devices outside the scope of the dramatic monologue. *Maud* comes to the *right* conclusion through a reversal; the speaker gives up brooding and goes to fight in the Crimean War. The conclusion would be absurd enough in a narrative or play, since it abandons the problem instead of solving it. But it represents a particular abandonment of the dramatic monologue, since the speaker abandons his character as well as the problem. The reversal does show that Tennyson could not have achieved a *right* conclusion with the dramatic monologue. Some external force, corresponding to the miracle of grace in Pope's poem, was necessary; for left to its own logic, the speaker's character could have led only to madness and suicide—a conclusion of sheer character revelation, proving nothing morally.

The Ring and the Book achieves completeness through juxtaposing dramatic monologues, creating a master context in which each dramatic monologue is to be read. But such a total organization works against the single perspective and thus against the organization of each dramatic monologue. For the juxtaposition of dramatic monologues turns them into dialogue; we can no longer give entire assent to any single perspective, but must adopt a general perspective by which to judge among the utterances. Browning helps to establish this general perspective by abandoning the dramatic monologue entirely—by speaking in his own voice in the first and last Books in order to establish the *right* judgments, and by bringing the poem to a *right* conclusion with the Pope's monologue which is, according to the distinction I have drawn, less a dramatic monologue than a soliloquy. Not only is the Pope addressing himself, but he is wrestling with the truth rather than pursuing a strategy. And his judgments, even about himself and his own motives, are clearly something more in the master context than one man's opinion; they are clearly *right* and therefore expository.

The Pope's monologue is a soliloquy to the extent that *The Ring and the Book* approaches the condition of drama in having a general perspective for which the Pope can speak and which gives his speech authority, making it not merely another point of view but the resolution of the poem. To the extent that the Pope does not, however, gain authority from an ethos to which we give assent for reasons outside the poem, to the extent that he has only as much authority as he has earned through superiority of mind and character, we would not consider the poem to be morally resolved and the Pope's speech would remain a dramatic monologue. The issue demonstrates again, as in *Maud*, that the dramatic monologue must at some point be abandoned where logical completeness is desired.

The issue also demonstrates that drama, in the old sense of the complete action, becomes impossible where we do not bring an effective ethos to the poem. It suggests that our ability to read dramatic monologues depends on the modern habit of allowing the literary work to establish its own moral judgments. The habit is, indeed, necessary for reading modern literature where we can never know what the moral judgments are going to be, but it would have surprised our ancestors who expected to find, at least in their dramatic literature, Truth rather than points of view. The complete structure of traditional drama is a sign that it imitates or illustrates a complete idea; whereas the incomplete structure of the dramatic monologue is a sign that it projects a partial and problematical idea, a point of view. It is significant that when we misread old plays it is usually because we have lost sight of the ethos out of which they were written, and that we almost always misread in the same way. Instead of subordinating the points of view of the characters to the general perspective and allowing the plot to determine our judgments, we allow the central character to have his way with us; we see the play through his point of view and as an episode in his career. We turn the complete drama into an incomplete one. We turn it into a dramatic monologue.

5

Character versus Action in Shakespeare

THE reinterpretation or, as some critics would have it, the misinterpretation of Shakespeare in the nineteenth century is worth reviewing not only for the light it throws on that elusive thing, the *real* Shakespeare, but also for the light it throws on the difference between the mind of Europe before and after the Enlightenment. For it is because they had lost sight of that traditional ethos from which the Enlightenment separates us that nineteenth-century readers read Shakespeare as they read the literature of their own time. They read him not as drama in the traditional Aristotelian sense, not in other words as a literature of external action in which the events derive meaning from their relation to a publicly acknowledged morality, but as literature of experience, in which the events have meaning inasmuch as they provide the central character with an occasion for experience—for self-expression and self-discovery. What such a reading suggests is that drama depends for its structure on belief in a single objective moral system, and dissolves without that belief into monodrama—into the nineteenth century's substitute for poetic drama, the dramatic monologue.

Thus, the nineteenth-century reading of Shakespeare gives great weight to the soliloquies, which are just the moments when the point of view of the central character seems to obliterate the general perspective of the play. The dramatic monologue is largely modelled on the Shakespearean soliloquy; for in the Shakespearean soliloquy as they read it, nineteenth-century poets thought they had found the form by which they could objectify and dramatize their essentially subjective and lyrical impulse. It is significant, therefore, that in our time, when the effort of Shakespeare criticism has been to restore to the plays their Elizabethan ethos, the soliloquies have been alleged to be not characteristic and self-expressive at all but just those moments when the speaker steps out of character to make an expository utterance, to speak not for his own particular perspective but for the general perspective of the play.

As we are nowadays given to understand, Shakespeare's soliloquies are those moments in the play that correspond to the choruses of Greek tragedy, moments when the action stops for narration, moral judgment or general reflection. Hamlet in "O, what a rogue and peasant slave am I!" judges himself by the traditional code of honour, even seeing himself through the eyes of a hypothetical accuser:

> Who calls me villain? breaks my pate across?
> Plucks off my beard and blows it in my face?
> Tweaks me by the nose? . . .
> 'Swounds, I should take it! for it cannot be
> But I am pigeon-livered and lack gall. (II, ii, 599-604)

And spurred on to action after the play-within-the-play has confirmed the King's guilt, he stops to describe—with what must be understood as either the most exaggerated self-consciousness or else the descriptive technique of a narrator—the appropriate character of revenger he is going to assume, as well as the appropriate setting for the revenge:

> 'Tis now the very witching time of night,
> When churchyards yawn, and hell itself breathes out
> Contagion to this world. Now could I drink hot blood
> And do such bitter business as the day
> Would quake to look on. (III, ii, 406-10)

Lady Macbeth, too, in the soliloquy in which she calls upon the spirits to "unsex" her and fill her full of "direst cruelty," describes her new character of murderess not from a murderess's but from the general moral perspective. And she, too, conceives the murder in its appropriate setting, the croaking raven and "thick" night. Macbeth on his way to murder Duncan stops to describe the hallucinatory dagger he sees before him. This would be an excellent example of particular perspective were he absorbed in the hallucination; but he has a perfectly external awareness of ambiguity:

> Art thou not, fatal vision, sensible
> To feeling as to sight? or art thou but
> A dagger of the mind, a false creation,
> Proceeding from the heat-oppressed brain? (II, i, 36-39)

even comparing the hallucinatory dagger with his own, which he draws from its sheath. He is perfectly aware of the moral significance of the hallucination, that the dagger with its "gouts of blood" belongs to the realm of the living hell he is about to enter; and in going on to describe for the murder an appropriate setting, he describes the landscape of that realm making abundantly clear the moral judgment he is turning against himself:

> Now o'er the one half-world
> Nature seems dead, and wicked dreams abuse
> The curtain'd sleep. Now witchcraft celebrates
> Pale Hecate's offerings; and wither'd murther,
> Alarum'd by his sentinel, the wolf, . . .
> Moves like a ghost.   (II, i, 49-56)

The twentieth-century scholarship that has made us aware of this self-descriptive convention in Shakespeare—the convention "whereby the good characters," to quote E. E. Stoll, "speak of themselves frankly as good and the wicked as wicked"[1]—has changed our understanding of Shakespeare's plays by restoring to us the world-view out of which the plays were written. For if, on the one hand, the self-descriptive convention can be considered as merely primitive, as a sign of the still imperfect emergence of the dramatic form from the lyric and narrative, it can also, on the other hand, be considered as the entirely adequate expression of an absolutist world-view. There is surely something deeper involved than a stage convention when the whole imaginative fabric of *Macbeth* is determined by the fact that the two protagonists call their deed a murder and summon up a universe of blood to bear witness against them. "Macbeth and Lady Macbeth themselves call it a murder," Stoll says in his essay on Shakespeare's criminals, "because it is a murder because public and poet could see it in no other light—not in *their* [the Macbeths'] light, to be sure." "In short," he concludes, "the doctrine of the point of view simply had not arrived. There was as yet no Ibsen in the drama, no Henry James in the novel, no *Ring and the Book*."[2]

The point of view had not arrived because people had no

---

[1] *Shakespeare Studies* (New York: Macmillan, 1927), p. 102.
[2] pp. 366, 376.

yet learned, in literature at least, to separate truth from the public view of truth. Though Machiavelli had already broached the idea, it was not yet understood that experience might be categorized according to some other scheme, a scheme by which the same act might be called something other than murder. In other words, the point of view was conceived not as the result of a particular world-view but as a relative position on the moral scale, a scale recognized by hero and villain alike. A case in point is the Elizabethan dramatists' misunderstanding of Machiavelli. Machiavellian characters like Marlowe's Jew of Malta and Shakespeare's Iago announce their villainy, recognize the moral scale by taking for themselves the lowest position on it; whereas Machiavelli had precisely questioned the scale and proposed new virtues according to quite another scale.

Thus, the character in traditional drama cannot be wholly absorbed in his particular perspective, but keeps one eye on the general perspective from which he must take the judgment of his actions. This is the crucial difference that separates us from so much pre-Enlightenment literature, causing us to "romantically" misread as the scholars tell us. It is difficult for us to understand the lack of protest among Dante's sufferers in hell, or that Dante's sympathy for Francesca implies no criticism of the Divine judgment against her, or that our sympathy for the fate of the tragic hero ought not to imply criticism of the gods and their ways. Apparently, the moral order was accepted as fixed in a way that we now accept only the natural order; and the combination of suffering and acquiescence was probably the secret of the old tragic emotion—an emotion we talk a good deal about but which always, I suspect, eludes us. For we have been trained to expect the particular perspective to be carried to its logical conclusion in self-justifying values. But the traditional character only half represents himself and half helps to expose the moral meaning of the play. He acts out his own story in order to reinforce the moral order.

It is largely, then, on the soliloquies that the issue hangs between the twentieth-century anti-psychological interpretation of Shakespeare, as represented by Stoll, and the nineteenth-century psychological interpretation, which is best summed up I think in A. C. Bradley's *Shakespearean Tragedy* (1904). The issue hangs on the soliloquies because dialogue is necessarily characteristic, whereas we have really to choose between reading the soliloquies from a particular or from the general perspective. From a particular perspective, we read the speaker's account as a characteristic distortion; we sympathize but do not believe him, and have therefore to employ intricate psychological concepts of self-deception and subconscious motivation to understand the self-revelation the speaker does not intend.

Hamlet's soliloquies become self-deceiving pretexts for inaction; and though he chides his delay, and gives as a reason for not killing the King at prayers that he wants to kill him at a time when he can destroy his soul as well as his body, we do not by Bradley's reading believe him but understand him to be rationalizing his reluctance to act. And though Iago announces his evil intentions and alleges several evil motives—ambition, jealousy, lust—we neither believe in these motives nor in a devil figure of pure unmotivated evil. Bradley rejects the devil figure as the far-fetched because psychologically unintelligible interpretation. And it is far-fetched, of course, if we read Iago's soliloquies as characteristic rather than as expressing the general moral perspective. For he seems, if we look for a characteristic statement, too objectively aware of his moral category to be engrossed in it as a *psychological* devil would have to be.

A moral devil could of course consider himself the representative of evil. But Bradley does not account for Iago morally, as the negative pole of the moral scale, but psychologically, as deficient in the moral sense. He follows Hazlitt and Swinburne (and by implication Coleridge, though he is less happy with him) in finding Iago's real motive to be largely nonmoral and aesthetic: possessed of a genius for intrigue, Iago must express his genius by manipulating the plot quite for its own sake and even if, to stir things up, he must play the villain himself. Hazlitt calls him "an amateur of tragedy in real life . . . [who] getting up his plot at home, casts the principal parts among his nearest friends and connections";[1] while Swinburne calls him "an inarticulate poet," a poet who instead of writing his poem lives it: "He has within him a sense or conscience of

[1] *Characters of Shakespear's Plays* (London: Taylor and Hessey, 1818), pp. 55-56.

power incomparable; and this power shall not be left, in Hamlet's phrase, 'to fust in him unused.'"[1]

Coleridge presents a problem in this connection since he gave birth to the famous description of Iago as a "motiveless malignity"—a phrase Bradley calls misleading because it seems to support the devil figure he and presumably Coleridge reject. Yet in its context the phrase denotes, I think, a psychological conception, though enigmatic and of a depth we are only now catching up with. The full phrase is "the motive-hunting of a motiveless malignity," from which we may infer that Iago lacks the motives he ascribes to himself in the soliloquy Coleridge is discussing (I, iii, 389)—hate, jealousy and ambition, motives the world recognizes. But Coleridge suggests in the rest of the paragraph that Iago shares the deeper motive beneath these apparent motives, the desire for self-realization and contact with others, and that it is a sign of his emotional deficiency that in him the deeper motive does not take the ordinary expression. For though Iago tries to explain himself to himself as motivated by passions, Coleridge speaks of his "passionless character": "It is all will in intellect; and therefore he is here a bold partizan of a truth, but yet of a truth converted into a falsehood by the absence of all the necessary modifications caused by the frail nature of man."

The truth in question is Iago's assertion that we can do what we will with ourselves (I, iii, 322); but his belief in the efficacy of the will turns, in its application, to falsehood and destructiveness because undirected by human sympathies toward the ordinary human goals. We can thus connect Iago's emotional deficiency with his desire to be a man of passion and to manipulate the passions of other people, and see that desire as motivated by his desire to assert his own humanity and to make contact with the humanity of others. We are in a position to suggest a resolution of the brilliant intuition which Coleridge himself lacked the concepts to resolve—just because destructiveness as a social gesture of the emotionally underdeveloped, as a function even of their need for love, is accounted motive enough in our latest depth psychology. But does not Coleridge, in his own dark way, intimate as much in the paragraph's final sentence, where he leaves an impression of Iago's frightening

[1] *A Study of Shakespeare* (London: Chatto and Windus, 1880), pp. 177, 179.

pathos: "Yea, whilst he is still allowed to bear the divine image, it is too fiendish for his own steady view,—for the lonely gaze of a being next to devil, and only not quite devil!"[1]

Those last words should make clear at any rate that Coleridge does not support the devil figure. For the devil, as Stoll gives us to understand, does evil because it is evil; he acts with a full knowledge of and acquiescence in the moral scale. But evil is an accident of Iago's deeper purpose as Coleridge conceives it; it is the failure of his purpose. He does evil not out of knowledge but out of lack of knowledge, out of a limited perspective. He is therefore human and his actions are psychologically intelligible, even if we require the deepest possible psychology to understand them.

It was precisely to explain the psychological enigma of Coleridge's "motiveless malignity" that Hazlitt and Swinburne looked for a deeper motive than had yet been understood. But they did not look deeply enough. They tried to make Iago less unpalatable in order to account for his pathos, whereas it requires the more articulated romanticism of our own time to recognize what Coleridge really had in mind—the most monstrous possible Iago in whom pathos and psychological intelligibility are nevertheless to be found. Coleridge's Iago is not the devil for the same reason that the motiveless malignities in Dostoyevsky, Gide and Faulkner are not.

It is significant that Coleridge ignores the last two lines of Iago's soliloquy, since these are just the lines that support the view of Iago as a self-describing devil who as spokesman for the general perspective judges himself by the morality he violates:

> I have't! It is engend'red! Hell and night
> Must bring this monstrous birth to the world's light.
>
> (I, iii, 409-10)

If we read these lines as expository, we must read the whole soliloquy as expository and the psychological reading collapses. We must believe that Iago's motives are what he alleges; or at least, as Stoll suggests, that the alleged motives are "conscious pretexts" devised by Iago to deceive not himself but the world. The issue between the psychological and anti-psychological

[1] *Lectures and Notes on Shakspere and Other English Poets*, collected by T. Ashe (London: George Bell, 1884), pp. 387-88.

reading hangs on whether we understand the soliloquy to mean what Iago intends or something other than he intends.

"One must constantly remember," says Bradley, "not to believe a syllable that Iago utters on any subject, including himself, until one has tested his statement."[1] "The soliloquy," says Stoll, ". . . is the clue given to the audience, and must be the truth itself. There must even the liar speak true, and it is to knock the props from under Shakespeare's dramatic framework to hold that Iago's soliloquies are lies—that he lies to the audience, to himself."[2] The very reasons Bradley gives for doubting Iago's utter evil—his "perception, however dim, of the goodness of goodness," "his uneasiness and his unconscious desire," betrayed in the soliloquies, "to persuade himself that he has some excuse for the villainy he contemplates"[3] —are for Stoll signs of the self-descriptive convention: "The conscience darkly working within him is no more than . . . familiarity with the true moral values." Iago is the devil because he adheres to the same world-view as the other characters, and describes himself accordingly: "Instead of denying the devil a conscience or moral sense, as we should do, for good and all, it is according to Shakespeare's lights to give him one, but perverted, turned upside down. Iago thinks as we do, but is as we are not."[4]

Stoll impresses us as historically accurate if only because he describes a world-view so radically different from ours, but Bradley has the virtue of accounting for Shakespeare's greatness and for our continued interest in him. (Stoll leaves me wondering why in the world we still read Shakespeare, unless it is because we misread him.) Fortunately, we do not for our purpose have to decide the issue. It is enough that the issue indicates the extent to which dramatic structure dissolves along with belief in a single objective moral order. For once we stop judging by an external standard, we stop understanding the character by what he does and says. We start understanding him from inside, through sympathy. And once we start sympathizing, the central character is no longer the Aristotelian "agent" of the action but the creator of its meaning. Drama, in

---

[1] *Shakespearean Tragedy* (London: Macmillan, 1904; New York: Macmillan, 1949), p. 211.
[2] *Shakespeare Studies*, p. 388.
[3] pp. 234-35. [4] p. 385.

other words, gives way to monodrama, to the dramatic monologue.

Sympathy would seem to have been responsible in the first place for the psychological interpretation of Shakespeare, and it is no coincidence that the new interpretation made its first appearance in the latter eighteenth century when we note the decline of the dogmatic and the beginning of the sympathetic or humanitarian attitude. Our reading of a Hamlet soliloquy depends, after all, on whether we give more emphasis to Hamlet's moral problem or to his experience in facing the problem. If the moral imperative is uppermost in our minds, we are likely to agree with Hamlet when he chides his delay; we are likely to be concerned with his delinquency and to hope that his confession of guilt will advance him toward the fulfilment of his duty. But if we do not find the moral imperative compelling, we are likely to be less concerned with Hamlet's guilt than with his suffering from the sense of guilt; and we are likely to hope not so much that he will do his duty as that he will free himself from the sense of guilt. Nor will the uncompelling moral imperative strike us as a sufficient motive for so much suffering; in which case we will seek out an underlying motive, less abstract and external, more psychological and even biological, more consonant in other words with our assumptions about the mainsprings of human action. An abstract morality lurking in the dim periphery of our attention can hardly compete with the vivid human being filling the stage. Or to put it conversely, where dogmatic sanction recedes, sympathy rushes in to fill the vacuum.

Modern sympathy is even better illustrated when we see it turned upon Shakespeare's villains, for there it is clearly at odds with the plot. All the subtleties of nineteenth-century Iago criticism are attempts to account for the fact that, in spite of Iago's villainy, we find him attractive. We admire him because he has a strong and clearly defined point of view, and we sympathize with him because he is on the stage and claims our attention. To the extent that he is there to be understood, we try to understand him; we give him our sympathy as a primary condition anterior to judgment.

Iago was *understood* in the traditional interpretation as well, but he was understood as congruent with his moral category. When the moral imperative is, however, less compelling than the sheer appeal of the human being on the stage, sympathy overflows the weakened confines of the moral category; so that the modern reader finds in Iago a life that exceeds the moral category and is not to be accounted for by it. The modern interest—what we mean by *character* in fact—is in just that which is incongruent with the moral category. The modern reader can sympathize with any character, regardless of his moral position in the plot, provided only that he is sufficiently central to claim our attention, and has a sufficiently definite point of view and sufficient power of intellect and will to hold our interest. Thus, sympathy is likely to be more important than moral judgment in the modern interpretation not only of Iago but also of Shakespeare's Richard III, Macbeth, Shylock and Falstaff, and Marlowe's Tamburlaine, Faustus and Jew of Malta. If we have no sympathy for the execrable Aaron of Shakespeare's *Titus Andronicus*, it is not because he is wicked but because he is too crude and stupid to command our interest. Where we do find Elizabethan villains attractive, it is in the same sense and for the same reason that we admire Browning's duke in *My Last Duchess*.

We know how the decline of the moral sanctions against Jews and usurers has, by turning out sympathy toward Shylock, turned *The Merchant of Venice* from a crude comedy into a pathetic if not tragic drama;[1] and how the modern audience, unable to keep uppermost in its mind a distinct idea of the social limitations Malvolio has violated in daring to aspire to a Lady's hand, soon begins to feel sorry for him. Since the comic effect depends specifically on the exclusion of sympathy, it is even more important in comedy than in tragedy that we keep the offended mores in mind—which is why fewer comedies than tragedies survive, and why the comedies that do survive

[1] There has been, however, no decline in the sanction against tyrannical fathers, who still make excellent butts for comedy provided they are top-dog not under-dog as, in our eyes, Shylock is through his Jewishness. Stoll objects of course to the pathetic Shylock. But I see no alternative if *The Merchant* is to be played at all. A modern audience would not relish the red-wigged, hook-nosed caricature of the Elizabethan stage, nor would they enjoy participating in the unanimous baiting of the lone Jew. The alternative to the modern misinterpretation would seem to be an historically accurate but dead document.

do so through the pathetic or psychological interest that modern readers think they find there.

Falstaff's comic effect has not been impaired. But that is because his comic role has been made philosophical by the modern elevation of his character, an elevation which Stoll attributes to the decline of the chivalric code of honour. We laugh with Falstaff when he makes the common-sense attack upon honour ("Can honour set to a leg?"), because we see him as the witty philosopher of a rival world-view. But according to Stoll, the Elizabethans laughed at him for his transparent attempt to justify his cowardice. They saw him as a self-describing coward turning the general perspective against himself by poking sarcastic fun at himself. Stoll even suggests that Falstaff might have winked at the audience as he "descanted on the duty of discretion."[1] Such humorous self-betrayal would have been no more unpsychological than the startling self-betrayal of Shakespeare's villains in the tragedies.

But whether or not we are willing to go along with Stoll on this point (there is, after all, reason to believe that the laugh on chivalry had begun by Shakespeare's time), the issue between the psychological and anti-psychological interpretations of Falstaff is whether as coward, lecher and glutton he is the butt of the comedy and deservedly outwitted in the end; or whether he is the maker of the comedy, playing the butt for the sake of the humour which he turns upon himself as well as everyone else—whether he is, in other words, victorious in all the wit combats whatever his circumstantial defeat. It is essentially the issue of Hamlet and Macbeth criticism, whether they confront their difficulties or create them; and of Iago criticism, whether he is the villain or as maker of the plot merely playing the villain. In other words, are the characters agents of the plot with only as much consciousness as the plot requires; or have they a residue of intelligence and will beyond what the plot requires and not accounted for by it, so that they stand somehow above the plot, conscious of themselves inside it? The latter view assumes that we can apprehend more about the characters than the plot tells us, assumes our sympathetic apprehension of them.

[1] *Shakespeare Studies*, p. 468.

The Falstaff question has been only less important than the Hamlet question in establishing the psychological interpretation of Shakespeare. Both Hamlet and Falstaff began to appear in their new complex and enigmatic character in the 1770's, the decade of Werther and of a European Wertherism that owed much to an already well-established sentimental tradition in England. Of such a propitious age for psychological criticism, Maurice Morgann, the projector of the new Falstaff, was one of the advanced spirits—liberal in politics, humanitarian in sentiment, and in literature endowed with the new sensibility.

Morgann's sensibility is abundantly illustrated in the *Essay on the Dramatic Character of Sir John Falstaff* (1777), where the perceptions are far in advance of the dialectic. It is his fundamental sympathy for Falstaff that Morgann is trying to explain when he undertakes to prove that, in spite of cowardly actions, "Cowardice *is not* the *Impression*, which the *whole* character of *Falstaff* is calculated to make on the minds of an unprejudiced [i.e. sympathetic] audience." And it is on the ground of experience that he makes the novel distinction between our "*mental Impressions*" and our "*Understanding*" of character— whereby "we often condemn or applaud characters and actions on the credit of some logical process, while our hearts revolt, and would fain lead us to a very different conclusion." The "Understanding" takes cognizance, he says, of "*actions* only," and from these infers "*motives* and *character*; but the sense we have been speaking of proceeds in a contrary course, and determines of *actions* from certain *first principles of character*, which seem wholly out of the reach of the Understanding."[1]

Unfortunately, Morgann is a bit frightened by the revolutionary nature of his case, and tries to prove it to his eighteenth-century readers on their own rationalistic and moral grounds. His essay is therefore valuable for its scattered insights rather than for the hair-splitting, text-citing argument destructive of the dramatic and comic context which he employs in order to uncover in the *actions* he says do not *matter* evidences of Falstaff's courage. It would have required the dialectical equipment of the next century for Morgann to have granted the moral case against Falstaff and accounted for his sympathetic *impression* of him by quite another order of value. Yet the other

[1] Ed. W. A. Gill (London: Henry Frowde, 1912), pp. 4-6.

order of value is certainly implied by Morgann's distinction between the *first principles* of character which we apprehend sympathetically and its manifestations which we judge. It is also implied by his distinction between "*Constitutional Courage*" and the "Courage founded upon *principle*." The latter is moral courage, which comes of conformity to "the prevailing modes of honour, and the fashions of the age." But the former is an existential courage, which "extends to a man's whole life, makes a part of his nature, and is not to be taken up or deserted like a mere Moral quality."[1]

It follows—though Morgann does not specifically articulate the conclusion—that our judgment of Falstaff's moral courage must be problematical because based on a shifting idea of honour; whereas our apprehension of his *constitutional* courage must be certain because based on what he is in himself. Only the double apprehension of character could have given rise to Morgann's perception that character may be incongruous with action, that "the *real* character of *Falstaff* may be different from his *apparent* one," and that an author may give wit, dignity and courage to a character made to seem ridiculous, ignoble and cowardly by all external appearances.[2] The recognition that our *impressions* of a character and even of certain of the character's sentiments and actions may be contradictory of his moral category yet "we know not why, natural," leads to the essential method of all psychological criticism in that it compels us "to look farther, and examine if there be not something more in the character than is *shewn*."[3]

Now it is just the habit in Shakespeare criticism of looking for more than is shown that makes Stoll see red, since he contends that this is to treat the character as historical and that there can be no more in a fictitious character than *is* shown. It is true enough that psychological criticism treats the character as though he had a life of which the action presents only a portion; yet Stoll defines the issue, I think, inadequately. For if we conceive the play as larger than the plot, the part of character uncovered by psychological criticism falls not outside the play but outside the moral categories of the plot. The plot, which we understand through moral judgment, becomes a

[1] p. 23. [2] pp. 14, 148-50.
[3] p. 153.

clearing in the forest; while the play shades off to include the penumbra of forest fringe out of which the plot has emerged, a penumbra which we apprehend through sympathy. Such a conception makes room for psychological criticism by dissolving the limits of character and of the play, by suggesting that the limits are always in advance of comprehension. That is how we come by the modern idea of a masterpiece as an enigma whose whole meaning can never be formulated. Comprehension becomes an unending process, historical and evolutionary; while the play itself moves inviolate down the ages, eluding final formulation yet growing, too, in beauty and complexity as it absorbs into its meaning everything that has been thought and felt about it.

According to this conception, Morgann remains within the play, though outside the categories of the plot, when he undertakes to justify Falstaff by an order of value contradictory of his moral position as comic butt outwitted in the end. The *first principles* of character from which we gain our favourable *impression* of Falstaff are those "qualities of a strong mind, particularly Courage and ability," which attract us in spite of the character's vices. They are sufficient to "discharge that *disgust* which arises from vicious manners; and even to attach us . . . to the cause and subject of our mirth with some degree of affection."[1] But a character without courage and ability cannot long command our interest. That is why Morgann can grant all the other vices attributed to Falstaff, but not cowardice: if we "reckon cowardice among his other defects, all the intelligence and wit [i.e. *ability*] in the world could not support him through a single play."[2] The issue is not moral, it is not that cowardice is the gravest sin; rather it would seem to be whether Falstaff is to exist at all. He is "saturated," says Morgann, "with every folly and with every vice not destructive of his essential character,"[3] with every vice, in other words, except cowardice and stupidity which would be destructive. "Courage and Ability are first principles of Character, and not to be destroyed whilst the united frame of body and mind continues whole and unimpaired; they are the pillars on which he stands firm in spight of all his vices and disgraces."[4]

[1] pp. 11-12.
[2] p. 165.
[3] p. 149.
[4] p. 165.

But in what sense is cowardice destructive of character, when there are after all cowardly characters (Shakespeare's Parolles, Jonson's Bobadil)? Morgann's meaning can, I think, be understood in the terms we have established in this discussion. Courage and ability are necessary if Falstaff is to exist as a *character* in the modern sense, as something more than agent of the plot or representative of a moral category—as a pole for sympathy, with a consciousness in excess of the plot's requirements and a life outside the plot and proof against its accidents. The plot makes him out a coward, "but that is nothing," says Morgann, "if the character itself does not act from any consciousness of this kind, and if our Feelings take his part, and revolt against our understanding."[1] I take this to mean that Falstaff's intention is not to escape danger but to provide humour; just as in the psychological interpretation Iago's intention is to create the plot, and Hamlet's and Macbeth's to exercise their moral sensibility. To entertain so radical an idea, we must have apprehended in these characters a residue of consciousness which is as much a spectator of the action as we are, this consciousness being precisely the quality we apprehend through sympathy.

The fact that our *feelings* should have occasion to revolt against our *understanding* means that we judge this residue of consciousness by an order of value other than moral. Morgann's *courage* and *ability* are existential virtues, virtues which make for the sheer survival of the personality apart from any moral purpose toward which the personality is directed. He speaks at length of the indestructible nature of Falstaff, who, unlike Parolles and Bobadil, is never defeated and never even loses stature from his several disgraces. That is because the disgraces, like the "ill habits, and the accidents of age and corpulence, are no part of his essential constitution . . . they are second natures, not *first*." Falstaff's *first* nature is the "substance of his character [which] remains unimpaired," for "*Falstaff* himself has a distinct and separate subsistence."[2]

[1] p. 166.

[2] p. 177. "And hence it is," Morgann continues, "that he is made to undergo not one detection only, but a series of detections; that he is not formed for one Play only, but was intended originally at least for two; and the author, we are told, was doubtful if he should not extend him yet farther, and engage him in the wars with *France*." There follows the best

CHARACTER VERSUS ACTION IN SHAKESPEARE

Falstaff's courage, remember, is not moral but *constitutional*. It is not Hotspur's kind of courage. It is too bad that Morgann did not undertake the contrast with Hotspur, for it holds good under his interpretation—not to be sure as between cowardice and heroism, but as between two kinds of heroism. If Hotspur is the chivalric hero, Falstaff is the natural hero, the Hero of Existence. His is the courage to be himself, to realize his individuality. He is a hero because of his hard core of character, his fierce loyalty to himself, because he is more alive than other people. By this peculiarly modern reading, Falstaff and Hotspur would represent opposite kinds of heroism both of which go down to defeat; while the Prince, who temporizes between the two extremes, appropriating from each the virtues he can turn to his advantage, becomes prudence triumphant.[1]

Although the eighteenth century could not supply the concepts and vocabulary by which Falstaff might be called a hero, Morgann is already dealing in the distinctive virtues of the new heroism when he attacks as mere prudence the moral virtues Falstaff lacks, and glorifies Falstaff on the ground of his imprudence.

It may not possibly be wholly amiss to remark in this place, that if Sir *John Falstaff* had possessed any of that Cardinal quality, Prudence, alike the guardian of virtue and the protector of vice; that quality, from the possession or the absence of which, the character and fate of men in this life take, I think, their colour, and not from real vice or virtue; if he had considered his wit, not as *principal* but *accessary* only; as the instrument of power, and not

explanation I have seen of Falstaff's "disgrace" at the end of *Henry IV Part II*. Since Falstaff interests us by his wit in extricating himself from detections and disgraces, Shakespeare leaves him in disgrace in order that he may get himself out of it in the next play. There is, indeed, no other way of leaving Falstaff, Morgann shrewdly observes, except to leave him dead. For there can be no conclusion of his story in terms of the plot, since his existence has been mainly outside the plot: "He was not involved in the fortune of the Play; he was engaged in no action which, as to him, was to be compleated; . . . he passes thro' the Play as a lawless meteor" (p. 183). Thus, Shakespeare kills him off in *Henry V*, when he has decided not to use him any more.

[1] Although Bradley does not carry his reading of the play this far, he calls the Prince "perhaps, the most *efficient* character drawn by Shakespeare," and considers him an unpleasantly calculating person who planned from the start to reject Falstaff: "He is still his father's son, the son of the man whom Hotspur called a 'vile politician.'" ("The Rejection of Falstaff," *Oxford Lectures on Poetry*, London: Macmillan, 1926, pp. 256-57.)

as power itself; . . . he might, without any other essential change, have been the admiration and not the jest of mankind.[1]

Without using the word, the passage effectively describes Falstaff as a hero in the new sense; it contains in brief the whole ethical attitude of the next century. The attack on prudence is the beginning of the romantic ethics. Hypocrisy (the denial of one's own nature) is its worst sin, sincerity (another name for existential courage) its prime virtue. Morgann's Falstaff has the virtues Blake was to recommend in *The Marriage of Heaven and Hell*: "Prudence is a rich, ugly old maid courted by Incapacity," "He who desires but acts not, breeds pestilence," "The road of excess leads to the palace of wisdom." *Excess* explains Falstaff's nature; his girth, his appetites, his laughter, even his style of wit and the rich redundancy of his language—all derive their character from excess; yet they are not for that reason vices, as they would be according to the Aristotelian ethics of the Golden Mean. According to the new ethics, Falstaff's excesses are at once the cause of his failure and of his distinction.

For he commits what Shelley was to call the "generous error," the error of those who try to live life by a vision of it, thus transforming the world about them and impressing upon it their character. This is the secret of Falstaff's appeal. His vision of life takes over whenever he is on the stage; and everyone on stage with him, most notably the Prince, is drawn into his characteristic atmosphere. The only characters who resist his influence are those who, like the King and Hotspur, never confront him. Yet Falstaff's genius for creating his own environment is dangerous, since the single vision of life cannot be identical with reality and must eventually collide with it. That is why the "generous error" distinguishes the Hero of Existence from what Shelley calls the "trembling throng," who "languish" and are "morally dead," who live eclectically because they have not the courage to live out the implications of their own natures, who are too prudent to venture all on what must turn out to have been a noble delusion.[2]

Dr Johnson, who saw where Morgann's kind of criticism was leading, said of him: "Why, Sir, we shall have the man come

[1] pp. 20-21.
[2] See the Preface to *Alastor* and the last stanza of *Adonais*.

forth again; and as he has proved Falstaff to be no coward, he may prove Iago to be a very good character."[1] Johnson thought he was indulging in witty hyperbole, but the admiration for Falstaff was in fact to be accompanied in the next century by an admiration for Iago and for all characters alive enough to take over the scene, to assert their point of view as the one through which we understand the action. The new existential rather than moral judgment of character was to dissolve dramatic structure by denying the authority of the plot—making the psychologically read play, like the dramatic monologue, depend for its success upon a central character with a point of view definite enough to give meaning and unity to the events, and the strength of intellect, will and passion, the imaginative strength, to create the whole work before our eyes, to give it a thickness and an atmosphere, an inner momentum, a life.

It is, however, in the isolation of character from plot that we can best see the psychological interpretation of Shakespeare as dissolving dramatic structure and leading us toward the dramatic monologue. For in concentrating on the part of character in excess of plot requirements, and in claiming to apprehend more about character than the plot reveals, the psychological interpretation isolates character from the external motivation of plot (such as money, love, power). It makes of character an autonomous force, motivated solely by the need for self-expression. The psychological interpretation of Falstaff rests, for example, on the assumption that Falstaff does not employ his wit for practical advantage, that he makes no secret of his true nature and therefore does not really expect to deceive the other characters but merely to draw them into his jests. Deny this assumption as Stoll does, and you have a Falstaff who menaces the other characters and vies for advantage in the same way as the rival factions of the play's historical episodes. Such a Falstaff must be judged morally and laughed at as a base clown who is deservedly humiliated and outwitted at every turn.

But Morgann's Falstaff employs his wit not as the "instrument of power" but as "power itself." And Hazlitt's Falstaff is

---

[1] James Boswell, *The Life of Samuel Johnson, LL.D.* (London: J. M. Dent, 1901), III, 230.

less interested in sensual gratification than in his own "ideal exaggerated description" of the life of sensuality and freedom, of a world-view he has taken it upon himself to dramatize.

> His pulling out the bottle in the field of battle is a joke to shew his contempt for glory accompanied with danger, his systematic adherence to his Epicurean philosophy in the most trying circumstances. Again, such is his deliberate exaggeration of his own vices, that it does not seem quite certain whether the account of his hostess's bill, found in his pocket, with such an out-of-the-way charge for capons and sack with only one halfpennyworth of bread, was not put there by himself as a trick to humour the jest upon his favourite propensities, and as a conscious caricature of himself. He is represented as a liar, a braggart, a coward, a glutton, &c. and yet we are not offended but delighted with him; for he is all these as much to amuse others as to gratify himself. He openly assumes all these characters to shew the humourous part of them. . . . In a word, he is an actor in himself almost as much as upon the stage, and we no more object to the character of Falstaff in a moral point of view than we should think of bringing an excellent comedian, who should represent him to the life, before one of the police offices.[1]

Falstaff has no motive other than to exercise his genius for comedy.

Hamlet is in the same way isolated from the plot, when Coleridge explains the intricacies of his character not by referring us to his function in the plot but by referring us to "Shakspere's deep and accurate science in mental philosophy" and to the "constitution of our own minds." Thus, Hamlet's "wild transition to the ludicrous" is explained not as a madness deliberately assumed to deceive the King but as "the expression of extreme anguish and horror." And Hamlet's delay is explained not as due to external obstacles which prevent him from executing the revenge but as due to an "overbalance of imagination" which indisposes him for action.[2] Hazlitt goes even farther by making the delay entirely a matter of Hamlet's preference: "it is more to his taste to indulge his imagination in reflecting upon the enormity of the crime and refining on his schemes of vengeance, than to put them into immediate practice."[3]

[1] *Characters of Shakespear's Plays*, pp. 190-91.
[2] *Lectures on Shakspere*, pp. 471-73.   [3] *Characters*, p. 109.

The Iago of the psychological interpretation is the Shakespearean character most isolated from plot; for ever since Coleridge's characterization of him as a "motiveless malignity," it has been generally agreed that Iago has nothing to gain from the intrigue he devises to destroy Othello. "He is quite or nearly as indifferent to his own fate as to that of others," says Hazlitt; "he runs all risks for a trifling advantage; and is himself the dupe and victim of his ruling passion—an insatiable craving after action of the most difficult and dangerous kind." He devises the intrigue "as an exercise for his ingenuity" and "to prevent *ennui*."[1] Mere motivation, says Swinburne, would spoil the character of Iago: "A genuine and thorough capacity for human lust or hate would diminish and degrade the supremacy of his evil. He is almost as far above or beyond vice as he is beneath or beyond virtue. And this it is that makes him impregnable and invulnerable."[2]

This last statement carries the isolation of character from plot as far as it will go. The effectiveness of character is made to depend on its inaccessibility to the rational and moral categories of the plot. Falstaff, Hamlet and Iago are geniuses whose only purpose is to express their genius. They are creators of the play who must be judged not as we judge men of action but as we judge artists, by the virtuosity of their creations. It matters less whether they are right than that they accomplish what they set out to be and do—that Falstaff conquer with his wit, that Hamlet gain spiritual ascendancy through his moving and profound exploration of moral experience, and that Iago's intrigue be bold, ingenious and successful.

Such a theory is in its ultimate implication destructive of drama. It destroys the play as an entity distinct from its parts, having a logic, meaning and unity of its own to which the parts are subordinated; for it destroys the objective principles which relate the events and characters to each other and to the whole. By leaving events subject to the will of character, it destroys the logic inherent in the events themselves. And by giving unconditional sympathy to sheer vividness of character, it destroys the moral principle which apportions sympathy among the characters according to their deserts. It leaves an anarchic free-for-all in which the characters compete for a sympathy

---

[1] *Characters*, p. 55.   [2] *A Study of Shakespeare*, p. 179.

that depends on the ability to command attention, with the strongest character able to assert his point of view against the general meaning.

What such a theory does is to break down the barriers that hold sympathy in check, subordinating it to the general meaning. It allows sympathy to become a law unto itself, the law of dramatic structure in fact; so that we no longer have the logical unit Aristotle spoke of, with its beginning, middle and end, but rather a succession of whatever characters and events happen to fall within the purview of the character who has captured our sympathy. Instead of a play which is complete because of the working out of its own logic, we have a play whose limits are defined only by the perspective of a central character. Hence the controversy between the anti-psychological critics, who insist that there is only as much character as appears in the play, and the psychological critics, who insist that dramatic characters can be treated as though they were historical, that it is legitimate to speculate upon their lives before and after the play. The question is whether the character is part of a definitive unit, the play; or whether the play is merely an episode in the character's career, an episode whose beginning and end shades off into the rest of his biography. To the extent that perspective replaces logical completeness as the principle of organization, we are moving away from drama toward the dramatic monologue.

There has always been in drama a certain tension between the point of view of each character and the play's final meaning which assigns values to the points of view. And among the audience there has been a corresponding tension between the inclination to be interested in each character out of sheer curiosity and the necessity to judge the characters morally. But character has always given way in drama to general meaning; whereas the nineteenth century preferred to weight the balance in the other direction, to allow the individual point of view and the inclination to be interested in it to have their way against the general meaning. That is what the nineteenth century did with its reading of Shakespeare, where it may not have had the right to, and what it did where it undoubtedly had the right—with its own literature, as in the dramatic monologue.

The dramatic monologue brings to the surface what is underground in drama; what in drama resists the law of the form becomes the law of the dramatic monologue. The sympathy which pulls against the meaning of drama is the meaning and whole *raison d'être* of the dramatic monologue. External and moral relations are still there, but pushed off-stage; they are now the underground and resisting element, the foil against which meaning defines itself. For the meaning of the dramatic monologue derives not from the absorption of the particular in the general but from the defiance of the general. The meaning is not the law which puts character in its place; the meaning *is* character in its unformulated being, in all its particularity.

6

The Lyrical Element: Character as Song

TO appreciate the victory of character over action in the dramatic monologue we have only to consider the motives for which the speakers undertake to speak. Although the utterance is dramatic because entirely strategic, we find that the motive for speaking is inadequate to the utterance, that the utterance is in other words largely gratuitous—it need never have occurred. The result is that the dramatic situation, incomplete in itself, serves an ultimately self-expressive or lyrical purpose which gives it its resolution.

Why, for example, does Browning's duke tell the story of his last duchess to, of all people, the envoy of his prospective duchess? The duke's utterance is undoubtedly strategic in that he does not tell the story in the interest of truth or to add to the envoy's store of information, but clearly to make an impression, to manipulate the envoy. Yet the story can do the duke no good but only harm in the business at hand, the arrangement of the marriage and the dowry. The duke's motive cannot be accounted for by the dramatic situation. It remains ultimately mysterious. But insofar as it can be accounted for at all, his motive is to assert his point of view for no purpose that the dramatic situation can tell us anything about, but simply to overcome the envoy by enveloping him within the duke's orbit of value. It is to make him participate in the duke's organization of the world, not to convert him to it (the envoy is no more converted than we are) but to give him the same sense that the poem gives us of the duke's pressing actuality.

Even where the speakers' motives come closer to the business at hand—as where the bishop wants to convince his sons to give him the magnificent tomb he plans, or Andrea del Sarto wants to convince Lucrezia to spend the evening home with him—there remains a superabundance of expression, more words, ingenuity and argument than seem necessary for the purpose.

Browning has been criticized for this superabundance. Yet it is just the gratuitous nature of their utterance that constitutes the speakers' "Song," for the speakers of dramatic monologues *burst* into utterance in the same sense that the verb is used in connection with song. Just as in opera the singer only wants occasion to burst into an aria the expressiveness of which can hardly be justified by the dramatic situation; so in the dramatic monologue the dramatic situation is less the adequate motive than the occasion for a total outpouring of soul, the expression of the speaker's whole life until that moment. The bishop and Andrea reconstruct the course of their lives—all they hoped for, all they achieved and failed to achieve, even projecting their hopes into eternity. All for what? For the sons who must have heard all this before and will not be illuminated or convinced by it one way or another; and with even less reason (the bishop is, after all, making his deathbed statement) for a routine quarrel with the indifferent Lucrezia.

The impression of gratuitousness is heightened by the fact that the speakers never accomplish anything by their utterance, and seem to know from the start that they will not. Lucrezia goes out after all, and it is clearly implied that the bishop's sons will not build him the tomb he wants. The speakers' misgivings are expressed in their pleading tone: Andrea's "do not let us quarrel any more," "bear with me for once," "all shall happen as you wish," and the bishop's "is Anselm keeping back?" "My sons, ye would not be my death?" "Nay, boys, ye love me." It is as the perfectly consistent result of what has been developing all along that Andrea finally gives Lucrezia the permission to depart that he has withheld only long enough to make his utterance. And the bishop finally articulates the fear that has been haunting him all along, the fear that he is not to be immortalized by immortal materials for his tomb but must pass into dissolution with mere perishable

> Stone—
> Gritstone, a-crumble! Clammy squares which sweat
> As if the corpse they keep were oozing through—
> And no more *lapis* to delight the world!

Fra Lippo Lippi does, it is true, convince the guards who have stopped him in the streets after curfew to let him pass on, but it hardly required his biography as well as a whole theory of art and of the relation of physical to spiritual reality to accomplish that. The question was no doubt settled by his reference at the very beginning to a certain Cosimo of the Medici, a friend. It is also true that Don Juan convinces his wife that his love for her is not compromised by his flirtation with Fifine, but at a cost in argument far beyond what in this case the reader no less than Elvire requires. And then Don Juan negates his own argument by returning in the end to Fifine.

It is a favourite device with Browning to have the speaker negate in the end his own argument. Cleon establishes with convincing logic that mankind has reached a point of self-consciousness where existence is no longer endurable without some assurance of personal immortality through direct revelation, but he rejects in the end the barbarian Jew, Paulus, who claims to bring such revelation. The speaker in *How It Strikes a Contemporary* perceives and admires, he even exaggerates, the transcendental virtues of the poet, but he makes clear in the last two lines that he will have no part of such virtues for himself:

> Well, I could never write a verse,—could you?
> Let's to the Prado and make the most of time.

Bishop Blougram withdraws support from his Christian argument by demonstrating in the end that his motive has not been to convert Gigadibs, to convince him of what the argument purports to be about, but to impress him, show him that the bishop is not taken in by the Church but, with eyes as wide open as Gigadibs', chooses the better bargain. All this to get Gigadibs

> To discontinue—not detesting, not
> Defaming, but at least—despising me!

The bishop ends with a direct challenge to Gigadibs. He will give him letters to all the Catholic and some non-Catholic reviews in London, Dublin and New York; he will afford him the means to publish his "lively sketches," even to expose the present "eccentric confidence," in order to prove, first, that from his vantage in the Church the bishop wields more power than Gigadibs in Gigadibs' own world of journalism, and second, that Gigadibs can do the bishop no harm so impregnable is his position. Thus, the bishop reveals that he has confided in Gigadibs as an affront, to show contempt for his judgment; just as the duke of *My Last Duchess* shows contempt for the envoy's judgment. The bishop's design upon Gigadibs is in fact similar to the duke's. For the bishop casts doubt upon the validity of his argument, in order to reveal that he has used it to overcome Gigadibs by the sheer display of personal virtuosity.

The speaker's negation of the argument is carried farthest in *Mr Sludge, "The Medium,"* where the speaker is Browning's most despicable character and in every way least qualified to be believed. Sludge appears from the start as an untrustworthy scoundrel, leads us to think better of him through his persuasive argument, and finally reveals himself as even baser and more vicious than had originally appeared. The poem opens with Sludge on his knees before his patron, Hiram H. Horsefall of Boston, who has just caught him cheating in a séance. Sludge begs not to be exposed, trying to win his point by referring to Horsefall's dead mother whose breath Sludge feels upon his cheek. Horsefall is not to be exploited that way any more, and almost chokes Sludge to death in his rage. Sludge then offers to tell all about his tricks if Horsefall will pay his passage to England and not expose him; and after some haggling about price, a bargain is struck.

Horsefall agrees to the bargain out of curiosity, since he does not need the confession for proof of Sludge's guilt. His role becomes at this point less dramatic, less that of active opponent, more that of interested auditor, and the whole long argument that follows has a gratuitous quality. Since it is established from the start that Sludge is to have his quiet departure for England, he expends more ingenuity and takes a higher, more difficult line than is necessary for his apparent purpose.

He admits he is a cheat, but embarks upon a lengthy review of his career to show that far from having victimized Horsefall and his friends, he has been their victim. They enticed him into the "medium" trade by their anxious credulity and the rich rewards they offered him for telling them what they wanted to hear. They were the most aggressive promoters of his imposture, proselytizing for him and defending him against all rational objections, but leaving him to pay the moral price of their spiritual comfort.

All this is convincing enough, and Sludge might have stopped here. Although he has been more concerned to defend himself than to tell about his tricks, he has certainly done as much as he is going to do in fulfilment of his side of the bargain. But spurred on to self-display by the impression he seems to be making on Horsefall ("How you do tease the whole thing out of me!" he complains coyly in response to the leading questions Horsefall has begun to ask), and apparently spurred on by a genuine desire for self-knowledge ("Really, I want to light up my own mind"), Sludge undertakes the supreme test of his ingenuity—to re-establish with all the facts against him the validity of his discredited trade.

> I don't unsay
> A single word: I cheated when I could,

and yet

> This trade of mine—I don't know, can't be sure
> But there was something in it, tricks and all!

For somehow, in spite of his intention, he manipulates the truth:

> I've told my lie,
> And seen truth follow, marvels none of mine.

The fact is he has a sixth sense he cannot understand. Although he uses tricks to get the séance started, things take over of themselves after that in a way he cannot understand. Perhaps he is made to believe he cheats because he would die of fright if he knew what hand guided his. His lie is "quick with a germ of truth" because it does not replace the truth, it makes the truth accessible. He compares his cheating to the self-desecration for a worthy end, the "strange secret sweet self-sacrifice," which in certain ancient Egyptian rites the initiate undergoes to achieve a state of purity. And he compares it to the art of the poet who ignores the facts, or the prose-writer who shapes them to his end, all to make the truth appear. Since in his séances Sludge makes operative man's visions of the ideal—"the Golden Age, old Paradise/Or new Eutopia"—he is greater than the poets, for he "acts the books they write."

Thus, Sludge makes the minimum argument for the reality of spirit. As in *Blougram*, the argument is superior to the motive and the truth in question superior to both, but Sludge achieves his glimpse of truth from an even lower level than Blougram's. He stands somewhere between Blougram and Caliban in the relative inadequacy of his mind and experience to the truth in question, and his utterance is less reliable than theirs because he is less disinterested—he has a tight spot to talk himself out of. Nevertheless, we take his argument seriously because of its intrinsic merit (it is, after all, similar to other arguments in Browning which we do take seriously), and because there remains in it the superfluous element—Sludge does not have to say all that to win his point. It comes as no surprise that Horsefall finally gives him everything he wants, and even more, in the way of money, for the bargain was struck at the start and the extra gratuity is not something that it required Sludge's last word to win. But Horsefall goes no further. When in the end Sludge tests the extent of his success by referring again to Horsefall's "sainted mother" in order to see if he has regained his former hold over him, Horsefall makes it clear that he has not. So for all his talking, Sludge winds up pretty much where he started. It is just the ineffectiveness of his strategy that causes us to disallow it in judging his argument, the argument being so obviously incommensurate in size and ingenuity with its intended effect. We also judge him apart from his strategy. For the superfluity of his argument indicates that he is carried away by it, that his self-revelation is unintentional and to that extent sincere.

We are surprised, therefore, when after Horsefall's departure from the room, Sludge repudiates his own argument more thoroughly than any other speaker in Browning. He curses Horsefall with a viciousness we are not prepared for, and immediately plans the most vicious possible revenge. Having exploited Horsefall's devotion to his dead mother, Sludge plans to say that Horsefall killed his mother and that when Sludge accused him of it, Horsefall attacked him, was thrashed, and howling for mercy begged Sludge to leave the country and save him from disgrace. With this story and the money Horsefall has given him, Sludge plans to resume the "medium" trade in England. Is Horsefall, he asks in the last line, "the only fool in the world?" By the last line alone, Sludge shows that his argument with all its transcendental implications was pure strategy. He even regrets it as strategy:

> Where was my head? I ought to have prophesied
> He'll die in a year and join her: that's the way.

The effect is to cast as much doubt as possible upon the argument. Yet the argument gives off its own light which casts doubt upon Sludge's declaration of motive. For whatever of truth, beauty and sincerity the argument contains, came after all from this same snarling cur who now repudiates it. Thus, the speaker and his utterance are, if not quite contradictory, at least in disequilibrium with each other; while both the speaker and his utterance are in disequilibrium with the business at hand, the dramatic situation. The result is to throw each element on its own to be judged intrinsically; while their meaning, their relation to each other, remains in question.

Far from being a fault, this disequilibrium is precisely the genius of the dramatic monologue, the thing to be worked for. It is the disequilibrium of its structure that distinguishes the dramatic monologue from a speech in drama or narrative. For the superfluity and unaccountability of the dramatic monologue are antithetical to the structure of drama and narrative, where the point is precisely to achieve economy and accountability. To the extent that an utterance is *dramatic*, we expect it to reveal as much as we need to know about the speaker's character, and we expect to find its justification and meaning in the situation to which it is the strategic response and in its effect upon the situation. We expect the dramatic utterance to alter things in some way, to leave us in the end in advance of where we started.

It is the lyric instead that arises as an expression of pure will, an expression for which the dramatic situation, if any, provides merely the occasion. Since the lyric is not a strategically limited response to a specific situation, it seeks to be total in its expression—to express, as Browning suggests in his *Essay on Shelley*, the whole soul of the speaker as "the nearest reflex" of "absolute Mind." Nor does the total expression of the lyric get anywhere; the lyric digs as deeply as it can, to paraphrase Browning, where it stands.[1] For all its affinity to drama, the dramatic monologue has an affinity to the lyric in just the respect in which the lyric is antithetical to drama.

But why does the speaker of the dramatic monologue express himself? In order to learn something about himself as a way of learning something about reality (Browning's "absolute Mind"). Whether the speaker is St Simeon adding up the sum of his mortifications, or Ulysses explaining his personal reasons for the voyage to mariners who will undertake it in any case, or Rizpah repeating the traumatic events of her son's execution and her theft of his bones to the evangelical lady who knows it all and wants only to hear Rizpah's confession of repentance, or Andrea del Sarto playing out his pathos to the unresponsive Lucrezia, or Sludge *lighting up his own mind*—the speaker does not use his utterance to expound a meaning but to pursue one, a meaning which comes to him with the shock of revelation. The speaker's pursuit of meaning accounts for the tone of improvisation in the best dramatic monologues, as well as for the speaker's rapt absorption in what he is saying and his strange lack of connection with the auditor. The meaning the speaker pursues is precisely his Song, his life's meaning. To prolong that illuminating music, he prolongs his utterance— losing sight of its ostensible motivation and of the person towards whom it is ostensibly directed.

It is in pursuit of his Song, his "Love Song," that Eliot's J. Alfred Prufrock passes through those "half-deserted streets," filled with sexual portent, to that drawing-room where the ladies' talk of Michelangelo makes it all too easy to avoid the sexual question; so that Prufrock finally retreats to the sea-chambers of fantasy, where he can spend the rest of his life listening to mermaids singing. The lyrical element, which is in other dramatic monologues the extra quantity, is the substance of Eliot's poem; for Prufrock does not merely say more than the situation requires, he does not direct his utterance to the situation

[1] "Not with the combination of humanity in action, but with the primal elements of humanity, he [the subjective or lyric as distinguished from the objective or dramatic poet] has to do; and he digs where he stands— preferring to seek them in his own soul as the nearest reflex of that absolute Mind, according to the intuitions of which he desires to perceive and speak." (Published with Shelley's *Defence of Poetry*, ed. L. Winstanley, Boston and London: Heath, 1911, p. 131.)

at all. His utterance is not even contemporaneous in tense with the situation, since he speaks not to alter the situation but to extract from it the pattern of his life. Whereas the speaker's whole life, past and future, emerges in other dramatic monologues as an inference from his strategy in the present-tense situation; in *Prufrock*, we infer the present-tense situation and the speaker's strategy from an utterance almost entirely in the present-perfect and future tenses.

The poem's crucial situation, the broaching of the sexual question, appears as anticipation: "there will be time," "how should I begin?" and as recollection: "would it have been worth it after all?"—but never actually happens. Even the details of the tea party appear as part of a pattern: "I have known the eyes already," "I have known the arms already," "I have measured out my life with coffee spoons." And once Prufrock leaves the tea party, there is no situation at all nor even the implication of a present tense, but pure pattern. There is the pattern of the future: "I shall wear white flannel trousers, and walk upon the beach," blended with the pattern of the past: "I have heard the mermaids singing," to make in the final lines the distillation of a life significantly without any present:

> We have lingered in the chambers of the sea
> By sea-girls wreathed with seaweed red and brown
> Till human voices wake us, and we drown.

Prufrock is clearly speaking for his own benefit. Yet he does not, like the soliloquist, address himself; he addresses his other self—the "you" of the first line, "Let us go then, you and I," and the second party of the "we" in "We have lingered." Prufrock's other self figures as the auditor who watches Prufrock's performance at the tea party and to whom Prufrock tells what he learns through the performance about his life. In introducing the speaker's other self as auditor, Eliot makes explicit what is implicit in all the dramatic monologues. All those inadequately motivated and ineffectual utterances are addressed ultimately across the dramatic situation and across the ostensible auditor to some projection of the speaker for whom the superfluous element of the utterance is intended. That is why it makes so little difference, as long as the speaker's attention is directed outward, whether the dramatic monologue has or has not an ostensible auditor; for ultimately the speaker speaks to understand something about himself.

It is the speaker's ultimate purpose that accounts for the curious style of address of the dramatic monologue. Not only does the speaker direct his address outward as in dialogue but the style of address gives the effect of a closed circuit, with the speaker directing his address outward in order that it may return with a meaning he was not aware of when sending it forth. I say a closed circuit because the utterance seems to be directed only obliquely at the ostensible auditor, and seems never to reach its ultimate goal with him. Nor does the essential interchange take place with the auditor; for even where the auditor's remarks are implied, the speaker never learns anything from them and they do not change the meaning of the utterance. If the speaker represents one voice of a dialogue, then his other self is the essential second voice in that it sends back his own voice with a difference.

Thus, Prufrock *comes to see* the pattern of his life through a series of revelations culminating in the vision of the mermaids. But we have to understand the revelations as passing across an implied strategic utterance, if we are to understand that Prufrock is not describing the pattern of his life but discovering it. By omitting the strategic utterance, leaving only the essential interchange between Prufrock and his other self, Eliot carries the lyrical element in the dramatic monologue to its limit. Go a step farther, take away at least the implication of the present-tense situation, and the poem ceases to be a dramatic monologue. It becomes a traditional lyric, the logically reworked recollection of an idea rather than the dramatic presentation of how through a particular dialectical situation the idea comes to be perceived.

Yet it is interesting to note how little dramatic situation suffices to make a poem a dramatic monologue. We know nothing of Prufrock's lady, his relation with her, the question he is to ask, or of what passes between them at the tea party. There is only enough dramatic situation to serve as springboard for Prufrock's self-realization and self-revelation. And here again Eliot is merely carrying to an extreme a characteristic of all dramatic monologues, since it is precisely by subordinating the situation to what the speaker gets out of it in the way of experience that the dramatic monologue achieves its characteristic disequilibrium. The inadequacy of the speaker's motive as well as his repudiation of the utterance envelop the situation in ambiguity, with the result that we are unable to judge it and must treat it as merely the agency by which the speaker learns what he tells us about himself.

But Eliot does not go as far in subordinating situation to experience as Browning himself in "*Childe Roland to the Dark Tower Came.*" Eliot at least implies a precise situation of which he does not choose to disclose all the details; whereas Browning's poem is about a quest of which we do not know the purpose or whether in the end the knight succeeds or fails. It is the whole point of the poem that there is nothing more precise to be known, that the poem is about the sheer questing—the experience not the situation. There is no question of an inadequate motive, because the knight has no motive beyond the quest itself. To fail as the other knights before him will be success enough, since he will at least have come to the end of the journey. The forward movement is automatic, magical; it leads to failure, but is in itself a kind of success. Yet it marks no sort of progress. When the knight finally achieves the Dark Tower, it is not because the forward movement has brought him there but because of a transformation of consciousness.

His journey across the devastated landscape must be treated as experience, because it cannot be judged morally or logically. The moral categories cancel each other out, leaving the journey outside the realm of good and evil. It is a "hoary cripple, with malicious eye," who directs the knight

> Into that ominous tract which, all agree,
> Hides the Dark Tower.

The knight's first thought is that the cripple lies and sets a trap for him. But it turns out that the cripple has told the truth. Yet the knight's suspicion is justified, too; for when the Dark Tower comes upon him, it is with a click "as when a trap shuts." The cripple sends him to his doom and to the triumphant accomplishment of his quest.

The journey cannot be judged logically, because the details of it mark no sort of progress. To the extent that they mean anything, they mean the same thing over and over—defeat, sterility, death; and since their very existence is unaccounted for, they appear not as the expected development of a theme but as each time a shock, a unique experience. Whether the detail is the "one stiff blind horse . . . however he came there," or the "sudden little river . . . as unexpected as a serpent," or the water-rat the knight spears crossing the river ("ugh! it sounded like a baby's shriek"), or the "savage trample" of an old struggle, unaccountable in such a place and with

> No foot-print leading to that horrid mews,
> None out of it

or the abandoned instruments of torture, or the great black bird that brushes the knight's cap with its wing, "perchance the guide I sought"—all these details, with the possible exception of the last (the passing of the bird seems to open the knight's eyes), are presented for their sensational value. If we are dealing here (as some interpreters say) with the landscape of hell, it is not an allegorical hell of moral significance; it is a psychological hell the details of which do not develop an idea of hell but give duration to the experience.

When the Dark Tower is finally achieved, the knight does not go to it; it comes upon him, suddenly, unaccountably, as an illumination. Mrs. Orr, in her *Handbook to the Works of Robert Browning*, sees that the poem is rendered mysterious by the fact that "The Tower is much nearer and more accessible than Childe Roland has thought."[1] She calls this a "discrepancy," but it is perfectly right, indeed necessary, once we realize that the poem follows the structure not of situation but of experience. For it is when the knight has decided he is as far as ever from the end that the black bird passes and his vision is transformed. He somehow grows aware, in spite of the dusk, that the plain has given place all around to mountains; no progress this way, he thinks, then he hears the trap click shut—and he *sees*.

> Burningly it came on me all at once,
> This was the place!

"Dotard," he accuses himself as though the thing had been there before him the whole time,

> a-dozing at the very nonce,
> After a life spent training for the sight!

[1] (London: George Bell, 1937.) Her remarks on *Childe Roland* all appear on pp. 273-74.

> What in the midst lay but the Tower itself?
>> The round squat turret, blind as the fool's heart,
>> Built of brown stone, without a counterpart
> In the whole world.

What he sees is not his physical surrounding but a transformation of it, as darkness gives way to light and silence to noise, as the mountains turn into giant spectators of his destruction, and he hears in the tolling of bells the names and stories of the friends who preceded him on the quest, and sees them in a sheet of flame ranged to meet him.

> Not see? because of night perhaps?—why, day
>> Came back again for that! . . .

> Not hear? when noise was everywhere! it tolled
>> Increasing like a bell. Names in my ears
>> Of all the lost adventurers my peers,—
> How such a one was strong, and such was bold,
> And such was fortunate, yet each of old
>> Lost, lost! one moment knelled the woe of years.

> There they stood, ranged along the hill-sides, met
>> To view the last of me, a living frame
>> For one more picture! in a sheet of flame
> I saw them and I knew them all. And yet
> Dauntless the slug-horn to my lips I set,
>> And blew. "*Childe Roland to the Dark Tower came.*"

What is this but the experience of understanding as distilled from what is understood? The final stanzas should enable us to see through retrospect that everything leading up to them has been about the experience of the ominous mystery understood in the end. It is not an allegorical interpretation to say that the poem is about the experience of destiny, as awful presage and as awful yet triumphant understanding of the very worst.

Childe Roland is not an allegory in that it says nothing of the nature of destiny or even, I think, of the moral value of man's confrontation of destiny. The triumph in the end I would call existential rather than moral. For the trek has been loathsome, the knight has hated it every step of the way, and the Dark Tower turns out not only sinister but hateful—"squat." The slug-horn blast is not for any good perceived, nor is it the just reward for a noble quest. There is no reward, and the quest can hardly be called noble since it has been pursued without motive and, as it turns out, for an unworthy goal. The blast is, I think, a blast of defiance in that it contains both the knight's praise of himself for having endured and discovered and his dispraise of what has been endured and discovered. The triumph, such as it is, is not moral since there has been no good in the intention or the result; it is a triumph of the knight's own personality. He has added a new side to his nature, he has exercised and expanded his will and consciousness, he has transmuted a hateful reality into experience and thus into a triumphant acquisition. The details of the poem are not allegorical just because they are not representative of an idea but of a perception. They are evocative—used to make us see what the knight sees, so we can respond as he does and thus participate in his growth of consciousness.

Such a reading is not in its main lines new, since it has always been the critical consensus that *Childe Roland* cannot be read allegorically. Browning himself said that the poem had come to him "as a kind of dream" which he had to write then and there: "I did not know then what I meant beyond that, and I'm sure I don't know now."[1] DeVane calls the poem a "fantasy, that might almost be called a nightmare"; William Lyon Phelps speaks of it as a "wholly romantic poem" that "means nothing specifically except a triumphant close to a heart-shaking experience"[2]; while Mrs Orr, who comes closest to dealing with its organization, has this to say:

> We can connect no idea of definite pursuit or attainment with a series of facts so dreamlike and so disjointed: still less extract from it a definite moral; and we are reduced to taking the poem as a simple work of fancy, built up of picturesque impressions which have, separately or collectively, produced themselves in the author's mind.

These quotations should make clear, however, the advantage of reading the poem in our particular context. For it is one thing to dismiss the poem as simply an experience, and another to apply to it the systematic concept of a poetry of experience— to find through a comparison of it with other dramatic mono-

---

[1] Quoted in DeVane, *Browning Handbook*: (New York: Appleton-Century-Crofts), p. 229. (London: John Murray), p. 204.
[2] *Browning, How To Know Him*, (Indianapolis: Bobbs-Merrill, 1937) pp. 237, 232.

logues that it fits into a structural pattern, that it has a rationale in its irrationality and an order in its disorder.

Thus the "discrepancies" noted by Mrs Orr in the geographically ambiguous nearness and accessibility of the Tower, in the ambiguous moral meaning of the "sinister-looking man" who seems to lie but tells the truth, and in the ambiguous objectivity of the country the knight traverses ("as he describes the country through which he passes, it becomes clear that half its horrors are created by his own heated imagination, or by some undefined influence in the place itself")—these "discrepancies" are signs of the ambiguity with which the dramatic monologue, generally, seeks to envelop the dramatic situation. And here as elsewhere the effect of the ambiguity is to shift attention from the situation to the speaker, to make it impossible to judge the situation; so that we look to the speaker for the rationale of the poem, while regarding the situation as in every way problematical and therefore a projection of the speaker, the agency of his self-revelation.

Without inherent moral meaning and pursued through a country of which we can only be sure that it is what the knight sees, the quest cannot be read as a self-contained chain of events but only for what it tells us about the speaker; while the nearness and accessibility of the Tower makes the end of the quest seem more an illumination than the end of a journey. The geographical "discrepancy" imitates in its effect the psychological phenomenon of illumination, in that it makes for the suddenness of the discovery and the sense of the discovery as a transformation of what was already known.

The whole movement of the poem from presage to illumination is an example of the characteristic movement of the dramatic monologue in a straight line—toward the intensified restatement of what has already been said. Such illumination of what is already known gives the effect of having come not as a result of the dramatic situation but through some private purpose of the speaker which cuts across the dramatic situation. Since neither the duke's design on the envoy, nor Andrea's on Lucrezia, nor Sludge's on Horsefall seem to deflect them from the inevitable line of their self-revelation—a self-revelation which does not serve their strategic purpose—the utterance is in its ultimate effect a private dialogue of the speaker with himself, leading to a private illumination. The discovery of the Tower in *Childe Roland* is comparable in its effect to the illumination at the end of *Karshish* ("The very God! think Abib") which bursts upon us with the same *éclat* and reveals Karshish to have been the whole time talking to himself, working toward this illumination—although ostensibly addressing quite another line of thought to his teacher.

This brings us to the style of address, which in *Childe Roland* has puzzled the commentators and is indeed hardly understandable without a systematic comparison of it with the style of address of other dramatic monologues. Mrs Orr concludes that the knight must have escaped the general doom of his predecessors, since he after all "lives to tell the tale"; while Phelps, relying rather more on sensibility, prefers to think that "the monologue is murmured by the solitary knight as he advances on his darkening path."[1] Mrs Orr's reasoning must be judged fallacious since nothing in the poem, other than the telling of it, indicates that the knight survives—indeed, he says that his predecessors are ranged "to view the last of me"—and there is no indication that the poem is being told to anyone or that it deals, though it is in the past tense, with a past-tense situation. Phelps comes closer to the truth, though his account deprives the utterance of any purpose or any quality of dialogue. It requires comparison with other dramatic monologues, as well as with the dramatic lyric and the lyrical drama, to understand that the knight is directing his utterance outward to a projection of himself, and that he is speaking not to tell himself what he in an articulated way knows but in order to work toward the articulated realization of what he knows only as presage.

Phelps, who is obviously aware of the present-tense effect of the utterance, does not account for the fact that it is in the past tense. The fact can, I think, be accounted for by comparing *Childe Roland* with *Prufrock*, where the genesis of a perception through a present-tense situation is dramatized by an utterance almost entirely in the present-perfect and future tenses. In *Childe Roland*, as in *Prufrock*, the disparity of tense between the utterance and the situation enhances the disequilibrium be-

[1] *Browning, How To Know Him*, p. 233.

tween them; it shows the utterance as not directed toward the situation, as not concerned with altering it, but as ultimately self-directed because concerned with extracting from the situation a pattern for self-understanding. The making of the pattern is a present-tense process which necessarily reduces the situation to the past, so that the disparity in tense isolates from the dramatic business of the quest the knight's pattern-making dialogue with himself.[1]

But the pattern cannot be understood, either in *Childe Roland* or *Prufrock*, as a rational pattern leading to an extractable idea. The pattern is rather the shine that comes off the events, the peculiar vibration by which we recognize them as expressive and as therefore in that sense significant. The pattern is the Song the events give off, their effluence or aspiration toward the purely expressive condition of music. *Childe Roland* is Browning's materialization of that wild snatch of song in *Lear* from which the poem takes its title.[2] Just as that single line means little as an idea, so it means intensely and all-inclusively as the expressive distillation of many possible ideas. Browning projects one of these possibilities through the circumstances of his poem; but the circumstances remain only half-substantial, the mere projection of a possibility—meaning only partially and inconclusively in the ordinary sense, and for the rest meaning in the sense that the title *means*, as a vibration. Thus, the circumstances threaten at every moment to turn back into Song, which is what they do when in the end the knight comes out not with an idea, with an answer limited to the circumstances, but with an

---

[1] We might say that the whole utterance occurs in the mind of the knight during the moment of illumination, except that the utterance develops as in other dramatic monologues without preordained direction—the knight does not, articulately at least, seem to know the outcome.

[2] "See Edgar's song in LEAR," says Browning beneath the title. The song occurs at the end of Act III, Sc. iv, and is worth considering in context. Edgar is disguised as a naked madman, Poor Tom. Lear encounters him on the heath with a storm raging all around and when for Lear the whole moral order is cracking. Lear has been calling Poor Tom a "philosopher" and finally addresses him as "good Athenian." Gloucester says to Lear, "No words, no words! hush." And it is then that Edgar, for no reason and in answer to nothing but as if to utter the antithesis of philosophy and words, breaks out with: "Child Rowland to the dark tower came." It is only this line which has sublimity; the last two lines are equally a *non-sequitur* and yet *mean* little in any sense: "Fie, foh, and fum!/I smell the blood of a British man."

answer which at once answers nothing and yet exceeds the circumstances—when he comes out with a blast of Song, the very song out of which the poem had its inception. The poem begins in Song and moves through circumstances only to dissolve back into Song.

Since the knight makes the pattern by *seeing* the landscape as vibrating with significance, he stands in the same relation to the poem as the poet in that he finds in the circumstances the Song which he himself has brought to them. The Song is thus the knight's own nature which he passes through the circumstances to externalize; so that the Song is both the question and the answer, the result of the quest and the motive for undertaking it. The knight passes through the circumstances to discover as experience the self he already knows as presage; just as Prufrock takes his other self on that odyssey to tell himself about himself.

Both Prufrock and the knight know from the start that they will fail. But Prufrock must act out his failure in order to hear the Song of it from the mermaids who are products of his own fancy; and the knight must blast forth his own music, after having discovered the Tower through a transformation of his own vision. The fact that there is progress, that the Song at the end is something different from the Song at the beginning, is a sign that the speakers need the circumstances in order to reveal themselves. Both speakers adopt at the end a self-revealing posture which is the dramatic counterpart of the final outburst of Song, and this posture—Prufrock's "I grow old" and the knight's dauntlessness—could only have been produced by the circumstances. The combination of posture and Song, the one dramatic the other lyrical, is the meaning of the poem, the meaning being what the speaker both reveals and discovers about himself.

On the one hand, the Song gives rise to the circumstances; on the other hand, the circumstances provide not only the occasion for expression but also the words—the speaker learns through the circumstances what the Song is to be. A comparison with other dramatic monologues illuminates the outward movement of the address and discovery in *Prufrock* and *Childe Roland*. But the illumination is thrown both ways; for Prufrock's address to his other self, and the knight's discovery of what he already knows, illuminate the essentially circular movement of all dramatic monologues. They enable us to see the effect toward which all those devices for achieving disequilibrium are directed —that it is the whole technique of the dramatic monologue to set one element of the poem against the other in order to cast doubt upon the validity and meaning of each, in order to render the circumstances and ideas only half substantial so as to break up the normal progress of drama outward and return us at every point to the speaker for the rationale of the poem.

The result is to make the outward movement of the poem a device for returning inward, to make the dramatic situation the occasion for lyric expression ; so that in effect the speaker directs his address outward in order to address himself, and makes an objective discovery in order to discover himself. No matter how dramatic the dramatic monologue is, no matter how far outward it moves, its development is lyrical in that the speaker does not develop outward toward an external ideal, he does not change moral direction as a result of the circumstances; he rather makes the circumstances a part of himself as he develops inward toward an intenser manifestation of his own nature.

If it is the whole technique of the dramatic monologue to be thrown off balance, to project circumstances and ideas which cannot stand on their own feet and are not the adequate counterpart of the poem's meaning, it is in order that the whole weight of the poem may fall upon the speaker. It is to establish the speaker's existence, not his moral worth but his sheer existence, as the one incontrovertible fact upon which the poem can rest and from which it can derive the substantial core of its existence; so that the speaker is not just a part of the poem, another element with the circumstances and ideas, he *is* the poem.

Like the poem, the speaker is larger than the situation and includes it; he not only acts in the situation but contains within himself, as feeling, the residue of meaning not dramatized by the situation. Since this residue of meaning is the lyrical element of the dramatic monologue, the fact that the speaker resolves the disequilibrium between situation and meaning from his position outside the situation indicates that the dramatic monologue is resolved not dramatically but lyrically, not by the completeness of the situation but by a completeness that resides within the speaker.

Characterization in the dramatic monologue must thus be understood as not only a feature of the dramatic element but as the source of the lyrical element. This means that the dramatic monologue must use at the same time two opposite methods of characterization. It uses the method of drama, where character is manifested through utterance and action and is determined by what Aristotle calls *ethos* or moral bent. But it also uses the method of the lyric, where the manifestation of character is not by Aristotelian standards *characterization* at all, since it is total rather than determinate and therefore self-expressive and self-justifying rather than teleological and moral. It is to the extent that the characterization is lyrical that we cannot judge the speaker of the dramatic monologue or find in his utterance the counterpart to everything we understand about him. For the lyrical characterization manifests an area of existence outside the poem, sympathy being the means by which we apprehend such an area—we supply it with our own existence.

In *My Last Duchess*, it is because the duke's motive for telling the story is inadequate, and because the situation is never resolved in that the utterance is not quite directed to the auditor and does not accomplish anything, that we look for a resolution in the duke's life outside the poem. We see the situation as an episode of a life still in the process of articulating itself, and as only equivocally objective because called into being to further the process of self-articulation. The poem is a dramatic monologue rather than a first-person narrative just to the extent that the story is subordinated to the self-articulation.

Prufrock takes his other self along to project it into the role of lover at the tea party, while he remains outside to discern the bald spot on the head of the would-be lover. It would be wrong to say that Prufrock simply learns he is unheroic, his final Song is too little satiric and too full of feeling for that. The disparity between his desire and its dramatic realization makes him more aware than ever of the primordial urge which is his life. What he learns is to articulate his life precisely by playing an inadequate role—by donning a mask, as Yeats would put it, a mask which would be according to Yeats not only inadequate but Prufrock's opposite. Certainly, in moving from the would-be lover at the tea party to the timid old gentleman in white flannels, Prufrock moves farther from his original desire. Yet it is through the fancy of the timid old gentleman that he creates his "love song." All the speakers of dramatic monologues are inadequately represented by their dramatic characterizations; yet the dramatic characterizations must manage to suggest, if the dramatic monologue is to be successful, their total life.

The point then of characterization in the dramatic monologue would necessarily be to suggest as much as possible of the speaker's life outside the poem, to make us so aware of the inadequacy of the dramatic characterization that we look beyond it. This necessity accounts for the kind of speakers we find in the best dramatic monologues, speakers who excel in passion, will or intellectual virtuosity—in existential courage, the courage to be themselves. All the qualities necessary to the successful speaker are existential in that they must be sufficiently extraordinary in their development to command our admiration in and for themselves, regardless of the moral direction they happen to take. The speaker must, in other words, evince more life than the situation requires, in order to suggest that life outside the poem which makes him larger than the situation.

There is a kind of existential hierarchy by which the speaker is justified not because he is more right than the other characters—he seldom is—but because he is more alive. The dramatic monologue is constructed around a fundamental disproportion in size and vividness between the speaker and the other characters, a disproportion which is in the successful dramatic monologue so wide that the speaker partakes of another order of existence. He is the only character who is characterized lyrically, and therefore the only character whom we know from inside—in whom we feel the pulse of life as our life just to the extent that his life derives not from the situation but from a source of existence which we ourselves supply. The speaker is for this reason the only completely concrete character in the poem, his concreteness being the counterpart of our own. The other characters, instead, derive their life from the speaker. They exist as he sees and describes them, so that their existence partakes of the problematical quality of a visual and intellectual construction.

That is why it matters less that the evangelical lady is less right than Rizpah, or that the sweet-tempered duchess is more right than the duke, than that the speakers are in both poems so much more vivid and interesting than their opponents—that the speakers are the life with which the poems deal, while their opponents exist as the pragmatic constructions by which the speakers reveal themselves. We have seen what happens in drama when, through the intention of the author or the misinterpretation of the reader, one character achieves a stature and vividness out of all proportion to the rest; so that the whole play becomes an instrument of his self-revelation, while for the sake of his self-revelation he is exonerated from the judgments that apply to the other characters. The drama becomes a lyrical drama and ultimately a dramatic monologue. Conversely, when the speaker of a dramatic monologue describes characters either more vivid than himself or at least not appreciably less vivid, the speaker becomes a narrator and the poem a first-person narrative. That is what happens to Browning's *The Flight of the Duchess*, which for all its fine points is not successful as a dramatic monologue because the speaker—although he is one of Browning's noblest male characters—is of the same order of existence as the other characters. He has not a life large enough to dominate and exceed the poem.

For one thing he is not a paradoxical character, and the paradoxical character of the speaker indicates his disproportionate largeness. Since paradox is the form by which the inexpressible gets expressed, the fact that the speaker is both villain and aesthete like the duke of *My Last Duchess*, or vulgarian and aesthete like the bishop who orders his tomb, that he is like Rizpah or Porphyria's lover a criminal because he loves, or like St Simeon a saint because he does not love, that he is right with the wrong reasons like Blougram, or like Sludge wrong with many right reasons—such contradictions suggest that the whole truth about the speaker lies outside the facts, in an area of existence where all contradictions are resolved.

But the contradictory qualities are not the fundamental paradox, we merely pick them out as a way of articulating our sense of the fundamental paradox. Contradictory qualities can, after all, be contained within a dramatic characterization; whereas the fundamental paradox stems from the two modes of characterization, which are incompatible. On the one hand, the speaker is characterized as an articulated personality engaged in moral action, as distinctly other than ourselves and to be judged. On the other hand, he is "characterized" (if the word can be used) as sheer consciousness, as the primordial unarticulated self-justifying life which we share with him and in fact supply. The speaker is ourselves and not ourselves, to be judged and not judged. He articulates himself, engages in action, only to dissolve the action and the self-articulation in the stream of his unarticulated life; he learns his lesson in order to become more himself than ever. The thing we sense as we read the dramatic monologue, the thing that accounts for the peculiar effect which is the starting-point of our whole discussion of the form, is that the speaker has one foot inside the poem and one foot outside, that even as he engages in the action he is as much a spectator as we are.

This does not mean that he turns the general moral perspective upon himself, as we have seen the soliloquist do. For it is just in the matter of moral judgment that the speaker of the dramatic monologue is oblivious and committed to his own strategy. He is like us not in his judgment of the situation but in his reason for being in it, in that he enters into the situation for the same reason that we read the poem—deliberately, for an experience. His perspective must be, as a matter of fact, as far as possible from the general if the situation is to figure both for him and us as an experience rather than as the illustration of a principle. It is by rendering the categorical generalization inapplicable that the speaker's particular perspective leads us back to the most uncategorical possible generalization—the undifferentiated life common to us all; and it is this reference to a concrete life (rather than an abstract principle) outside the poem that makes the situation an experience. It is, in the same way, because the speaker himself is so much particularized, because his characterization through contradictory qualities renders inapplicable the publicly recognized categories of character, that we find in him a pole for sympathy—since it is between the categories that we find the counterpart of our own life.

The speaker's paradoxical particularity universalizes him, in other words, as sentience just because it makes it impossible to generalize him as concept. As the sign of his particularity, the particular perspective is therefore the sign of his universality and of the fundamental contradiction between the two modes of his characterization. The particular perspective shows the speaker as both involved and not involved in the situation, as too particular and too universal for categorical meaning. On the one hand, the incompleteness and distortion of the view show the speaker under the most severe physical limitation; on the other hand, they show the situation as only partially and equivocally seen, referring us outside the poem for the complete meaning. The particular perspective is thus the visible track between the lyrical and the dramatic characterizations, between the Song and the situation. Even as it defines the situation and the speaker as actor in the situation, it marks the circular route by which both actor and situation came into being and by which they will return.

The particular perspective also marks the reverse route by which the reader understands the poem. If the speaker reveals himself by moving into conditions, it is through conditions, through seeing what the speaker sees within the limits of his perspective, that we apprehend his total life and therefore our own. The particular perspective is the channel through which the life we share with the speaker takes on a form other than our own; and we project our life into that channel for the same reason that the speaker projects his, to gain an awareness of that life, an experience.

Such being the purpose, the narrower the channel the better, the more particular the perspective the better. For the more aware we are of the inadequacy of the dramatic characterization, of the disparity between it and the lyrical characterization, the more we become aware of the lyrical characterization. In the same way, the more aware we are of the disparity between ourselves and the dramatic characterization, of how far we are projecting ourselves and of how limited a manifestation of our life the projection is, the more aware we become of the life we have left behind us and of the distance the speaker has projected, since he derives from that same life. It is, in other words, where the dramatic characterization offers the least possible justification for sympathy, where the speaker is most unlike us, that we are most sharply aware of our own life in him as accounting for our sympathy—and most sharply aware, having found our own life in him, of his life too.

That is why the characteristic effect of the dramatic monologue is so much more apparent in a poem like *My Last Duchess* than in, say, *Rizpah*. It is not easy to see that our sympathy for Rizpah does not depend upon our moral approval of her, but the duke's self-justifying life forces itself upon us against all the facts and all the conclusions to be drawn from them, against what we usually consider the meaning. The speaker is more alive to the extent that he is less meaningful. And in the same way, the thing the speaker sees is more alive to the extent that it is distorted and incomplete, to the extent that it excludes ideas by appearing as incongruent with the average and therefore as *seen* in its ultimate concreteness. This movement away from rational meaning toward the intensest concreteness accounts for the evocative quality of the dramatic monologue. For it is to the extent that the dramatic monologue excludes from its meaning the middle ground of ideas, marking the narrowest possible track between the most particular possible fact and the widest possible life, that it does not so much make a statement about an idea, a place, an age, as it evokes their "spirit."

How then do ideas figure in the dramatic monologue? More than any other poetic form, the dramatic monologue deals with ideas—being the appropriate instrument of an age of ideas, of a self-conscious culture every aspect of which has been abstracted to be compared with every other as an idea. Yet it is in just such a culture that ideas are most likely to provide the content of literature—to act as the contending forces, the *dramatis personae* as it were—but cannot determine meaning. To determine meaning, ideas must have the general assent that we nowadays give only to scientific ideas about nature. Where such assent is lacking and ideas are problematical, we must fall back for meaning upon the perceptive or genetic process by which ideas are evolved, upon psychology and history in speculative thought and upon character and biography in literature.

Blougram's ideas about the Church and Caliban's ideas about the nature of God are not the meaning of those poems. The poems render the ideas problematical if they do not indeed negate them. Yet the meaning is not that Blougram and Caliban are wrong; the poems would hardly be interesting if they presented ideas simply to refute them. The meaning is a total movement in perception, and the ideas are, along with the seen objects, the facts of character out of which the new perception is made.

Ideas, then, are used for the same purpose and effect as character and perspective—not to mean but to be evoked, brought alive as aspects of a life articulating itself through perception. It follows that wrong ideas are more likely than right ideas to refer us to the life outside the poem, for the same reason that the reprehensible speaker and the extraordinary perspective refer us to it—as minimizing our rational relation and enhancing our sympathetic or life-perceiving relation to the poem. For it is clear when we let wrong ideas have their way with us that we are interested in them not logically, as ideas, but genetically, as a kind of articulation life can take. As a point of view, the most wayward ideas can present a worthy foil for our judgment, our disapproval only serving to emphasize their necessary because characteristic quality.

The meaning of the dramatic monologue is what the speaker comes to perceive. But the thing he comes to perceive is something more than the sum of what he sees and thinks. It is also a new surge of life, an advance on the dramatic characterization with which we start because an infusion into it of the lyrical characterization—of that part of the speaker's life outside the poem which he has managed, through what he sees and thinks in the course of the poem, to articulate. The meaning of *Blougram* is the strength of will and intellect Blougram reveals through his manipulation of the Christian argument; and the meaning of *Caliban* is the life-persistence, the biological vitality and cunning which Caliban finds in the swamp world and in what he deduces from the swamp world about the nature of the god, Setebos. The meaning is Caliban as he stands revealed in what he sees and thinks. But it is—and this is why the dramatic monologue reaches its climax in the succinctly drama-tized restatement of what has already been said—the trans-formed Caliban of our final impression, the Caliban who bursts upon us in the end as a revelation, with a new intensity and largeness that justify him as more himself than ever.

The meaning is the Song of Caliban, the expression of

Caliban's whole soul as it breaks through and exceeds the conditions of the poem. Indeed, the knight's slug-horn blast at the end of *Childe Roland* represents the ending of all dramatic monologues; they all end with the speaker's triumph over the conditions of the poem, with his acquisition of the poem as a new side of his own nature. The dramatic monologue is essentially a poem of learning, since more is known at the end than at the beginning, and the thing known has validity and importance not in itself but as an acquisition of the speaker. The disequilibrium of the dramatic monologue is in this sense a dynamic equilibrium. The speaker catches up in the end with the total life out of which the whole poem rises, he resolves the poem lyrically by learning his Song. The situation or argument ends in an *impasse*; but the resolution comes from a breaking through to a new dimension of vision, from shifting the argument to a larger context, a deeper level of intensity.

Ultimately, of course, the same thing is learned in all dramatic monologues, as in all dramatic lyrics and lyrical dramas. They all mean the same thing—the greatest possible surge of life. But in the step before the ultimate, we distinguish the life of a Blougram from that of a Caliban, the final transcendent perception being in fact possible only through the characteristic perspective. It is St Simeon's hatred of life and blurred vision of the people at the base of his pillar that accounts for his vividly hallucinatory vision of the angel offering the heavenly crown, and that leads us to perceive in the hallucination the bursting forth of his deepest desire, the meaning of his whole life and thus of the poem. And it is the organist's intimate vision of the church, his devotion to dust and cobwebs, that accounts for his transforming perception of Master Hugues' arid old organ fugue, and that leads us to perceive the music beneath the contrapuntal sophistries—because we perceive the love and imagination that have gone into the making of the organist's perception, the life beneath his threadbare exterior. Although *Abt Vogler* works in reverse, in that the ordinary follows the transcendent perception, it is our sense from the start that the extemporizer's rhapsodic vision is temporary and illusory and therefore characteristic (a sense confirmed when the vision passes), that leads us to perceive it as a counterpart to the extemporized music and as a climactic expression of his soul.

As in all poetry of experience, the final perception is a fusion of subject and object, an instant when the speaker sees and understands the object because, seeing it through his own perspective, he sees and understands himself in it. But the perception cannot be stopped at this penultimate step; it cannot be extracted as an objective entity, an idea leading to other ideas. It cannot achieve completeness but remains tied by perspective to the speaker, enjoying a tremulous existence only as long as it is being perceived and then giving way before the need of the speaker's self-articulating life to achieve its own completeness by absorbing the new perception into itself. It is at the point where the life established by the particular perspective becomes so strong a surge as to lose its form, that the speaker reaches his apotheosis of perception and self-perception, becoming more himself than ever only to dissolve his own particularity and the particularity of what he sees in the general stream of being.

CONCLUSION

The Poetry of Experience

TO sum up our discussion of the poetry of experience, we can hardly do better than review the distance travelled from traditional literary practice. As the "classical" description of that practice, Aristotle's *Poetics* has much to teach us about modern literature—just because it so illuminatingly does not apply. We realize, in fact, once we consider the full implication of Aristotle's theory, that to write a new *Poetics* describing the high literature of the period since the Enlightenment we would have to turn Aristotle upside down. Our popular literature is another matter, and it is a tribute to the eternal validity of Aristotle's principles that they are abandoned only by the literature which seeks to be true to the modern situation, to a culture without a metaphysically objective morality. Where aesthetic pleasure is bought at the price of truth, where for the sake of entertainment writer and audience are willing to assume the objectivity of either a sentimental or a merely legal morality, there—as in all the kinds and degrees of our melodrama from the well-made play and best-selling novel down through the detective story and Western to the comic book—the literature of action, as described by Aristotle, still flourishes.

Since it is largely the victory of character over action that distinguishes the high literature of modern times, the best sign of its difference from the literature of action is to be found in Aristotle's description of the *dramatis personae* as "agents" of the plot. What Aristotle calls Character (*ethos*) is only one of the two distinguishing qualities of the agent, the other being Thought (*dianoia*). "Character is what makes us ascribe certain moral qualities to the agents," says Aristotle.

> Character in a play is that which reveals the moral purpose of the agents, i.e. the sort of thing they seek or avoid, where that is not obvious—hence, there is no room for Character in a speech on a purely indifferent subject. Thought, on the other hand, is shown

in all they say when proving or disproving some particular point, or enunciating some universal proposition.[1]

Character is the direction in which the agent exerts force; while Thought would seem to be the rhetorical and intellectual equipment with which he exposes and defends his moral direction.

Character, however, reveals only the kind of purpose that advances the plot. That is why it reveals only the kind of purpose which is *not obvious*, and why there cannot be room for Character in a speech *on a purely indifferent subject*. A biologically or socially conditioned purpose (the desire for life or to be well thought of) would presumably be *obvious* and therefore not moral and Characteristic. To be moral and Characteristic, the purpose must depart from the norm as a personal distortion; it must be particular, it must have been chosen. In other words, Character itself is revealed only where the agent pursues a strategy that advances the plot. Since a speech *on an indifferent subject* would be one that does not advance the agent's strategy, it could not reveal the agent as a Character but only as a rhetorician—a spokesman for the Truth, to be judged not morally but for his style and intelligence.

The conception seems to be of an original *right* flow of rhetoric which, when it is deflected to a particular purpose, reveals Character but which, left undeflected, reveals the *right* ideas from which it flows—Truth and the play's meaning. One sign of Aristotle's conception of *right* rhetoric is the fact that he does not give the rules for Thought in the *Poetics*, but refers us instead to his *Rhetoric* since Thought "belongs more properly to that department of inquiry."[2] And he tells us in another place that Thought "is what, in the speeches in Tragedy, falls under the arts of Politics and Rhetoric; for the older poets make their personages discourse like statesmen, and the modern like rhetoricians." One is struck by the lack of any idea of characteristic discourse, but Aristotle warns us not to "confuse it [Thought] with Character."[3] The strict separation is still another sign that the agent's utterance and ideas are not conceived as in our sense characteristic, but as *right*. The poet learns to make them *right* by consulting a *Rhetoric* and a *Politics*, while

[1] Trans. Ingram Bywater in Vol. XI of *Works*, ed. H. D. Ross (Oxford: Clarendon Press, 1924), Chap. 6, pp. 1450a-1450b.
[2] 19, 1456a.   [3] 6, 1450b.

the difference between agents would seem to lie in the ends to which they turn their *right* rhetorical and intellectual equipment.

Such a conception is foreign to us, since we look to utterance and ideas as identifying marks of character. But then character has come to mean mainly personal idiosyncrasy, whereas for Aristotle it seems to be entirely a moral quantity. The agents, he tells us, "are necessarily either good men or bad—the diversities of human character being nearly always derivative from this primary distinction, since the line between virtue and vice is one dividing the whole of mankind."[1] To understand how this differs from the modern conception of character we have only to consider Blake's criticism of Aristotle's statement.

> Aristotle says Characters are either Good or Bad; now Goodness or Badness has nothing to do with Character: an Apple tree, a Pear tree, a Horse, a Lion are Characters, but a Good Apple tree or a Bad is an Apple tree still; a Horse is not more a Lion for being a Bad Horse: that is its Character: its Goodness or Badness is another consideration.[2]

We might conclude from Aristotle's statement that the relativity of goodness and badness, the deviation in other words from the moral ideal, would be the one deviation, the *primary distinction*, by which character is defined—all other qualities remaining as norms. Yet even the amount of moral deviation would seem to be restricted in correctly portrayed Characters; for in listing the four points to aim at in portraying Characters, Aristotle lists as "First and foremost, that they shall be good."

> There will be an element of character in the play, if (as has been observed) what a personage says or does reveals a certain moral purpose; and a good element of character, if the purpose so revealed is good. Such goodness is possible in every type of personage, even in a woman or a slave, though the one is perhaps an inferior, and the other a wholly worthless being.

This last grudging concession leads directly into the second point to aim at—*appropriateness*, that a Character have the qualities appropriate to his station. Thus, we are told that "it is not appropriate in a female Character to be manly, or clever"; and we can go on to infer that it would not be appropriate in a slave to be haughty or in a king to be servile.

---

[1] 2, 1447*b*.
[2] "On Homer's Poetry," *Poetry and Prose*, ed. Keynes, p. 582.

Although it is conceded that goodness can cut across social categories, appropriateness establishes for the non-moral qualities a rule of *rightness* according to station that corresponds to the rhetorical rules of *rightness* according to purpose. The non-moral qualities categorize rather than in our sense characterize; their purpose is to identify the Character with his category rather than, as in modern characterization, to distinguish him from it. Since the fourth point, *consistency*, warns us not to change categories in midstream, it also works to keep the Character within his category in order to make him rationally understandable.

The third point, however, is interesting because it is as Aristotle recognizes exceptional: "The third is to make them like the reality, which is not the same as their being good and appropriate, in our sense of the term."[1] This point expresses perfectly Blake's conception of character, and would in any modern rules for characterization come first and foremost. The interesting thing is that Aristotle recognizes the reality of Character as something other than the categories by which Character is understood. It is not clear whether he recognizes that the reality may be in direct opposition to the categories. For he states the third point in the one vague sentence I have quoted and never alludes to it again, possibly because he could not fit it into his system.

What then is his system, and how does his conception of Character fit into it? His conception fixes all the qualities of Character as norms, except for moral purpose which remains the single variable. The result is to reduce Character to a quantity, a weight on the moral scales, and to exclude from judgment (except judgment of their aesthetic *rightness*) all those personal idiosyncrasies which do not lend themselves to moral measurement. Such a conception makes admirable sense once we remember that "Tragedy is essentially an imitation not of persons but of action. . . . In a play accordingly they do not act in order to portray the Characters; they include the Characters for the sake of the action."[2] Where action is the end, we require a conflict of purposes; and for the action to have meaning, the purposes must have relative values—we must be able to evaluate one as better than another. It follows that the action will be clearer and less interrupted to the extent that we eliminate

[1] 15, 1454*a*. [2] 6, 1450*a*.

qualities which confuse the lines of force and our evaluation of the forces. Personal idiosyncrasies, which endow a man with charms or defects having nothing to do with moral purpose or value, are just such superfluous qualities.

Whitehead, in *Science and the Modern World*, calls the Greek tragedians "the pilgrim fathers of the scientific imagination" because they conceived a moral order operating with the same impersonal universality as, say, the laws of Newton. "Their vision of fate, remorseless and indifferent, urging a tragic incident to its inevitable issue, is the vision possessed by science. Fate in Greek tragedy becomes the order of nature in modern thought."[1] Whitehead seems to have in mind the Greek idea of *hybris* and *nemesis*, presupposing an original cosmic balance which, when it is upset by the moral deviation of the tragic hero, restores itself as inevitably as water seeks its own level. Man can set the cosmic mechanism in motion through the moral deviation which Aristotle calls Character, but the consequences are beyond his control. Thus the perfect, because completely "scientific," tragic plot is that of *Oedipus Rex*, where the mechanism of justice is unmistakably autonomous. What Oedipus thinks is going on is quite different from what the audience knows to be going on; and by his very action in trying to escape the decree of the oracle, he rushes headlong to his doom. Events work themselves out according to their own laws, independently of any human will. Oedipus' purpose brings results opposite from what he intends; yet no one is responsible for the inversion.

Aristotle says nothing of all this, possibly because he could not be expected to recognize as, in the esoteric sense, Fate (any more than we would speak of Gravitation as Fate) what was for him the rational arrangement of events in imitation of the way things are. Only we moderns, who have taken morality out of nature, out of the realm of the objective and autonomous, and psychologized it, making it a study of the values people place on things—only we find it un-*natural* and therefore supernatural that events should grind out a justice quite other than Oedipus' idea of justice. But if Whitehead is right in placing such a strictly mechanical construction on Greek tragedy, then

[1] (New York: Macmillan, 1926), p. 15; (Cambridge: Cambridge University Press, 1926), p. 12.

Aristotle's analysis becomes an even more coherent system, especially as regards the subordination of Character to action.

The laws of science are universal only because they deal with a single abstraction from things, their measurements. The Law of Gravitation does not take into account what things are falling, their value, why they have fallen and what will happen to them when they hit the ground. In the same way, the moral order is universal only to the extent that people figure as moral quantities. Restore the moral quantity to its original conditions amid the unmeasurable qualities that make up the bulk of human personality as we conceive it, take into account the person's wit, charm, intelligence, strength of will, and his whole biography stretching back through childhood into the womb, and you have a case so particular as to require a law of its own, as to be in fact a law unto itself; for no moral generalization will apply.

But a moral generalization must apply where events are the object of imitation and therefore the producer of meaning. For events have no meaning in themselves. They produce meaning by conforming to a prescribed moral pattern, by illustrating a moral generalization; and to do this they must be reduced to the categories in which the generalization deals. If they have a meaning beyond what the generalization requires, it is because they have been conditioned by character to the point of particularity where the generalization no longer applies. They then derive meaning from character; they illustrate the agent's character. That is why where action rather than character is the primary object of imitation, the events must have only as much meaning and the agents as much character as the generalization requires. And this limited meaning and character must figure as moral quantities in a moral equation, if the action is to be complete, if we are to feel satisfied that events have worked themselves out and a balance been achieved.

How then are the moral quantities of the agents determined; how are the agents, in Aristotle's sense, Characterized? Here the rule of appropriateness becomes important. For rank is the public and conventionalized recognition of moral gradation. The social categories of king and subject, husband and wife, parents and children, are also moral categories in that they carry with them expectations as to behaviour and a definite code of privileges and duties which can be used to measure the degree of virtue or defection. The measure is precise just because the proprieties for each rank are different. Cowardice in a slave would be indulged with laughter, but would be so serious a flaw in a king that it would probably be ruled out as disintegrating his kingliness and therefore his character. On the other hand, excessive pride would be so intolerable in a slave as to be ruled out; whereas it is a perfectly appropriate flaw in a king, who would have to learn to curb his entirely kingly pride. In prescribing that Characters be good and be appropriate, Aristotle limits the amount they may deviate from the behaviour expected of their ranks.

The de-objectification of morality in the modern era is intimately associated with the de-objectification of rank, and both have had the same democratizing effect on literature as on society. Just as moral judgment by rule will not do for us moderns (at least in our contemplative moments), but we must judge a man in all the particularity not covered by the rule, allowing him to generate the law by which we judge him, submitting him in Nietzsche's phrase to his own test; so we are no longer willing to accept rank as a guarantee of moral worth. Indeed, the whole effort of modern literature (and this is especially true of the novel as the specifically modern vehicle) has been to turn rank upside down, finding respectability a sham and nobility in the most unlikely places.[1] The characters of our serious literature must earn our good opinion. We cannot simply label them with a social and moral category and get on with the story; we must know all about them as unique individuals in order to follow the modern story.

But the good classical plot (whether in the Classics or in our popular drama and fiction) can be adequately recounted without telling anything more about the characters than their rank and whether they live up to the behaviour expected of their rank. It is enough to speak of a good king or a wicked queen, of a wife who betrays her husband, or a mother who

[1] It can be objected that the inversion constitutes in itself a ranking. But it is only after the old hierarchy has passed into obsolescence that the attack upon it becomes an orthodoxy. Our best literature usually turns its attack upon the latest orthodoxy, though fashionable non-conformism, or the socially approved attack on the dead dog, is a characteristic of our "middlebrow" literature.

deserts her child, of an itinerant cowboy for that matter, or a detective, for us to understand the moral meaning in terms of the expected behaviour of the social category.[1] We give a perfectly comprehensible account of Aeschylus' *Oresteia* when we say that the king is murdered by the wicked queen and her lover, who usurp the throne, but that the prince avenges his father by killing the guilty pair and, after a period of penance for the murder of his mother, secures the throne. The summary omits any account of emotion, but no further particularization of the characters is required (and the trilogy gives little more beyond naming them) to understand the logic of the action as well as the moral evaluations, just because rank stamps the characters with value.

In spite of Hegel's idea that tragedy deals with the conflict between good and good, between incompatible moral obligations, the obligations are never quite equal. If they were, the action would come to a standstill; there could be no movement toward a *right* conclusion. Although Orestes, like Hamlet, must summon up all his moral strength to accomplish the revenge, there is no more question of a moral dilemma than in *Hamlet*; for duty to a father and king clearly takes precedence over duty to a mother and queen, especially when the father has so clearly been wronged by the mother. Yet it is Agamemnon's advantage in rank that gives him the moral advantage over Clytemnestra; for though there is much reason, as the chorus admits, in Clytemnestra's defence of her crimes, her defence is not quite valid. She pleads that she has taken a lover in revenge for Agamemnon's involvement with other women at Troy, and that she has killed him in revenge for his sacrifice of their daughter, Iphigenia, to insure fair winds for the Greek fleet sailing to Troy. But we gather from the moral emphasis of the trilogy that Clytemnestra's defence is invalid, because a

---

[1] It is significant that our literature of action has had to retreat to the social categories which still carry an implicit moral meaning—the categories of the immediate family (the courting couple, husband and wife, parents and children) and the categories on the social periphery, between law and lawlessness (the detective and cowboy versus the criminal), or between us and the enemy (the soldier). But what moral meaning is implicit in our more usual public categories—businessman, farmer, labourer, or even teacher, minister, Senator? Thus our high literature cannot be, like the high literature of old, *public*; it cannot deal with rulers and heroes in their public capacity.

husband's betrayal of his wife is a far less serious offence than a wife's betrayal of her husband, and because a father and king may take the life of his daughter whereas it is a heinous offence for a wife to kill her husband and king.

The very fact that Clytemnestra must die for her crime, whereas a short period of torment at the hands of the Furies compensates for Orestes' murderous deed, is a sign of the quantitative difference between the two murders; as is the logic of the action, by which Clytemnestra's murder of Agamemnon represents the low point, and Orestes' return to Argos and murder of Clytemnestra represents an unmistakable incline and return to equilibrium. The whole moral scheme of the trilogy is made explicit in the final trial of Orestes before Athena. In answer to Orestes' defence: "A husband and a father, both, she slew," his accuser, the Leader of the Furies, replies, "And death hath purged her. Shalt not thou die too?"—thus suggesting that the murders are of equal moral weight. Apollo then takes up Orestes' defence to resolve the trilogy by showing that the murders are not of equal weight. In reply to the Leader's assertion of the rights of motherhood:

> 'Twas Zeus who bade thee charge
> This man to avenge his father and cast down,
> As nothing worth, his mother's sacred crown?

Apollo asserts the superior rights of kinghood and manhood:

> Are these the same? That a great man, raised high
> By royal scepter, given of God, should die,
> And die by a woman's hand—

as well as the superior rights of fatherhood over motherhood:

> The mother to the child that men call hers
> Is no true life-begetter, but a nurse
> Of live seed. 'Tis the sower of the seed
> Alone begetteth.[1]

[1]. "The Eumenides," *Complete Plays of Aeschylus*, translated with commentaries and notes by Gilbert Murray (London: Allen and Unwin, 1952), pp. 232-35. The fact that Gilbert Murray (in his note on the trial, pp. 261-62) and H. D. F. Kitto (in *Greek Tragedy*, London: Methuen, 1950, pp. 90-93) are unwilling to take this debate seriously is rather more a sign that the modern reader cannot take it seriously than that Aeschylus did not. We cannot know how seriously Aeschylus took it, but we do know that he offers no other resolution in terms of the mechanics of the plot. Although it is true that the vote of the jury is tied and Athena makes the decision to

The trilogy is saved from bare mechanics by qualitative reinforcement of the quantitative differences. Thus, in addition to Agamemnon's right to dispose of his daughter's life, it is also true that his motive in sacrificing her was entirely disinterested. He did it against his will, in obedience to divine command and for the good of the nation. Orestes' motive in killing Clytemnestra is likewise disinterested. He is commanded by the Delphic oracle to return and avenge his father's death. But Clytemnestra's motives are at best mixed. Whatever her justifiable motives for taking revenge, it is certain that she also acts to further her illicit love and to usurp the throne.

But what about the case where moral quality contradicts, instead of reinforcing, moral quantity—where the criminal's motives are better than the non-criminal's, or where the person of inferior rank has the moral advantage, where the mother, say, has been wronged by the father? These are the characteristically modern questions that inevitably occur to us. The answer would seem to be that the Greeks, and for that matter all ancient peoples, either did not conceive such questions or did not consider them suitable for literature. For where in traditional literature is the *moralized* revenge story in which the son accomplishes revenge against the father for the mother?[1] We

acquit Orestes, the decision is after all Zeus' as expressed through Athena, the argument is Apollo's, and the decision does not contradict the argument but reinforces it. Professor Kitto himself admits this when he says, against Clytemnestra's claim as a mother, that "organized society is patriarchal." "Kings hold their sceptres from Zeus; the murder of a King is a blow struck at authority and order. The marriage-bond is the keystone of society, and the authority of the husband is the counterpart of that of the King. (In this debate, both of the Olympians are for the male.)"

[1] The unmoralized story is another matter—as for example in the archetypal Oedipus situation reflected in the myth of the overthrow of Uranos by Kronos and of Kronos by Zeus, in both cases with the collusion of the mothers. No moral significance is attached to these revolutions; they simply establish the reign of Zeus, where the moral order begins. The Leader of the Furies cites, against Apollo's assertion of the supremacy of fatherhood and kinghood, the fact that Zeus overthrew his own father and king; but the victory of Apollo in the debate would indicate that the case is not in point. For it is to rationalize the moral order of Zeus, to suppress really the natural or biological myth, that the moralized myth gets established. In the old Irish legend of Cuchulain, the son is tricked by his mother into taking vengeance for her against his father. When he realizes he is fighting his father, he purposely misses aim, and is killed by his father who does not yet know who he is. The son dies cursing his mother. (See Lady Gregory's rendition, *Cuchulain of Muirthemne*, London: John Murray, 1902, Chap. XVIII.)

moderns equate the interesting with the exceptional case, with the incongruency of the particular to the general. But the traditional interest seems to have been in the congruency of the particular to the general. The interesting story seems to have been for the ancients what the significant experiment is for the modern scientist, the one that illustrates rather than confutes the rule.

Aristotle explains the classical interest in congruency by the distinction he draws between history and poetry. History, he says, "describes the thing that has been," and poetry "a kind of thing that might be. Hence poetry is something more philosophic and of graver import than history, since its statements are of the nature rather of universals, whereas those of history are singulars." Since poetry, like modern science, makes statements about universal truths, it describes particulars that are congruent with general laws. And its characters are likewise congruent with the publicly recognized patterns of action; they act appropriately, according to type. While the singular statement of history is "one as to what, say, Alcibiades did or had done to him," the universal statement is "one as to what such or such a kind of man will probably or necessarily say or do— which is the aim of poetry, though it affixes proper names to the characters."

Aristotle warns us not to be misled by the proper names into supposing that the characters of poetry are particular persons rather than illustrative types. The true function of proper names, he says, has become clear by this time in Comedy, where

it is only when their plot is already made up of probable incidents that they give it a basis of proper names, choosing for the purpose any names that may occur to them, instead of writing like the old iambic poets about particular persons. In Tragedy, however, they still adhere to the historic names; and for this reason: what convinces is the possible; now whereas we are not yet sure as to the possibility of that which has not happened, that which has happened is manifestly possible, else it would not have come to pass. Nevertheless even in Tragedy there are some plays with but one or two known names in them, the rest being inventions; and there are some without a single known name, e.g. Agathon's *Antheus*, in which both incidents and names are of the poet's invention; and it is no less delightful on that account.[1]

[1] 9, 1451*b*.

It is no less delightful because the historical content is not essential to tragedy, though it helps to convince by giving the illusion of historical actuality. The essence of tragedy is in the logical sequence of events, and this requires logical (that is typical) rather than actual characters. Note that Aristotle speaks of the replacement of particular by typical characters as a recent innovation—which is interesting since we think of the reverse movement, from types toward particularized characters, as modern. That is because we think of literature as a kind of counterpoint to science and philosophy, and therefore as largely a criticism of formulations; whereas Aristotle seems to have thought of it as working, along with science and philosophy, toward formulation. We see literary progress as an escape from philosophical rationalization toward historical empiricism. But Aristotle seems to have seen it as an escape from factuality toward rationality.

Of course, Greek drama can be congruent only to the extent that we remain aware of the world-view to which the characters and events adhere. Once we lose sight of the world-view out of which the plays were written, we read them psychologically as we have done with Shakespeare. In other words, we reverse Aristotle by giving the primacy to character over action. For the whole Aristotelian analysis, leading through congruency and appropriateness to the primacy of action over character, breaks down once we regard the characters as, in the democratic sense, people rather than as hierarchical categories of people. Unless we dismiss the proper names and regard the murders in the *Oresteia* as perpetrated against a daughter, a king and husband, a mother, and unless we are aware of the different degrees of loyalty owing to a king and husband as opposed to a daughter, and to a king and father as opposed to a mother—we cannot make the proper moral discrimination between the murders committed by Clytemnestra and Orestes, and we cannot therefore follow the logic of the action, the fall and rise in its fortunes. We must as a result look for the meaning of the trilogy in character rather than action.

For we do discriminate between the murders, if not morally then psychologically. And the interesting thing is that the very quality which elevates Orestes morally, that he acts for an abstract reason of justice, degrades him once we cease to feel the authority of the moral sanction; for he strikes us as acting in cold blood—without psychological motives, motives we can understand through sympathy. Once we lose sight of rank, the son's murder of his mother is likely to strike us as more horrible than the wife's murder of her husband, because more un-natural—especially if we consider Orestes' moral duty of revenge against the mother for the sake of the father as violating the son's natural hostility against the father for the sake of the mother. Clytemnestra, on the other hand, who is degraded morally because she acts out of lust and self-interest, gains in the psychological reading by just those motives. For they are psychological motives with which we can sympathize; they make her murder of Agamemnon a *crime passionnel*.

The moral relation of the two murders is thus reversed once we judge them not by the external hierarchy of moral and social values of which the action is an illustration but by the ability of Orestes and Clytemnestra to command sympathy. The whole meaning of the *Oresteia*, including the Aristotelian analysis of its structure, is in fact turned upside down once, losing sight of the hierarchical world-view out of which it was written, we allow sympathy to become the law of interpretation. We have had enough experience of the psychological reading of Shakespeare to understand how, with sympathy the law, Clytemnestra emerges as the central figure, simply because she is the most passionate and wilful figure and the initiator of the action.

Clytemnestra becomes the existential heroine, and the *Oresteia* her tragedy—the tragedy of a wife torn between hus-band and lover, and of a mother turned by grief for her daughter into a murderess, yet encountering in the end her own son as her murderer. I have manipulated the perspective towards the events to show how this would be tragedy in the modern manner, an imitation of character rather than action. For the conflict takes place inside Clytemnestra once the moral distinctions of the action lose authority, so that we become more concerned with Clytemnestra's problem in facing the action than with the action itself. The internal conflict proves nothing morally in the end; it simply puts Clytemnestra through her emotional paces. Such tragedy deals, in the modern manner, with the paradoxes of the unfettered will, proving nothing about external reality—instead of dealing, in the Greek manner, with the mysterious and inextricable union of will and fate by which will serves even against itself as the agent of fate, thus illustrating for all its freedom the inevitable moral working of things.

Compare, for example, to Aristotle's "Tragedy is essentially an imitation not of persons but of action," Pound's distinction between the moments of character revelation which are the poetic part of a drama, and the rest which is the prose part and therefore uninteresting. Or compare to Aristotle's statement Wordsworth's "the feeling therein developed gives importance to the action and situation, and not the action and situation to the feeling," or Browning's "My stress lay on the incidents in the development of a soul: little else is worth study," or

> Instead of having recourse to an external machinery of incidents to create and evolve the crisis I desire to produce, I have ventured to display somewhat minutely the mood itself in its rise and progress, and have suffered the agency by which it is influenced and determined to be generally discernible in its effects alone, and subordinate throughout, if not altogether excluded.[1]

And compare to Aristotle's rule of appropriateness Browning's description in *Bishop Blougram* of the modern interest in character, which sets forth in effect a rule of inappropriateness:

> Our interest's on the dangerous edge of things.
> The honest thief, the tender murderer,
> The superstitious atheist, demirep
> That loves and saves her soul in new French books—
> We watch while these in equilibrium keep
> The giddy line midway: one step aside,
> They're classed and done with.

They're done with because they have only as much character as the plot requires; whereas we mean by character just the element in excess of plot requirements, the element we call *individual* because it eludes and defies classification.[2] The para-

---

[1] Pound's *Letters* (see p. 81) and the prefaces to *Lyrical Ballads*, *Sordello* and *Paracelsus*.

[2] It is thus a sign of "seriousness" to criticize, as lacking in characterization, just those well-made plays and novels in which the characters stick to the business of exerting moral force, and behave according to the manners appropriate to their social class.

doxical defiance of classification does not so much describe the individual element by creating a new, more refined category, as it alludes symbolically to its ultimately enigmatic nature—to that unlit area behind the Aristotelian agent, in sensing which we sense what we mean by the character's *life*. This area provides the mysterious, life-giving dimension of those "three-dimensional" characters the reviewers of fiction are always talking about. It is the place where the irreducible core of character Blake has in mind exists independently of Aristotle's "primary distinction" between virtue and vice, and therefore independently of the action which, if it cannot give meaning to character, must take meaning from it.

"All human happiness or misery," says Aristotle,

> takes the form of action; the end for which we live is a certain kind of activity, not a quality. Character gives us qualities, but it is in our actions—what we do—that we are happy or the reverse. In a play accordingly they do not act in order to portray the Characters; they include the Characters for the sake of the action.[1]

But the high literature of modern times starts with an opposite ethical assumption. "This is the question," says John Dewey in his *Ethics*,

> finally at stake in any genuinely moral situation: What shall the agent *be*? What sort of a character shall he assume? On its face, the question is what he shall *do*, shall he act for this or that end. But the incompatibility of the ends forces the issue back into the question of the kinds of selfhood, of agency, involved in the respective ends. . . . When ends are genuinely incompatible, no common denominator can be found except by deciding what sort of character is most highly prized and shall be given supremacy.[2]

Ends become incompatible when we can no longer measure them by an external moral standard. In literature it is difficult, once we cannot take Hamlet's duty of revenge quite seriously, to see any one course of action as superior to any other. The interesting question becomes, therefore, what Hamlet shall take it upon himself to *be* in responding to the situation; and it is the sensitivity and complexity of his response that justifies

[1] 6, 1450a.
[2] In collaboration with James H. Tufts (New York: Henry Holt, 1908; London: George Bell, 1909), p. 210.

him, even though he bungles the revenge. In the same way, we cannot know what Hamlet *is* by referring to his rank as Prince and his role as hero of a revenge play. But we can, through using the action as an object for penetration rather than judgment, come to know the Hamlet who, as the counterpart of ourselves, sends the stage Hamlet into action—less to accomplish the revenge than to experience it. We can in a modern context understand the play by reversing Aristotle, by using the action to lead to sheer response, to what Aristotle calls "quality."

Since response or "quality" is in the traditional distinction among the genres precisely the point of the lyric, the reversal of the Aristotelian economy of means to ends makes the ulterior Hamlet the subject of a lyrical drama, a monodrama, a dramatic monologue called *Hamlet in Doubt* or *Hamlet in Torment*. Such a poem is not, however, a lyric in the traditional sense; it is a poem of experience. For response cannot, any more than moral value, be named or alluded to as an objective category. It cannot be described; it must be dramatized. We need the stage Hamlet in order to apprehend the ulterior Hamlet. Like the speaker of the traditional lyric, the ulterior Hamlet cannot, address us directly, describing what he feels. For that would be to put speaker and reader in different roles, with the speaker communicating what he already knows to the reader who does not know. But it is precisely the nature of the ulterior Hamlet, who is the counterpart of ourselves, that we stand in the same relation as he to the stage Hamlet. We apprehend the poem by feeling and learning what the ulterior Hamlet feels and learns.

The bird singing on the bough we know not why, or the cat poised to spring we know not why, each in itself, in its utmost intensity and with no meaning beyond itself, is a lyric. Introduce the second event, the spring of the cat upon the bird, and the song of the one and the crouch of the other are accounted for by the events; for the two events are connected by a moral or at least a logical meaning. Thus, we have drama. Unless— and this is how we move toward lyrical drama, monodrama, the dramatic monologue—the perspective toward the events is so distorted that the events lose their distinctness, becoming fused into one as a function either of the bird's song or the cat's movement. If we focus entirely on the bird, then the cat becomes a peripheral blur and it matters only that the bird's song changes and not that the cat has caused the change; while if we focus entirely on the cat, it matters only that he springs and not what he springs upon. The point would not be to side with the bird against the cat, but to admire the transition from joy to anguish in the bird's song or the superb economy of the cat's movement. This is how the lyrical interest in the song or the movement for their own sake, apart from meaning, can be perpetuated in spite of the succession of events. So in the poem about the ulterior Hamlet, the events blur as we follow for its own sake Hamlet's self-expressive Song.

In an age where there is no valid moral principle for connecting the events, where we are left with perspectives toward the events, the literature that takes the modern situation into account must approximate the dramatic monologue—as even in prose it is in varying degrees approximated in the short stories of Chekhov and Joyce and the point-of-view novels of James, Conrad and Proust, or in those plays like Chekhov's or novels like Virginia Woolf's or like Joyce's *Ulysses* where we have, as in *The Ring and the Book* and *The Waste Land*, several dramatic monologues in juxtaposition. The reason the literature of perspective approximates the dramatic monologue is that we can adopt the perspective of only one character at a time. Our sympathetic projection can give to only one character at a time that special order of existence through which we see the events, not from outside as discrete units logically connected but from inside where we see them in their "effects alone" as Browning puts it, their effects that is on the consciousness of the one character, and therefore as a flow.

The analysis of experience into events is a product of logical hindsight, implying that the events have a structure, meaning and purpose of their own; whereas experience takes its shape from the flow of consciousness, from what Browning calls "the mood itself in its rise and progress" when the events are merely inferred. The self-expression of the ulterior Hamlet is in this sense a Song, because it is a distillation from the events, sheer response, sheer flow of emotion. To be perceptible, however, the flow must channel itself through the events in order that it may finally overwhelm them in its own lack of definition, in a completeness which means nothing in the sense that it means everything.

The disequilibrium between the completeness of the flow of consciousness or life, and the incompleteness of the events that rise out of the flow and sink back into it, gives to literature a new shape—a shape by which the poetry of experience can be identified. The poetry of experience breaks through the Aristotelian succession of events to achieve the condition of the lyric. And it is by violating the Aristotelian rules for achieving logical completeness or limited meaning that it breaks through. Yet the poem remains both dramatic and lyrical because it must be dramatic in order to be lyrical—because it uses limited meaning, if not to resolve the poem, then at least as an event in the poem, an event to be dissolved in the tide of unlimited meaning.

We can thus see in the dissolution of the traditional genres a symptom of the dissolution of meaning in the traditional sense; so that the poetry of experience can be understood as the instrument of an age which must venture a literature without objectively verifiable meaning—a literature which returns upon itself, making its own values only to dissolve them before the possibility of judgment, turning them into biographical phenomena, manifestations of a life which as life is self-justifying. Such a literature does not give us a meaning in the sense of a complete idea which can be abstracted and connected logically with other ideas. It resolves itself by immersing its uncompleted idea in an advancing stream of life—by shifting the whole argument into the context of a larger and intenser life, by shifting to a new perspective, a new phase of the speaker's career. The next episode would not follow from the last but would have to be a new dramatic monologue starting all over again as experience, with the only advance in the largeness and intensity of the speaker.

The poetry of experience can therefore be opposed to what we might at this point call the poetry of meaning—the poetry described by Aristotle insofar as it appears as drama or literature of action. In the poetry of experience, the idea is problematical and incomplete because it must give way before the need of the life flow to complete itself. But in Greek tragedy— if Aristotle's analysis is correct—the life flow, as it appears in the forces exerted by the agents, is problematical and incomplete because it must give way before the need of the idea or meaning to complete itself.

It is indicative of the necessary opposition between the poetry of experience and the poetry of meaning that the outstanding modern opponent of the Aristotelian analysis of Greek tragedy should, in his own analysis, turn Greek tragedy into a poetry of experience. I mean Nietzsche, who by the original title of his book, *The Birth of Tragedy out of the Spirit of Music*,[1] declares tragedy to be not the illustration of an idea of the world, of an objective order of values, but a birth, a natural growth from the unarticulated life surge, from what he calls the "Primordial Unity" or "primordial pain" of which music is the expression. The musical or Dionysian element of tragedy is, according to Nietzsche's famous dichotomy, the empiric ground of the dramatic or Apollonian element. Tragedy originates in the dithyramb or choric song, which evokes the dramatic situation as a partial and problematical articulation of itself: "We have learned to comprehend at length that the scene, together with the action, was fundamentally and originally conceived only as a *vision*, that the only reality is just the chorus, which of itself generates the vision."[2]

The chorus is thus, like the speaker of the dramatic monologue, the creative principle of the poem, providing us with our entry into the dramatic situation; we believe in the action because it is what the chorus *sees*. And like the speaker of the dramatic monologue, the chorus generates the vision in order to understand its own song. For the dramatic situation does not make the final meaning: tragedy "attains as a whole an effect which *transcends all Apollonian artistic effects*."[3] Having been of ambiguous reality throughout, having threatened at every moment to dissolve, the dramatic situation finally does dissolve back into the song out of which it arose; so that tragedy completes itself not in drama but in song—meaning in the end not

[1] Later changed to *The Birth of Tragedy, or Hellenism and Pessimism*.
[2] Trans. W. A. Haussmann, Vol. III of *Complete Works* in the authorized English translation, ed. Dr. Oscar Levy (Edinburgh and London: T. N. Foulis, 1909), p. 69.
[3] p. 166.

an idea but nothing less than life in all its concreteness, what Nietzsche calls "the heart of the world." "The mythus conducts the world of phenomena to its boundaries, where it denies itself, and seeks to flee back again into the bosom of the true and only reality."[1] For "music is the adequate idea of the world, drama is but the reflex of this idea."[2]

> In the collective effect of tragedy, the Dionysian gets the upper hand once more; tragedy ends with a sound which could never emanate from the realm of Apollonian art. And the Apollonian illusion is thereby found to be what it is,—the assiduous veiling during the performance of tragedy of the intrinsically Dionysian effect: which, however, is so powerful, that it finally forces the Apollonian drama itself into a sphere where it begins to talk with Dionysian wisdom, and even denies itself and its Apollonian conspicuousness.[3]

Hence the tragic hero is always justified, for he emanates from a self-justifying life outside the dramatic situation with its moral judgment. Since it was originally Dionysus himself who was evoked by the dithyrambic chorus, the tragic heroes are really masks or aspects of the god—temporary and partial manifestations, in other words, of the primordial life surge. They take on an individual nature in order to articulate that life through moral action. But the action always ends in crime; for in the realm of moral concepts, the life surge manifests itself as evil since it must break up the conventional categories. This is the tragic paradox and accounts for the paradoxical nature of the tragic hero—the split between what I have called his lyrical and dramatic characterizations, between our sympathy for him and our judgment of him.

> And so the double-being of the Aeschylean Prometheus, his conjoint Dionysian and Apollonian nature, might be thus expressed in an abstract formula: "Whatever exists is alike just and unjust, and equally justified in both."[4]

The paradox is resolved by the destruction of the tragic hero which, along with the dissolution of the dramatic situation, gives us pleasure because it returns us to a realm where the hero is justified. Nietzsche finds the meaning of the Aryan or tragic,

[1] p. 168.   [2] p. 165.   [3] pp. 166-67.
[4] p. 80.

as opposed to the Semitic or moral, conception in "the sublime view of *active sin* as the properly Promethean virtue, which suggests at the same time the ethical basis of pessimistic tragedy as the *justification* of human evil."[1] Tragedy achieves this meaning because the destruction of the hero shifts the argument to a larger context, the context of what Nietzsche at this point calls "the eternal life of the will" or "the instinctively unconscious Dionysian wisdom":

> The metaphysical joy in the tragic is a translation of the instinctively unconscious Dionysian wisdom into the language of the scene: the hero, the highest manifestation of the will, is disavowed for our pleasure, because he is only phenomenon, and because the eternal life of the will is not affected by his annihilation.[2]

Nietzsche describes a poem of experience—a poem which originates in song and passes temporarily through drama in order to articulate the song and refer us back to the song for meaning. As singer of the song, the chorus contains the life and meaning of the drama; in generating the vision of the tragic hero, it endows him with its life. The chorus, then, corresponds to the poet and the poet-*cum*-speaker of the poetry of experience. It makes of the hero a pole for sympathy, so that the audience, which starts by identifying itself with the chorus, identifies itself also with the hero, apprehending his self-justifying life. The audience understands the drama in the same way and for the same reason that the chorus generates it and the hero goes through his paces in it, in order to perceive the life common to chorus, hero and audience.

But if Nietzsche shows the drama as lyrical, he also shows the lyric as dramatic. The lyric is an Apollonian or dramatic evocation, "a *symbolic dream-picture*," of a Dionysian or musical apprehension; and the "I" of the lyric is an actor in this dream-picture—a mask, even as the tragic hero is a mask, of the poet's essential life and thus of the life common to us all. The lyrist is therefore not subjective, but

> has already surrendered his subjectivity in the Dionysian process: the picture which now shows to him his oneness with the heart of the world, is a dream-scene, which embodies the primordial

[1] p. 78.   [2] p. 127.

contradiction and primordial pain, together with the primordial joy, of appearance. The "I" of the lyrist sounds therefore from the abyss of being: its "subjectivity," in the sense of the modern aesthetes, is a fiction.

Even if the "I" bears the name, character and personal concerns of the poet, the identity is only superficial:

In truth, Archilochus, the passionately inflamed, loving and hating man, is but a vision of the genius, who by this time is no longer Archilochus, but a genius of the world, who expresses his primordial pain symbolically in the figure of the man Archilochus: while the subjectively willing and desiring man, Archilochus, can never at any time be a poet.

But the lyrist may use an identity other than his own to dramatize the life surge:

It is by no means necessary, however, that the lyrist should see nothing but the phenomenon of the man Archilochus before him as a reflection of eternal being; and tragedy shows how far the visionary world of the lyrist may depart from this phenomenon, to which, of course, it is most intimately related.

In other words, the same art of evocation that generates the vision of the man, Archilochus, as a mask of Archilochus, the genius of the world or manifestation of the life surge, also generates the vision of the tragic hero as a mask of Dionysus. The same art that generates the dream-picture of the lyric generates the dramatic situation of tragedy. The distinction between the so-called subjective and objective poet is therefore invalid. For the subjective man is the non-poet; the poet as poet must be objective, released from private desire. The only valid distinction is between the Apollonian or epic poet, who contemplates images as things other than himself, who is "guarded against being unified and blended with his figures," and the Dionysian or lyric-dramatic poet, who *is* in what he contemplates, who projects his Dionysian life into Apollonian images in order to find himself in them, whose images are in fact

nothing but *his very* self and, as it were, only different projections of himself, on account of which he as the moving centre of this world is entitled to say "I". only of course this self is not the same as that of the waking, empirically real man, but the only verily existent and eternal self resting at the basis of things, by means of the images whereof the lyric genius sees through even to this basis of things.[1]

Nietzsche's Apollonian-Dionysian dichotomy corresponds to our distinction between the poetry of meaning, which the reader understands through judgment, through contemplating the images or events as objects complete with their own meaning—and the poetry of experience, which the reader understands through a combination of sympathy and judgment, through finding by an effort of creative insight his own life in the otherwise incomplete images or events. The distinction is not between an objective poetry of meaning and a subjective poetry of experience. It is between a poetry of meaning which is either subjective or objective in that the poet talks, as in ordinary discourse, either about himself or about other things, treating his topic in either case as an abstraction from experience, as an object complete with its own meaning—and a poetry of experience which is at the same time both subjective and objective in that the poet talks about himself and other things, finding his meaning in neither but evolving it through an interchange and final fusion between the two. The lyric and the drama fuse into the single Dionysian genre in the same sense that they fuse into the dramatic monologue as the single genre of the poetry of experience. And the relation in Dionysian poetry of tragic hero and lyrical "I" to the poet and the life common to us all corresponds to the relation in the dramatic monologue of poet, speaker and reader.

The dissolution of genres, as well as the dissolution of the distinction between the poet and his material and the poet and the reader, are best explained by what has been called the organic theory of poetry—the theory, which begins with romanticism, that a poem is not a deliberate rhetorical construction but a quasi-natural organism, a "birth" as Nietzsche calls it, a kind of plant which the mind puts forth in accordance with the laws of its own nature.[2] Such a theory is destructive of the older

[1] pp. 45-47.
[2] For a detailed account of the organic theory, see M. H. Abrams, *The Mirror and the Lamp: Romantic Theory and the Critical Tradition* (New York: Oxford University Press, 1953).

theory of genres. For it suggests, on the one hand, that there must be as many genres as poets and even as poems; and, on the other hand, that there can be only one genre, since the dramatic movement from poet into poem and the lyrical movement from poem back into poet remain always the same. The organic theory also breaks down the distinction between the poet and his material, because the material is what the poet puts forth; and between the poet and the reader, because to apprehend the poem the reader must put himself in the poet's place—he must make the poem an out-growth of his own mind as well.

Thus Wordsworth, in the Preface to *Lyrical Ballads*, describes poetry as "the spontaneous overflow of powerful feelings," as an outgrowth of the poet's excess life. And Coleridge—in a characteristic analogy which describes perfectly the disequilibrium or dynamic equilibrium of the poetry of experience—compares the mind to a living plant in that, absorbing into itself the atmosphere to which its own respiration has contributed, it grows out into its perception.[1] His description of the function of imagination in poetry is perhaps the most famous statement of the organic theory. The poem does not, according to Coleridge, derive unity from the consistency of its own elements but from the poet's imagination which "reveals itself in the balance or reconciliation of opposite or discordant qualities." The meaning, in other words, is not in the elements of the poem but in the certain "tone and spirit of unity, that blends, and (as it were) *fuses*, each into each"; it is in our awareness of the poet's "synthetic and magical power," our awareness of his presence in the poem. The conflicting elements exist in order to be reconciled as a sign of the poet's reconciling presence.[2]

For Wordsworth and Coleridge, then, as for Nietzsche, the poem exists not to imitate or describe life but to make it manifest. It is this purpose of evocation that unites the poetry of experience—from the romantic poems of Wordsworth and Browning, with their individualized speakers and objects, to the symbolist poems of Yeats and Eliot, with their archetypal speakers and objects. Since the archetype is a psychological

[1] *The Statesman's Manual* (London: Gale and Fenner, 1816), Appendix, pp. xiv-xv.
[2] *Biographia Literaria*, Chap. XIV, ed. J. Shawcross (London: Oxford University Press, 1907), II, 12.

concept designed precisely to elude the rationalistic concept of the type, the archetypal perception is no less psychological and no less empiric than the individualized perception—though it proceeds from a deeper level of consciousness, a level where the perception of self merges with the perception of life in general, where the individual event merges with the myth. The poetry of experience remains essentially the same whether the actor in it is Dionysus or a dramatic or autobiographical mask of Dionysus, and whether the events are the mythical events appropriate to Dionysus or the dramatic or autobiographical events appropriate to his individualized masks. In all cases we know the poem through sentience, and the poem's meaning is the sentience which it calls into awareness.

Whatever the validity of Nietzsche's essentially psychological reading of Greek tragedy—and I think that, along with Coleridge and other romantic theorists, he makes a mistake in trying to apply to all literature an analysis which describes post-Enlightenment literature—whatever its validity, his reading is, like the psychological reading of Shakespeare, undoubtedly valid as a description of the literature of the nineteenth century and after. It is significant that Nietzsche does not attempt to apply his reading to any specific tragedy. He himself admits that it will not apply to Sophocles and Euripides (just the poets Aristotle has primarily in mind), since they have already succumbed to the force which was to destroy all tragedy—to what Nietzsche calls "Socratism," the moral and theoretical as opposed to the tragic view of life. Nietzsche rests his case on generalized allusions to Aeschylus and to the largely hypothetical pre-Aeschylean tragedies, dismissing as untragic most of what we consider to be Greek tragedy.

He makes clear in no uncertain terms, however, where his reading does apply. He tells us that he has undertaken to trace the birth of tragedy in order to hail its rebirth—most immediately in the music-dramas of Richard Wagner, but ultimately in the poetry potential at least in the whole post-Kantian culture. Kant and Schopenhauer have, he says, in demonstrating the limitations of logical and empirical science, dealt a blow to Socratic culture. For they have made possible again a mode of apprehension which is concrete because able to embrace moral and logical contradictions.

With this [Kantian] knowledge a culture is inaugurated which I venture to designate as a tragic culture; the most important characteristic of which is that wisdom takes the place of science as the highest end,—wisdom, which, uninfluenced by the seductive distractions of the sciences, turns with unmoved eye to the comprehensive view of the world, and seeks to apprehend therein the eternal suffering as its own with sympathetic feelings of love.[1]

Tragic may not be the word to describe that force in our culture which, having gathered originally under the banner of romanticism, still seeks to counteract the *Socratic* force. Nor do modern anti-rationalists think of themselves as combating so ancient a heritage as the Socratic; they are more immediately concerned with combating the heritage left us by Newton and the Enlightenment. Modern anti-rationalism is in any case different from the original Dionysian situation which Nietzsche hypothesizes. For the movement, there, was from the life surge toward formulation (lyric tragedy did after all evolve into Sophoclean tragedy). But modern anti-rationalists seek, as the next step in history, to reverse the historical process, to recover through history the concreteness of vision which history has progressively destroyed. That is what distinguishes their self-conscious kind of sympathy, their deliberate attempt to recover a sense of attachment, from the instinctive, almost biological, sense of attachment which we may suppose to have existed in the original Dionysian situation. That is what makes the modern anti-rationalist movement so very modern and—rational.

[1] p. 140.

I have used the following editions of the poets:

BLAKE, WILLIAM, *Poetry and Prose*, ed. Geoffrey Keynes, centenary edition (London: The Nonesuch Press; New York: Random House, 1939).

BROWNING, ROBERT, *Works*, with introductions by F. G. Kenyon, centenary edition, 10 vols. (London: Smith, Elder, 1912).

BYRON, GEORGE GORDON, Lord, *Poetical Works* (London: Oxford University Press, 1945).

COLERIDGE, SAMUEL TAYLOR, *Poems*, ed. E. H. Coleridge (London: Oxford University Press, 1945).

ELIOT, T. S., *Collected Poems 1909-1935* (London: Faber and Faber; New York: Harcourt, Brace, 1936).

HOPKINS, GERARD MANLEY, *Poems*, edited with an introduction by W. H. Gardner (London and New York: Oxford University Press, 1948).

POPE, ALEXANDER, *The Rape of the Lock and Other Poems*, ed. Geoffrey Tillotson, Vol. II of the Twickenham edition of Pope (London: Methuen; New Haven: Yale University Press, 1954).

POUND, EZRA, *Personae* (London: Faber and Faber, 1952; New York: New Directions, 1950).

SHAKESPEARE, WILLIAM, *Sixteen Plays*, ed. G. L. Kittredge (Boston, New York, London: Ginn, 1946).

SHELLEY, PERCY BYSSHE, *The Complete Poetical Works*, ed. Thomas Hutchinson (London: Oxford University Press, 1947).

TENNYSON, ALFRED, Lord, *Works*, edited with memoir by Hallam, Lord Tennyson (London and New York: Macmillan, 1950).

WORDSWORTH, WILLIAM, *The Poetical Works*, ed. Ernest de Selincourt and Helen Darbishire, 5 vols. (Oxford: The Clarendon Press, 1940-1949).

—— *The Prelude* (Texts of 1850 and 1805), ed. Ernest de Selincourt (London: Oxford University Press, 1950).

YEATS, W. B., *The Collected Poems* (London and New York: Macmillan, 1955).

INDEX

INDEX

Ammons, A. R.   *Tape for the Turn of the Year*   N659

Austen, Jane   *Persuasion*   Introduction by David Daiches
N163

Behn, Aphra   *Oroonoko, or, The Royal Slave*   Introduction
by Lore Metzger   N702

Brace, Gerald Warner   *The Garretson Chronicle*   N272

Browne, Sir Thomas   *The Complete Prose of Sir Thomas
Browne* (Norman J. Endicott, ED.)   N619

Browning, Robert   *The Ring and the Book*   Introduction
by Wylie Sypher   N433

Burgess, Anthony   *A Clockwork Orange*   Afterword by
Stanley Edgar Hyman   N224

Burney, Fanny   *Evelina*   N294

Campion, Thomas   *The Works of Thomas Campion*
(Walter R. Davis, ED.)   N439

Conrad, Joseph   *The Arrow of Gold*   N458

Conrad, Joseph   *Chance*   N456

Conrad, Joseph   *The Rescue*   N457

Creeth, Edmund, ED.   *Tudor Plays: An Anthology of Early
English Drama*   N614

Darwin, Charles   *The Autobiography of Charles Darwin*
N487

Edgeworth, Maria   *Castle Rackrent*   N288

Eliot, George   *Felix Holt the Radical*   Introduction by
George Levine   N517

Fielding, Henry   *Joseph Andrews*   Introduction by Mary
Ellen Chase   N274

Fuller, Margaret   *Woman in the Nineteenth Century*   Introduction by Bernard Rosenthal   N615

Gaskell, Mrs. Elizabeth   *Mary Barton*   Introduction by
Myron F. Brightfield   N245

Gissing, George   *The Odd Women*   N610

Gogol, Nicolai V.   *Dead Souls*   Introduction by George
Gibian   N600

Gogol, Nicolai V.   *"The Overcoat" and Other Tales of Good
and Evil*   N304

Gosse, Edmund   *Father and Son*   N195

Gregory, Horace, TR. AND ED.   *The Poems of Catullus*
N654

Hamilton, Edith, TR. AND ED.   *Three Greek Plays*   N203

Harrier, Richard C., ED.   *Jacobean Drama: An Anthology*
N559 (Vol. I) and N560 (Vol. II)

Hawthorne, Nathaniel   *The Blithedale Romance*   Introduction by Arlin Turner   N164

1310

1310